DEVOTIONS®

▶ **January**

He is the Maker of heaven and earth,
the sea, and everything in them—
he remains faithful forever.

—*Psalm 146:6*

Gary Wilde, Editor | Margaret K. Williams, Project *Editor*

Photo © iStock | Thinkstock®

DEVOTIONS® is published quarterly by Standard Publishing, Cincinnati, Ohio, www.standardpub.com. Copyright © 2015 by Standard Publishing. All rights reserved. Topics based on the Home Daily Bible Readings, International Sunday School Lessons. Copyright © 2013 by the Committee on the Uniform Series. Printed in the U.S.A. All Scripture quotations, unless otherwise indicated, are taken from the HOLY BIBLE, NEW INTERNATIONAL VERSION®. NIV®. Copyright © 1973, 1978, 1984, 2011 by Biblica, Inc.® Used by permission of Zondervan. All rights reserved worldwide. Scripture quotations marked (*KJV*) are taken from the *King James Version*. Scripture quotations marked (*NKJV*) are taken from the *New King James Version*®. Copyright © 1982 by Thomas Nelson, Inc. Used by permission. All rights reserved. Scripture quotations marked (*NASB*) are taken from the *New American Standard Bible*®. Copyright © 1960, 1962, 1963, 1968, 1971, 1972, 1973, 1975, 1977, 1995 by The Lockman Foundation. Used by permission. (www.Lockman.org). All rights reserved.

Each One a Favorite

He loveth righteousness and judgment: the earth is full of the goodness of the Lord (Psalm 33:5, *KJV*).

Scripture: Psalm 33:1-9
Song: "Rock of Ages"

Haley helped herself to a big chunk of fudge and savored the wide smile on Grandma's face. But the real icing on the fudge was yet to come, when Grandma said, "Shhh! This piece is just for you. I made it *especially* for you!" Haley relished that moment of such personal favor. Sweeter than sweet indeed!

Only in succeeding seasons did Grandma Williams's lineage learn the fullness of her secret. True to Grandma's word, *each* child was her favorite—Haley and Rachel; Nathan, Alex, and Cory; Kerri and Christopher and Zaley.

I suspect Patsy Williams wants her descendants to model the same amazing "mantle of worth" that God designed for each of His own children. Perhaps it was like the surprise covering He'd made when Moses asked to see the Lord's glory. While Scripture doesn't say he was the sole believer who ever requested such favor, the Lord enclosed Moses in a special cleft and made glory—"all [God's] goodness"—pass nearby (see Exodus 33:19-22).

Since God is no respecter of persons, we too can boldly approach His throne of grace, one at a time, and taste the wonders of His goodness through the redemption of His only Son, Jesus.

Father, into Your holy presence I come to find the fullness of joy. I am thankful for Your loving presence through Your indwelling Holy Spirit. In Christ's name, amen.

January 1. **Kay King** of Eddy, Texas, teaches and writes from her "life verse," Psalm 45:1a, 1b (*LB* and *KJV*): "My heart overflows with a beautiful thought! . . . My tongue is the pen of a ready writer."

Oh, Give Thanks!

Oh, give thanks to the Lord, for He is good! (1 Chronicles 16:34, *NKJV*).

Scripture: 1 Chronicles 16:23-34
Song: "Thanks for Thy Word, O Blessed Redeemer!"

Being an atheist is so fashionable these days. Some of these folks actually take delight in mocking God, making Him seem small and vindictive. And I've observed that many atheists want to make everyone agree with them. For example, they may use laws and court decisions to impose their will. Or they'll rewrite history to portray believers as being unsophisticated or bigoted. Yet throughout history, when atheists seize control of countries, carnage and horror result.

How frightening to think what this world today would look like if it were not for God and His goodness. Imagine a world without access to the Bible, or with no knowledge of God's amazing love, wisdom, and plan of salvation for our lives.

Yet through God's gracious self-revelation we can see history as *His* story. We learn from the transformation of men and women throughout history who've loved Him. We learn from the wisdom and insight of prophets and apostles, from natural law, and from His grace. Ultimately, we see the Father through His Son, and we long to be like Jesus—to see the whole world be as blessed as we are in Him.

Lord, what joy to give thanks! You have saved me to the uttermost—saved me from myself and set me on higher ground. You are greatly to be praised! In Christ, amen.

January 2–8. **Maria Anne Tolar** and her husband live in Portland, Oregon. Along with her other writing projects, she is currently working on a young adult novel.

All That God Is

Give to the LORD the glory due His name (Psalm 96:8, *NKJV*).

Scripture: Psalm 96:7-9
Song: "There Is Glory in My Soul"

When I began memorizing Scripture, certain simple words began to mystify me. I thought I understood words like *faith, hope,* and *grace*—yet they all seemed to grow in complexity as I pondered various verses. Perhaps the most puzzling of all was this simple, astonishing word: *glory.* What does it mean, "Give to the Lord the glory due His name"?

We talk of the glory of victory, the glory that was Greece, the glory of achievement. We use the word in the sense that someone or some nation has "arrived," reached the pinnacle of accomplishment. There's no higher point than that.

Thayer's Greek-English Lexicon includes in its definition of *glory,* "a most exalted state." And a definition I recently read said this: "The glory of God is a reality expressing *all that God is.*"

Contemplating God's glory is only possible when it is all about God and not anything about us, when we go outside ourselves to see Him. I remember seeing, as a child in Idaho, the astounding spectacle of the sky at night, the heavens filled with billions of stars, the constellations immense in the dazzling sky.

I know now that the awe that filled me then was a glimpse at God's glory. His weighty majesty, His awesome power.

My God and King, Your Word says that the time is coming when "the earth will be filled with the knowledge of the glory of the Lord, as the waters cover the sea" (Habakkuk 2:14, *NKJV*). May that time be now, Lord! Through Christ, amen.

Justice to the Gentiles

He will not fail nor be discouraged (Isaiah 42:4, *NKJV*).

Scripture: Isaiah 42:1-4
Song: "Who Is on the Lord's Side?"

I tend to read too many news and political websites on the Internet. To make it worse, I even read the comments that follow the articles. Readers on both sides of the political aisle weigh in, one side praising, the other deriding certain presidents, senators, news makers. The more comments, the more controversy and name-calling. Yet some posters appear to have already given up the fight, moaning, "This nation is going down in flames. It's too late for us. All is lost. God help us!"

How humbling to see Isaiah's prophecy of the Messiah some 700 years before His birth. If anyone would be concerned about the future of the human race, it would be the Christ. If anyone should be appalled at the disintegration of justice, it would be Jesus. But unlike us, He's not arguing, shouting, threatening—or even taking much notice of the opposition. He has a focused mission: to establish justice in the earth.

He will see victory. He will not be deterred.

I wonder what would happen if we had the same heart as Christ's for the battles for the soul of our country. Could we keep our eye on the God-honoring outcome we envision, determined in advance that we won't fail nor be discouraged?

O Lord, may Your Spirit rest on me at all times. When I battle for good to prevail, help me keep my focus on Your mission and not on my own anger and frustration. Let me always remember: love is our only "weapon." Through Christ my Lord I pray. Amen.

Hold On!

He has made My mouth like a sharp sword (Isaiah 49:2, *NKJV*).

Scripture: Isaiah 49:1-7
Song: "Waiting for the Promise"

A poor farmer on a pathetic acreage believed that the Word of God spoken in faith changes circumstances. After planting a crop, he marched around his field, day after day, holding his Bible and proclaiming its promises of abundance and bounty over his land.

His daily walks turned into weeks of daily proclaiming God's promises over his barren land. Finally one day, he stopped, defeated. What he was declaring in no way resembled what he saw. Nothing looked any better. "Lord, I feel like a liar," he confessed.

The farmer, Charles Capps, then said he heard these words as clearly as if someone stood next to him: "How can it be a lie if it is my Word?" Chastened, he continued to proclaim the Word, and in due time that year the land yielded its very first bountiful harvest—the first of many.

Mr. Capps put his faith into action with unusual actions. We wouldn't all do it that way. And most of us aren't contending with barren, unproductive acreage these days. We have other crosses to bear. Yet the principle holds: hold to His promises.

Dear Lord, my heart needs cultivating by hearing Your Word, over and over, until what I proclaim becomes what I see. I know I shouldn't presume on Your Word, but I can trust it. May my heart learn that Your promises are more than just words. They are the truth to live by, day in and day out. In Jesus' name, amen.

Help of the Helpless

Now may the God of hope fill you with all joy . . . that you may abound in hope (Romans 15:13, *NKJV*).

Scripture: Romans 15:7-13
Song: "Abide with Me"

Two years ago, I determined to memorize 50 Bible verses in a month. I wanted to build my faith, so I remember thinking, *I don't want any verses about hope; after all, anyone can merely hope.* When I began memorizing today's verse, I thought I'd made a mistake—I'd even copied it down wrong. It seemed to say, "May the God of hope fill you with hope." I'd expected it to say, "May the God of hope fill you with faith, power, victory."

When we don't see the sick healed, revivals started, our cities claimed for Christ, we might wonder why our faith isn't strong enough. We seldom wonder whether we've failed to abound in hope. But Scripture says, "Faith is confidence in what we hope for" (Hebrews 11:1). The city I live in has a homeless problem. It has a growing population of drug addicts, alcoholics, and the mentally ill. Others see these folks—and perhaps they see themselves—as utterly hopeless. But without hope no person can begin to change or even imagine change. Without hope, there's hardly a will to live. How startling to think that every sinner's salvation, every character transformation, every good thing—including faith—begins with hope.

What great breakthrough do you abound in hope for this day?

Lord, how well You understand us and our needs! Give me a heart of compassion for the needs of the helpless and hopeless. May I pray without ceasing that the people who dwell in darkness may see Your great light. In Christ, amen.

Show and Tell

Worthy is the Lamb who was slain (Revelation 5:12, *NKJV*).

Scripture: Revelation 5:11-14
Song: "The Wonderful Cross"

The most frequent advice given to writers is: Show, don't tell. In some respects, the Gospels follow this approach. Jesus is *shown* throughout His ministry, teaching, healing, feeding multitudes, and performing all manner of miracles. We see His power and grace and love in action; we hear His insight and wisdom.

Then there are His death, burial, and resurrection. The truth of it isn't merely shown; it is told and foretold. Old Testament prophecies suddenly become clear. Paul, Peter, James, and John write letters and make converts, establishing church doctrine by telling the meaning of the cross. Paul says, "I determined not to know anything among you except Jesus Christ and Him crucified" (1 Corinthians 2:2, *NKJV*).

On the cross, Jesus was punished for our sins, making us righteous before a holy God. He took away our diseases, delivered us from evil, gave us abundant life. No movie on earth could actually "show" those miracles that happened on the cross, but Scripture clearly reveals them. Even as He hung on the cross, suffering for our sins, He was providing blessing after blessing to all who would trust in Him and believe. What has been *shown* to us is clearly something for us to show others—in our deeds and in our words.

Father, I want to worship You as You deserve. May I daily grow more aware of Your goodness, grace, and compassion. Help me to rejoice daily in the victory of the cross on my behalf. How thankful I am in this moment! In the name of Jesus, amen.

Lessons from Nature

Oh, sing to the Lord a new song! Sing to the Lord, all the earth (Psalm 96:1, *NKJV*).

Scripture: Psalm 96:1-6, 10-13
Song: "This Is My Father's World"

Outside the window of my office is a layered hill, barren now in winter, the remnant of autumn leaves covered in mud. But in the summer, my view is blocked by intense foliage, the overgrown trees and lush green of the Pacific Northwest.

When I should be productive, I sit instead with binoculars, trying to identify the birds that visit. I watch late in the fall for the return of the thrushes in their Halloween colors of orange and black, and in the summer for the spotted towhee and lovely red-breasted robins. They all have their own unique songs to sing, as well.

Why was there a need for such intricate color combinations, for distinct warbles and whistles? Why do some tiny birds have eyes ringed in white and come arrayed in such amazing patterns and color combinations? Why was there a need for such exquisite individuality, as though each was crafted with care by a great artist?

Is it not sad that we often miss the glories of our Creator's creation? We even seem to ignore our fellow humans. And yet: "What is man that You are mindful of him? . . . You have crowned him with glory and honor, and set him over the works of Your hands" (Hebrews 2:6, 7, *NKJV*).

O Lord, when I look out across Your wondrous creation, may I see Your might and power, Your goodness and mercy. And let my heart sing! Through Christ, amen.

He Loves a Celebration

Be joyful at your festival—you, your sons and daughters, your male and female servants, and the Levites, the foreigners, the fatherless and the widows who live in your towns (Deuteronomy 16:14).

Scripture: Deuteronomy 16:13-15
Song: "I Will Celebrate"

I recently spent six weeks in a small mountain-resort town where it snows 6 months out of 12. During two weeks of my stay, the town celebrated Winter Carnival, their 50th one! Parades, fireworks, ice sculptures, ski races, hockey games, and more were scheduled back-to-back for 14 days.

There's a lot of nightlife attached to the festival too. Concerts and dance parties last well into the wee hours, and heavy drinking accompanies it all. For a few who move from true celebration into a decadent party spirit, there are arrests and incidents that eventually remove the joy for them.

God instituted celebration. The Festival of Tabernacles was a time for God's people to rejoice after the bounty of harvest had been stored away. Thus God received the glory for His goodness to His people. The fact is, God loves true celebration when His children rejoice in creation and in their relationship with the Creator.

So let us rejoice daily. Come, celebrate God's goodness!

Dear Lord, I desire to enter into joyful celebration of all Your good works. I receive Your provision for my life. I rejoice in You. Through Christ, amen.

....

January 9–15. **Jan Pierce** is a retired teacher and freelance writer. She and her husband are the founders of Teams India, a ministry to support Christian work in India.

He's Ready to Forgive

When we were overwhelmed by sins, you forgave our transgressions (Psalm 65:3).

Scripture: Psalm 65:3, 4
Song: "Wonderful Grace of Jesus"

The gospel message is quite simple: The Lord stands ready to forgive our sins. We need only to repent, call on His name, and receive His forgiveness.

What a relief! But isn't it hard to recognize our own sins? Somehow our own behavior slips beneath the radar as we diligently focus on the behavior of others. But soon the weight of guilt comes crashing down on our shoulders.

I taught first grade for many years, and I observed that 6- and 7-year-olds are blissfully ready to hang their friends by their thumbs for their transgressions. Billy cutting in line? Take his recesses for a week! But when caught in their own shortcomings, they, with totally straight faces, recommend leniency. Yes, it's funny—even endearing. But in their innocence little children mirror our adult tendency to let ourselves off the hook.

Our sin matters, though. Our words and actions have a profound effect on those around us. That's why our choices and decisions must be evaluated in light of God's standards. And guess what? When we look at them honestly, we'll once again be overwhelmed by our need of a Savior. Bearing the weight of our sins is hard, heartbreaking work. The good news? Father God is waiting for us, arms wide open, ready to forgive.

Heavenly Father, shine Your light on the darkness in my life so I can come before You humbly to receive forgiveness. You alone are good. In Jesus' name, amen.

Outdoor Medicine

The whole earth is filled with awe at your wonders; where morning dawns, where evening fades, you call forth songs of joy (Psalm 65:8).

Scripture: Psalm 65:5-8
Song: "For the Beauty of the Earth"

Time spent outdoors is so good for the soul. Hiking, bird-watching, gardening, strolls on a beach . . . all immerse us in the soul-lifting glories of God's creation.

David, the shepherd boy, spent countless hours outside watching over the sheep. David loved God, believed in His goodness, and saw His handiwork in all creation. David spent time in that creation, soaking in the beauty of skies and landscapes. He spent outdoor time where God is the Creator and less time indoors with man's handiwork. Isn't that why he overflowed with songs of praise to the Lord?

Romans 1:20 tells us that merely observing creation should give us insight into the goodness of God. His power and His divinity are strikingly apparent in nature. If we say we can't find God, we have no excuse—because the intricacies and majesty of creation cry out His name.

Take a look out your window. What do you see? The skies, the trees, the mountains, or maybe the sea? Do you catch a glimpse of a bird flitting by? The brilliant colors of flowers? Every bit of creation was made by our loving, creative Father.

O God, today I'll take a dose of outdoor medicine. And I will join all the universe in praising You who made it all. I praise You for the beauty all around me, and I thank You for the endless wonders within all of us made in Your image. In Christ, amen.

A Glimpse of the Greatest Love

Say to God, "How awesome are your deeds! So great is your power that your enemies cringe before you. All the earth bows down to you" (Psalm 66:3, 4).

Scripture: Psalm 66:1-5
Song: "Jesus Paid It All"

My father served as a medic during the four years of World War II, assisting in surgeries and caring for the injured near combat zones. He witnessed the death of his best friend and received the Purple Heart for moving into a firefight to pull two injured men to safety. On the long trip home by ship at the end of the war, he cared for shell-shocked victims—those so traumatized by the horror of battle that they lost their ability to cope. My father was a hero who risked his own safety to save others.

Dad's service came with a cost, though. He was a quiet man, rarely sharing his feelings. But I saw him cry when he spoke of the war; his heart was broken by what he'd seen.

We love heroes because they demonstrate selflessness. They mirror the ultimate sacrifice ever given when God gave up the life of His Son to take the punishment for the sins of mankind. What better way to express love than by rescuing others—enduring their pain, their suffering?

We may never fully understand the cost to our heavenly Father in sending Jesus. But when you next read the story of a military hero, remember God's sacrifice too. He gave His best to restore our lives.

Thank You, **Dear Lord,** for Your gift of life. My freedom and my place in Your kingdom came at a great price. I'm forever grateful. Through my Lord Jesus, amen.

From All the Nations

They will bring all your people, from all the nations, to my holy mountain in Jerusalem as an offering to the LORD (Isaiah 66:20).

Scripture: Isaiah 66:18-23
Song: "There Is Nothing Too Good to Be True"

My husband and I travel to India and support Christian ministries there. It is exciting and humbling to hear the stories of those who once lived in fear of their gods but now trust Jesus. Many of these converts enjoy revealing the Bible verses that most affected their decision. Quite often a key passage is Matthew 18:12-14, in which Jesus is portrayed as leaving the 99 sheep in search of a single lost lamb. How powerful is the love of God, who cares for one tiny stray!

Another passage of Scripture that grateful converts share is Psalm 23, which shows the Good Shepherd caring for the "lamb's" every need. New Christians are openly baptized, joyous in their new faith, even though their public proclamation may be dangerous.

In India, conversion from one belief to another can be very costly. Those who find Jesus often leave friends and families behind and suffer accusations of "breaking caste," a form of betrayal. They know they may be beaten or even killed for their new faith. Yet those who take the good news of salvation to distant lands will reap a harvest, and the believers will be as an offering before God the Father. How beautiful!

Good Shepherd, thank You for Your love and gentle care. As I look forward to the day I'll see You face-to-face, please continue to sustain and protect all those who are entering the waters of baptism across the world. In Jesus' name, amen.

Benefits of a Clean Heart

Repent and be baptized, every one of you, in the name of Jesus Christ for the forgiveness of your sins (Acts 2:38).

Scripture: Acts 2:37-47
Song: "Thou Christ of Burning, Cleansing Flame"

An hour's drive from my home sits the quaint town of Aurora, Oregon, the site of a utopian Christian commune that flourished from 1856 to 1883. At its peak, it boasted 600 people, German and Swiss immigrant families who traveled the Oregon Trail from Missouri.

The Aurora colony was a success, though it lasted only until its leader, Wilhelm Keil, passed away. The 54 families who populated Aurora loved God; they worked hard to produce crops, furniture, and textiles and were hospitalble.

When Peter preached to the people, their hearts were stricken with remorse at killing the Lord. "What can we do?" they cried. Peter's response was stark and simple: repent.

And look at the fruit of that repentance: devotion to teaching, fellowship, common meals and prayer, sharing of earthly possessions, joyful hearts, and praise to God. Who wouldn't want such a beautiful lifestyle?

While harmonious Christian fellowship is available today, it can be elusive. Sin and selfishness can creep in and cause havoc. Peter pleaded with the people to save themselves from such things. It is good advice for us as well.

Dear Heavenly Father, You offer me a beautiful, rich life in Your family, the church. Thank You for the bounty You place before me. Help me to live in peace and harmony with my fellow believers. Through Christ I pray. Amen.

Want or Plenty?

You crown the year with your bounty, and your carts over-flow with abundance (Psalm 65:11).

Scripture: Psalm 65:1, 2, 9-13
Song: "O the Riches of My Savior"

Because I travel to India and witness abject poverty firsthand, I often marvel that so many Americans live below the poverty level. Here in the U.S., one of the richest nations in the world, huge numbers of families live with hunger, inadequate health care, poor education, and a culture of "not enough." How can that be?

In *The Glass Castle,* a beautifully written memoir, Jeannette Walls chronicles her life as one of four children painfully neglected, growing up with an alcoholic dreamer father and a selfish, mentally ill mother. The children were so severely neglected that it was a miracle they clung together. Yet late in the story, Jeannette's mother reveals that she owns a piece of land worth nearly a million dollars. All the years of hunger and want were totally unnecessary.

Sometimes our lives mimic that sad narrative. We live in God's kingdom and have available a life of spiritual abundance. We have more than enough, yet we live as if we're dirt poor.

And in the natural realm, what can we do to meet the needs of the poor around us? Can we give, share our knowledge, and love even better? Can we give a cup of cold water to those in need?

Lord, thank You for abundant life. Give me eyes to see the needs of those around me. Soften my heart to embrace a life of generosity. Through Jesus, amen.

Judgment and Promise

You covered it with the watery depths as with a garment; the waters stood above the mountains (Psalm 104:6).

Scripture: Psalm 104:5-9
Song: "Cleanse Me"

Have you ever tried to give a bath to a cat? With thick rubber gloves on his hands, my husband held our struggling feline while I tried to pour on water and shampoo, scrub, and rinse. The poor thing needed cleaning, but he didn't want anything to do with water, thank you very much! He gwrabbed the faucet and clawed and wiggled to free himself, but we finally accomplished our objective. After he'd dried off, he strutted around clean.

God covered the world with water to cleanse it from sin and give it a fresh start. When we bathed our cat, it was also to cleanse and give a fresh start. But oh, how he fought us!

And didn't many of us do that? Not seeing the depth of our sin, not eager to be cleansed, giving up the dirt of our lives seemed daunting. But when we did, when we fully submitted to our Lord in baptism, we knew that we had been cleansed and were "like new" with a fresh start. I'm thankful God chose such an overwhelming immersion, both physically and emotionally, so we could look back and identify the moment He washed us.

Almighty and Everlasting God, please forgive me when I can't see the sin in my life. Open my eyes to my selfishness and shortcomings, and instill a desire in my heart to submit to Your will. I know You always have my best in mind, and I want to please You in my words and actions. In the name of Christ I pray. Amen.

January 16–22. **Janet Mountjoy** and her husband are retired after ministering with churches for 35 years in Wisconsin, Nebraska, North Dakota, Florida, and Missouri.

Act of God—Naturally!

He waters the mountains from his upper chambers; the land is satisfied by the fruit of his work (Psalm 104:13).

Scripture: Psalm 104:10-18
Song: "Praise to the Lord, the Almighty"

Our son-in-law drove into about six inches of water covering a familiar street, not seeing that the manhole cover had been pushed away amid the torrent. Driving into the open manhole caused a lot of damage to his car, but the insurance company wouldn't cover it. Why? You may have guessed it: an "act of God" had caused the downpour.

Have you ever noticed how bad things are called acts of God, while good things almost never are? We live in an age that thrives on news of the tragic and the terrifying, yet overlooks the good and the beautiful around us. Why is that? Are we so confident in ourselves that we must blame God when something is out of our control?

Why can't the world see and acknowledge that a newborn baby is an act of God? That a young couple falling in love or a healed marriage are acts of God? Why is it so hard to acknowledge that everything growing around us, feeding us, shading us, and blessing us with beauty is an act of God? Even in our son-in-law's accident, he was not hurt, although he could have been seriously injured. And we could see God's protective hand in his life. Now *that* was an act of God!

Lord, I ask You to act on my behalf, yet I often miss seeing how many times You do, indeed, intervene. Please open my eyes to Your loving touch today, and help me freely offer the praise You deserve. In Christ's name, amen.

One Thing I'm Not

He made the moon to mark the seasons, and the sun knows when to go down (Psalm 104:19).

Scripture: Psalm 104:19-23
Song: "It Is Well with My Soul"

My husband and I enjoy camping as a respite from the every-day world and its cares. When the sun rises, we rise. We enjoy our day, but at twilight, we begin to slow down and settle in. When it's too dark to see well, we go to bed (we never go to bed early at home). The sun going down gives us some gear-shifting time to relax and reflect.

It's a peaceful time. The fresh air, the smell of the woods, and the night sounds remind us that it's God's world, and He's in control. Through His creation, He gives us sweet rest.

God has created everything with a pattern, but we've pretty well messed up that pattern with our gadgets, technology, and busyness. It's impractical to wish us back to the time when we had no electricity, but God did give us daytime to accomplish our work and nighttime to rest.

These days, we seldom quit when the sun goes down, so occasionally it's good to go back to His design for a healthy and rested life. It's amazing how experiencing God's creation helps to clear our minds and give us time to meditate on the awesome power and love of our Creator. It puts things in perfect perspective: there is one God . . . and I'm not Him.

Lord, I will be still in Your presence in this moment. Forgive me when I get caught up in the hurry-and-worry life this world offers. May I recollect who You are and who I am in You, during a few quiet moments in my day. Through Christ, amen.

Worthy of Praise Forever

I will sing to the Lord all my life; I will sing praise to my God as long as I live (Psalm 104:33).

Scripture: Psalm 104:31-35
Song: "I Could Sing of Your Love Forever"

One night our small church decided to visit one of our charter members in her nursing home to celebrate her birthday. She was an Alzheimer's victim and didn't recognize any of us. She didn't remember whose birthday it was, even though she asked several times (and was thrilled each time to find it was hers).

She didn't seem to remember much about anything . . . until we started singing. Her eyes lit up, and she joyfully sang every hymn and song, knowing every word—even from verses that we didn't remember ourselves. It was a beautiful glimpse into her heart, revealing what lingered in her memory.

We were touched deeply that night. This woman's memory seemed to be gone. And yet she remembered her Creator. In her sweet and innocent way, she praised God with a spiritual depth that many of us have not yet attained.

God hadn't become important to her just that night or just that year. He wasn't even important to her only in those songs. Her relationship with Him had begun many years before and had continued, even though others in her life had faded. I'm sure she must have prayed as David did, "May my meditation be pleasing to him, as I rejoice in the Lord" (v. 34).

Father God, You are my breath and my life. I pray that the meditations of my heart will be pleasing to You, and that I will be able to sing praises to You as long as I live. In the holy name of Jesus, my Lord and Savior, I pray. Amen.

A Lifetime to Praise

Through the praise of children and infants you have established a stronghold against your enemies, to silence the foe and the avenger (Psalm 8:2).

Scripture: Psalm 8
Song: "O Lord, Our Lord"

When our children and grandchildren were born, the first song I sang to them was "Jesus Loves Me." They didn't understand what I sang, but in a short time, it became one of their favorites. It's moving to hear a little child singing and believing that Jesus loves him, even before understanding the awesome truth. As the children grew, other songs became their favorites, songs that took on new meaning as they experienced life.

My mother, who lived to be 99, could sing by heart most of the hymns she had sung in her younger days, like "Amazing Grace" and "I Come to the Garden Alone." She would also sing the newer praise songs like "You are My King" and "Lead Me to the Cross." She preferred the hymns, but joyfully sang all the songs because they all glorified God.

I loved sitting beside her and hearing her sing. During her last hours, our family gathered to sing with her (not *to,* but *with*).

What amazing gifts God gave us by giving us hearts and lips with which to praise Him. It's a timeless gift that we can use from the cradle to the grave, alone or alongside others.

Almighty and most merciful God, I thank You for the blessing of song with which to praise You. I pray that my heart and my lips will be as innocent as a child's, and that Your foes will be silenced by my praise to You. In the name of Jesus, who lives and reigns with You and the Holy Spirit, one God, now and forever, amen.

Valued by God

Look at the birds of the air; they do not sow or reap or store away in barns, and yet your heavenly Father feeds them. Are you not much more valuable than they? (Matthew 6:26).

Scripture: Matthew 6:25-34
Song: "A Shelter in the Time of Storm"

We lived in Fargo, North Dakota, during its worst winter—eight blizzards and 117 inches of snow, followed by an overland flood. We fed birds throughout that winter, yet realized that on the days the blizzards howled, it was impossible for them to find the food. We saw a few birds perched in leafless bushes and wondered how they could possibly survive. But as soon as the storms subsided, they'd be back, fluttering around the feeder and picking up other seed we'd thrown out for them.

Through that winter, we knew God provided for those little birds. They didn't ask for food; it was just there. That winter we were a part of God's provision, of course. But most of the time, He provided in other ways. And doesn't He do that for us?

We often beg God to intervene or provide. But how many times do we not even think to ask—because God takes care of us so consistently and generously that we don't give it a second thought; it's always there. What a loving Father we have, to provide even when we don't ask (and even when we don't thank Him). Because He values us even more than the beloved birds.

Heavenly Father, our wonderful provider, please open my eyes to the many things You provide for me every day—and give me a thankful heart. And may I see the needs of others as clearly as I could see the needs of birds in a storm. In the precious name of Jesus I pray. Amen.

Beautiful and Shareable

Praise the LORD, my soul. LORD, my God, you are very great; you are clothed with splendor and majesty (Psalm 104:1).

Scripture: Psalm 104:1-4, 24-30
Song: "Beautiful Savior"

During our weekly ladies' Bible study, the young children played right outside in our fenced-in backyard. In the middle of our study one day, they burst in with their hands full of tomatoes—*all* my tomatoes—some pink, most very green and tiny. They saw no wrong in what they'd done. They had merely found something beautiful and wanted to share it.

Isn't God's creation beautiful and "shareable"? We see His majesty in all He created. From the sunrise in the morning to the sunset of the evening, we see His handiwork. In the highest mountain and tiniest tomato, we see His power and gentleness.

Yes, God's heavenly creation clothes Him, and His earthly creation praises and is renewed by Him. Looking into the heavens is a reminder that if He can create and control the whole universe, He surely can know and work out the details in my life. How can we resist sharing that hope?

The kids never picked my tomatoes again. But that day is actually special in my memory. It was a display of God's creation, both in my tomatoes and in the innocent and generous little hands that picked them for gifts.

Father, I see Your majesty in everything You've created. Please help me to remember Your love and have confidence in Your power to work within the tiniest details of my life. Encourage me that I may encourage others with Your love. In Christ, amen.

Even If You Aren't Musical . . .

Let everything that has breath praise the Lord. Praise the Lord! (Psalm 150:6, *NKJV*).

Scripture: Psalm 150
Song: "Praise Him! Praise Him!"

Nearly 2,000 musical instruments exist in the world, but I can't play one of them. My two brothers took music lessons, though. One brother studied violin; the other studied steel guitar. The guitar player excelled and became a professional musician. The violin student gave up after a year of "fiddling" around instead of practicing faithfully. I pursued golf instead of music.

Psalm 150 offers good reasons to praise God and mentions a number of instruments with which to do it. But if we can't play an instrument, must we remain silent? Not at all! If we have breath—and we do—we ought to use it to praise the Lord.

It doesn't matter whether our voice sounds like that of a bullfrog or a chipmunk, when we use it to praise the Lord, it must sound as melodic to Him as a finely tuned orchestra.

Some of the most joyful, praise-full people I have known experienced so much pain that they could hardly move their feet or clutch a coffee mug. But they used their voices to tell of God's goodness. Which tells me that we have a choice: focus on our troubles and give voice to a mournful dirge, or focus on God and sing a joyful doxology.

Dear Heavenly Father, I praise You for who You are and for Your mighty deeds. May my life as well as my words praise You! In Jesus' name, amen.

January 23–29. **Jim Dyet** is a retired pastor and editor. He and his wife, Gloria, have been married 58 years and live in Colorado Springs. Jim enjoys golf and daily walks with his three dogs.

The Ultimate Witness

Where were you when I laid the earth's foundation? Tell me, if you understand (Job 38:4).

Scripture: Job 38:1-7
Song: "How Great Thou Art"

I like to play golf, although some non-golfers tell me it's foolish to chase a little white ball around on the grass. I simply shrug off the criticism. However, I must confess that a bad day of golf almost persuades me to agree with the critics. Still, I eagerly anticipate the next opportunity to play.

Some golfers have achieved a hole in one. I haven't, but maybe someday that little white ball will fly from a tee box and roll right into the hole. Yippee! But what if that blessed event happens when I am playing alone? Only those who know I am truthful would believe it happened.

Space exploration intent on discovering how the world began has cost millions of dollars, but the search has not supplied an answer. God alone was present when everything began, and He told us He created everything. He is the ultimate witness. Can we believe Him? (Hint: He cannot lie; see Titus 1:2.)

And what an amazing, beautiful world God created for our enjoyment and His glory! Although nature bears the marks of the fall in the Garden of Eden, it still reflects God's benevolence and glory. Let's take time today to enjoy and appreciate the wonder of God's creation. (Second hint: golf courses are beautiful.)

Father in Heaven, I thank You for the wisdom, power, and love You demonstrate in creating all things. As Your created and redeemed child, I want to join all nature in glorifying You today. I ask in Your Son's name. Amen.

The Pursuit of Wisdom

The LORD possessed me at the beginning of His way, before His works of old (Proverbs 8:22, *NASB*).

Scripture: Proverbs 8:22-31
Song: "Ye Servants of God"

Thomas Edison may have been a genius. But was he wise? About a century ago he championed the belief that DC (direct current) electricity was superior to AC (alternating current). He tried to discredit AC by demonstrating that it was more dangerous than DC. However, his attempt was foolish, futile, and cruel. He electrocuted a number of animals, starting with small animals and ending with an elephant named Topsy. To Edison's dismay, his country chose AC as the nation's electrical standard.

Unlike human wisdom that can lapse or be replaced by stupidity, God's wisdom neither lapses nor succumbs to foolishness. Further, God's wisdom is eternal. It "partnered" with Him in the creation of all things.

We live in a world where human beings and nations often relate to one another in unwise and uncivil ways. So it's wonderful to know that you and I can access genuine wisdom and use it to forge good relationships.

Of course, we gain wisdom by fearing the Lord (Psalm 111:10). That's why a highly educated person may possess a ton of information but not an ounce of wisdom. On the other hand, a believer who fears the Lord can possess and use wisdom, no matter his level of formal education. Let's walk wisely today!

Heavenly Father, You are the source of genuine wisdom. Help me draw from Your wisdom today so I will make decisions that honor You. In Jesus' name, amen.

Parting with Homegrown Sheep

The angel said to them, "Do not be afraid; for behold, I bring you good news of great joy which will be for all the people" (Luke 2:10, *NASB*).

Scripture: Luke 2:8-14
Song: "Worthy Is the Lamb"

Two young brothers, ages roughly 9 and 7, approached me after I had preached at a rural church. "Come, see our sheep," they said. So my wife and I followed the boys to a trailer in the parking lot, where two beautifully groomed sheep stood inside. The boys explained they were 4-H Club members and had raised the sheep to sell at auction. That afternoon they'd sell their homegrown sheep. Their words came slowly and softly, a clear indication that parting with their sheep would be heartrending.

It must be difficult for every 4-H Club member to part with an animal he or she has cared for so meticulously and lovingly. I'm sure God understands the sadness. After all, He parted with His dear Son, when He sent Him into the world to be our Savior. Until that amazing parting, throughout eternity God the Father and God the Son had enjoyed face-to-face fellowship.

How appropriate that the angels brought the good news of Jesus' birth to a group of shepherds! They were the first recipients of the announcement that the Lamb of God had been born.

How astounding is the love God bestowed on the world when He parted with His dear Son, the Lamb of God! What shall we offer Him in return?

Heavenly Father, thank You for parting with Your beloved Son, who made it possible for You to receive me into Your forever family. In Jesus' name, amen.

No Room at the Inns

When you beat your olive trees, you shall not go over the boughs again; it shall be for the stranger, the fatherless, and the widow (Deuteronomy 24:20, *NKJV*).

Scripture: Deuteronomy 24:17-22
Song: "Teach Me Thy Way, O Lord"

The first week of January may not be the best time to drive across western Kansas or eastern Colorado. Our neighbors, a fine Christian couple, found that to be true. Returning from Philadelphia, where they had spent Christmas and New Year's with relatives, they were returning to Colorado Springs, when a sudden, late-day blizzard shut down the interstate to the west and stranded them in a small Kansas town. Because all the motels were full, they resolved to hang out at the local Walmart until the interstate reopened in the morning.

My wife read about our neighbors' plight on Facebook and told me where they were stranded. Since I had preached in that town many times, I called a church family, asked if they could help my neighbors, and gave the family our neighbors' cell phone number. Soon our neighbors were settled into a warm home for the night.

Today's Scripture is just one of the Bible's many commands to help those in need, including strangers. I am grateful that Christians in a small Kansas town responded positively to help a couple of stranded strangers. By doing so, they demonstrated Christian love in action (and set an example for the rest of us).

Father, I can't meet all the needs that exist in the world, but help me do what I can to show others what it means to be charitable and hospitable in Your name. Amen.

Click Amen

The LORD is near to all who call upon Him, to all who call upon Him in truth. He will fulfill the desire of those who fear Him; He also will hear their cry and save them (Psalm 145:18, 19, *NKJV*).

Scripture: Psalm 145:13-21
Song: "I Will Call upon the Lord"

If I send a letter to my brother in Canada, he might receive it a week later. Now, thanks to e-mail, I can address a message to him, click Send, and he receives it instantly. E-mail also puts me in immediate touch with friends in the United States, Canada, my native Scotland, Germany, Australia, India, and the United Arab Emirates. I don't know how e-mail works, although I know satellites are involved. Fortunately, I don't have to understand; I just have to compose a message and click Send. It's amazing, to say the least.

Here's something I find even more amazing. I can call on God anytime with any praise, concern, request, or need. I suppose I don't have to "click" Amen at the end of my prayer, but I prefer to do so, and I have the assurance that God receives my message. He is near, He hears instantly, and He responds.

It seems incredible that a person might send numerous e-mail messages in a single day, yet fail to pray. If I had to choose between e-mailing or praying, I would choose to pray and forgo e-mail. Wouldn't prayer be your choice too?

Dear Father in Heaven, I thank You for drawing near when I call on You. May I stay in close fellowship with You at all times through prayer! In the name of the Father and of the Son and of the Holy Spirit, amen.

Heaven and Earth Praise the Lord

Praise the LORD from the earth, sea monsters and all deeps (Psalm 148:7, *NASB*).

Scripture: Psalm 148
Song: "All Creatures of Our God and King"

Psalm 148 summons people, animals, and inanimate objects to praise the Lord. I know people can praise the Lord, but how can animals and inanimate objects praise Him? Did the psalmist know something I don't?

Then I reasoned that the psalmist must have perceived animals and inanimate objects as praising the Lord by displaying His creative genius. For example, dolphins possess remarkable intelligence. Migratory birds fly long distances to their exact destinations. All animals instinctively care for their newborns. In cold climates, perennial flowers go dormant but come back to life in the spring. In all this, God's genius is praised.

Our three little dogs do not sing praises to the Lord, but their behavior reflects His intelligent design. They awake at the same time every day, and at 9:00 p.m. they tell me it's their bedtime. They also let me know when it's time for a walk. At precisely the same time every evening, they sit in front of my wife to inform her it's their mealtime. At 6:00 p.m., when I get comfortable in my recliner, they sit in front of me and stare at me, signaling they want their daily cheese bites.

In ways we may not understand, all of God's creation praises Him. Let's join the choir!

Heavenly Father, please open my eyes to see Your fingerprints in nature, and open my mouth to join all nature in praising You. Through Christ the Lord, amen.

I'm Doing My Part

After beginning by means of the Spirit, are you now trying to finish by means of the flesh? (Galatians 3:3).

Scripture: Galatians 3:1-5
Song: "Believe on the Lord Jesus Christ"

I introduced myself to Lynn. Like me, she was sitting in the nursing home lobby waiting to see an old friend. Lynn's friend was dying, and doctors could offer little hope of seeing another month. "I trust she knows the Lord," I said, casually.

"Oh, I'm sure she does," said Lynn without hesitation. "She has certainly done her part to get into Heaven."

Lynn then went on to explain how involved her dying friend was with her many charities, which opened the door for me to share with her what the apostle Paul had to say on the subject. "In essence," I concluded, "the Bible says that good deeds have nothing to do with our salvation. Paul told the Philippian jailer that the only thing he had to do to get into Heaven was to believe. That's the only 'doing' involved."

"Good works are commendable," I continued. "But the irony is that those who count on them to enter God's Heaven won't get past the gate."

A sigh of relief appeared across Lynn's face, as she realized that Christ's death on the cross didn't just *partially* pay her way into Heaven. It took care of the transaction completely.

Lord, I rejoice that salvation demands only belief on our part. All I have to do is receive the free gift of salvation, not work for it. Thank You, Lord, through Christ. Amen.

January 30, 31. **Paul Tatham**, now retired, was a Christian school administrator and teacher for 44 years. He continues to write for Christian publications and lead Bible studies.

Benefits of Obedience

Through your offspring all nations on earth will be blessed, because you have obeyed me (Genesis 22:18).

Scripture: Genesis 22:15-18
Song: "Bless Us Children Now"

Kevin was a bright kid with a problem. He readily caught on to new concepts that his middle-school science teacher presented and eagerly elbowed his way into any class discussion—whether he had anything worth saying or not. Let's just say that Kevin liked to dominate classroom conversations.

To make matters worse, Kevin could be downright rude. And because of his lack of social skills, Kevin wasn't popular with his teachers or his classmates. Other kids avoided him, and teachers prayed he'd be assigned to someone else's class.

Kevin frequented the principal's office on a monthly basis too, usually as part of a joint conference with his parents—along with a principal bent on persuading them that Kevin's classroom behavior verged on suspension, if not expulsion.

But the parents were as uncooperative as their son. They defended him with a "boys will be boys" attitude. Was it any wonder that Kevin felt at liberty to continue his wayward ways? He had never really learned to obey, nor grasped the benefits that accompany a teachable spirit.

Abraham's obedience to God resulted in both his salvation and the blessing of all mankind through the coming Messiah. There's a lesson plan for all of us.

Lord God, I confess that obeying You doesn't always come easily. Help me to see the heavenly benefits that make it all worthwhile. In Christ's name, amen.

thank you!

DEVOTIONS®

► **February**

And whatever you do, whether in word or deed, do it all in the name of the Lord Jesus, giving thanks to God the Father through him.

—*Colossians 3:17*

Gary Wilde, Editor | Margaret K. Williams, Project Editor | Photo © Liquid Library

DEVOTIONS® is published quarterly by Standard Publishing, Cincinnati, Ohio, www.standardpub.com. Copyright © 2015 by Standard Publishing. All rights reserved. Topics based on the Home Daily Bible Readings, International Sunday School Lessons. Copyright © 2013 by the Committee on the Uniform Series. Printed in the U.S.A. All Scripture quotations, unless otherwise indicated, are taken from the *HOLY BIBLE, NEW INTERNATIONAL VERSION®. NIV®.* Copyright © 1973, 1978, 1984, 2011 by Biblica, Inc.® Used by permission of Zondervan. All rights reserved worldwide. Scripture quotations marked (*NKJV*) are taken from the *New King James Version®.* Copyright © 1982 by Thomas Nelson, Inc. Used by permission. All rights reserved.

No Free Lunch

If the inheritance depends on the law, then it no longer depends on the promise; but God in his grace gave it to Abraham through a promise (Galatians 3:18).

Scripture: Galatians 3:15-18
Song: "Grace Greater Than Our Sin"

I bumped into Malcolm, a friend from church, at Home Depot. He was on a mission to purchase the perfect ladder to use in his lawn-service business. Several of the ladders were less expensive than the one he was examining, and I drew his attention to that fact.

"Yah, those are nice," he said. "But they don't last. Look at the hinges—cheaply made. You get what you pay for." According to Malcolm, if you want quality—something that will last—you have to pay top dollar. In other words, there's no free lunch.

And he was right. Virtually nothing in life that has real value comes free of charge. In fact, there's a high correlation between quality and price, and the closer an item gets to "free" the closer it gets to "worthless." No store just gives away quality stuff.

But there is one great exception to the get-what-you-pay-for rule: God's salvation. An eternal home in Heaven is far the most valuable thing anyone can ever own. Yet, amazingly, it's absolutely free of charge. It cost Jesus everything; it costs us nothing.

Thank You, **Lord**, for the priceless gift Your Son provided through the cross. The only requirement to receive it is that I be a repentant sinner. In Jesus' name, amen.

February 1–5. **Paul Tatham**, now retired, was a Christian school administrator and teacher for 44 years. He continues to write for Christian publications and lead Bible studies.

When the Lights Went Out

Even so the body is not made up of one part but of many (1 Corinthians 12:14).

Scripture: 1 Corinthians 12:12-18
Song: "Make Me a Blessing"

Ted Higgins was a retired electrician with a secret. A widower for the last 10 years, he continued to faithfully attend his beloved church alone. To skip a service was unthinkable to Ted. And he always arrived early, usually before everyone else.

Before greeting a few other early birds, Ted would dash down a side stairway into the basement and open the door to a small, dusty closet. With a little flashlight he always carried, Ted would open the electrical fuse box mounted on the wall, inspecting it quickly to make sure no fuses had blown since the last church service. If one had, he would replace it with an extra fuse he kept in his pocket. Over the years, Ted had replaced several fuses and managed to avert many electrical blackouts.

Then it happened. During a special evening service, the lights went dark, the sound system died, and the air conditioner slowly whined to a stop. Before anyone else could respond, Ted bolted downstairs and had everything up and running in less than a minute.

Ted had a talent, a gift, that he used in service to his fellow believers—quietly, behind the scenes. Every Christian also has a spiritual gift to offer. The question is, are you using yours?

Lord, I'm thankful that You have gifted each one of us. We all have some special ability that we can use to advance the kingdom of God. Help me to discover my gift and then use it to edify others within the body of Christ. In Jesus' name, amen.

Not Ashamed to Meet You

Continue in him, so that when he appears we may be confident and unashamed before him (1 John 2:28).

Scripture: 1 John 2:28–3:3
Song: "O the Bitter Shame and Sorrow"

Over 600 teenage students poured into the high school gymnasium from all four entrances and quickly took their assigned seats on the bleachers. It was the end of the school year, and they excitedly jabbered with each other about their summer plans. They also considered their prospects of being recognized in this, the annual Awards Day ceremony.

The principal stepped to the microphone, welcomed the students, and briefly challenged them with the benefits of hard work and dedication. "As you can see, I'm pleased to announce that we have more winners this year than in the past," he said, pointing to the trophy table spread before him.

The awards recognized outstanding accomplishments in academics, athletics, and citizenship. The ceremony dragged on for two hours, with so many plaques, trophies, and ribbons distributed that it seemed almost every kid in the school won something.

Except me. I kept listening for my name but finally surrendered to the inevitable: I was going home with nothing. I wasn't bitter, but I was ashamed.

When we Christians meet the Lord at the judgment seat of Christ (see 2 Corinthians 5:10)—Heaven's Awards Day—we will not suffer shame. We will be filled.

Lord, I don't want to leave that heavenly Awards Day with nothing to show for it. Help me use Your great gift of salvation to great effect each day. Through Christ, amen.

Take Off, Put On

As God's chosen people, holy and dearly loved, clothe yourselves with compassion, kindness, humility, gentleness and patience (Colossians 3:12).

Scripture: Colossians 3:12-17
Song: "The Fruit of the Spirit"

One of television's most popular series was *Downton Abbey,* a Public Broadcasting System hit that transports viewers back to a much simpler, more civil era.

Set in early twentieth-century England, in the fictional Yorkshire country estate of Downton Abbey, the story follows an aristocratic family and those who serve it. The opulent surroundings and a lifestyle of leisure amid dynastic wealth lulls the program's faithful fans into a kind of fantasy world of indulgence.

One of several attention-grabbing aspects of this pampered lifestyle is the number of wardrobe changes required. The lords and ladies are constantly changing their clothing, with the aid of the ever-ready "downstairs" staff. There are different outfits for meals, outings, and post-supper entertainments, so leading players are continually taking off and putting on.

In Colossians 3, Paul tells believers that they should be doing the same thing. Not with clothing, but with attitudes and habits. We need to take off such things as lust or a quick temper and replace them with the fruit of the Spirit—kindness, mercy, meekness, and such. We do this, knowing we're headed toward a heavenly estate that far surpasses Downton Abbey.

O Christ, keep my focus on things above, where my true citizenship lies. Give me courage to cast aside sin and put on Your matchless character. In Your name, amen.

Perfect Timing

When the set time had fully come, God sent his Son, born of a woman, born under the law, to redeem those under the law (Galatians 4:4, 5).

Scripture: Galatians 3:26–4:7
Song: "The Sure Foundation"

Often, the success or failure of something uttered or initiated hinges on timing. A joke can fall flat if it's offered at the wrong time. A new business can go belly-up in mere months if its investors misjudge the current business climate. It's the same all along Wall Street—it's all about *when* to make a move.

The Father sent His Son when the stage was perfectly set. I prefer the *King James* rendering, "when the fulness of the time was come." It smacks of precision. When angels heralded the birth of the babe of Bethlehem, the vaunted Roman Empire ruled the civilized world. Their disciplined armies controlled a vast swath of land from England to the Sahara, from Gibraltar to the Caspian Sea. They were in charge; they kept the peace.

Though highly regarded, and often feared, the Romans managed to keep anarchy at bay, standardize language, build thousands of roads, and impose a system of government that rewarded obedience while punishing lawbreakers.

Up until that time, there had never been an empire that could match Rome's successes. And that empire provided a perfect setting, and perfect timing, for the birth of a perfect Savior.

Father, Your timing is perfect. You know what to do and when to do it. I stand amazed at Your providential control over the affairs of the world, from the rise of nations to the remarkable precision of the planets. All glory to You, in Jesus' name. Amen.

Right on Time

May [God] grant you according to your heart's desire, and fulfill all your purpose (Psalm 20:4, *NKJV*).

Scripture: Galatians 4:1-7
Song: "Right on Time"

You had been going the extra mile at work for several weeks, working hard to get that job promotion. Much to your dismay, someone with less seniority got the position, and you were overlooked—again!

You know God has given you the gift and talent for writing, so you write . . . and write . . . Unfortunately, you've received more rejections than you'd ever care to admit—and sometimes you wonder if it's really worth all the hours and late nights.

Today's passage in Galatians gives me hope—particularly the first part of verse 4, *NKJV*: "But when the fullness of the time had come." Prophecies of the Messiah had flowed forth. People watched and waited . . . and waited. Did they ever grow tired of waiting for the Messiah to come?

But God didn't forget! In the fullness of time, He acted.

It's not easy waiting for dreams to become reality, but be encouraged. The God of the universe, who could be trusted to bring salvation for the entire world, at the right time, can be trusted to handle every part of our lives. And that includes the dreams He has given us, those we have yet to attain.

Father, I trust You, even with my dreams, because You care about every part of my life. Thank You for working all things together for my good. Through Christ, amen.

February 6–12. **Tyler Myers** lives in Jeromesville, Ohio, with his loving family and Golden Lab, Ben. He is a freelance writer in the Christian market and works at a print shop.

The Path to Prosperity

Keep the charge of the LORD your God: to walk in His ways . . . that you may prosper in all that you do and wherever you turn (1 Kings 2:3, *NKJV*).

Scripture: 1 Kings 2:1-4
Song: "Walk in Jerusalem"

If you posed the question "What's the path to prosperity?" you would likely get a number of different answers. Some people might tell you that getting a good education is the path to prosperity. Some folks believe you have to follow the money. Some people might think it all depends on whom you know.

Others would say, "The path to prosperity lies within yourself; blaze your own trail." And still others may declare, "There's no substitute for hard work. Roll up your sleeves, start at the bottom of the ladder, and work your way to the top!"

However, in our Scripture today, David gave his son Solomon a wonderful answer to our question. Interestingly enough, being highly educated, having a lot of money, knowing all the "right" people, making your own way, and working hard to get to the top didn't make the list. Rather, it's "Walk in God's ways."

That makes sense, doesn't it? As Jesus once said: "What profit is it to a man if he gains the whole world, and loses his own soul?" (Matthew 16:26, *NKJV*). Though it's not the world's way, it really is the only path to true prosperity.

Father, I'm glad that true riches come from You. Because of You, I am prosperous in the things that matter most. Thank You for all the wonderful blessings You have given to me down through the years. In Jesus' name, amen.

Strength Perfected

He said to me, **"My grace is sufficient for you, for My strength is made perfect in weakness."** Therefore most gladly I will rather boast in my infirmities, that the power of Christ may rest upon me (2 Corinthians 12:9, *NKJV*).

Scripture: 2 Corinthians 12:7-10
Song: "They Who Seek the Throne of Grace"

I have cerebral palsy, which affects my balance, coordination, vision, and walking. Thank God, I have a Christian family who is very loving, supportive, and understanding.

Even though the kind of cerebral palsy I have is milder than other kinds (which is a blessing), there are times when I have let my frustrations get the best of me. I am not proud of it, but I admit that I've had times of anger, despair, self-pity, and envy—especially when I make the mistake of comparing my life with someone else's. It's easy to think that others have it "so much better."

However, when I stop focusing on myself, put on the "garment of praise," and start focusing on God and His promises, I come back to reality. I recall the apostle's words in our verse today, and it's not long before my joy returns.

I don't understand all of God's ways. But my lack of knowledge doesn't, in any way, cancel out His goodness toward me. And it's great to remember that in my most imperfect moments, His perfection shines.

Heavenly Father, You love me unconditionally, caring for me every moment of every day. I can still rest in You, especially when I feel the weakest, knowing that Your plan for me is good and Your strength working through me is perfect. I could never thank You enough for that awesome reality! In Jesus' name I pray. Amen.

Just Not Worth It

What good is it for someone to gain the whole world, and yet lose or forfeit their very self? (Luke 9:25).

Scripture: Luke 9:23-27, 57-62
Song: "I'd Rather Have Jesus"

A rich and famous actor is often adored by millions. For that person, money is no object. He or she can live in a mansion, wear the classiest clothes, travel the world, and pamper the taste buds by wining and dining at the finest restaurants around. A famous rock star also has the kind of life many people dream of: having gold and platinum albums, playing to thousands of screaming fans, and having millions of followers on social media.

But all this fame and fortune will not slow down the inevitable: one day, to the sadness of family, friends, and fans galore, the rich and famous will finally take their last breath, like all of us will—and then the judgment.

Today I'm reminded that earthly fame and fortune—no matter how delightful—does not last. However, God and His kingdom do.

Of course, being rich and famous isn't a sin. It can even be a great blessing, especially for someone who sincerely loves the Lord. Imagine the joy of investing millions in the cause of the kingdom. As John Wesley once quipped, regarding the Christian and his money: "Earn all you can, save all you can, give all you can."

Heavenly Father, thank You for taking care of me, and especially for ministering to the desires of my heart. You and your eternal treasures are far greater than any earthly wealth and pleasures. In Jesus' name, amen.

Life and Peace

To be carnally minded is death, but to be spiritually minded is life and peace (Romans 8:6, *NKJV*).

Scripture: Romans 8:1-11
Song: "Peace, Perfect Peace"

OK, I confess: I have a habit of letting my mind wander—a lot! Don't get me wrong—it's not like I wake up every morning intending to be so scatterbrained, but it's so easy to do!

Sadly, what's *easy* to do often isn't what's *right* to do. Even though it's so easy to let my mind wander wherever it feels like going, when I do that, my mind—like a rebellious teenager—ends up wandering off into places it should never be. If left unchecked, things get worse—and then I find myself in a mental mess.

So what's the key, and how do I achieve victory in this mental battle? The last part of Romans 8:6 gives me the way forward: "to be spiritually minded is life and peace."

Filling my mind with Scripture, or having a Christian song in my heart, is invaluable to me in my quest for mental health and wholeness. Recalling my mind to Christ and His Word occasionally throughout my day is not always easy to do, but it's possible. And it's no doubt what Paul meant when he said in 1 Thessalonians 5:17, "Pray continually."

The bottom line? If I want the life and peace of mind that Romans 8:6 talks about, I must be intentional with how I use my mind—and think in ways that honor my Lord.

Heavenly Father, thank You for transforming my mind, by the power of Your Spirit. It's an ongoing process, and I want to submit to it each day. Through Christ, amen.

I Don't Have To!

We are debtors—not to the flesh, to live according to the flesh (Romans 8:12, *NKJV*).

Scripture: Romans 8:12-17
Song: "Victory in Jesus"

I just love food. Pizza, pastries, frozen yogurt, and chocolate are only some of the foods I crave. When I'm at an all-you-can-eat buffet—which is a joyous occasion of nearly indescribable proportions—self-control is quickly forgotten, as I continue to eat . . . and eat. Though my taste buds are in ecstasy, my voluminous eating is not without consequences; I am overweight, and I've committed the sin of gluttony so many times.

After all the times of being uncomfortable from stuffing myself, literally gasping for air while I put my shoes on, and not liking my overweight appearance, you would think I'd have a better handle on this problem. Sadly, not giving in is sometimes just as uncomfortable as eating too much.

Thankfully, Romans 8:12 gives me much-needed encouragement. Though I am a debtor, my debt is "not to the flesh, to live according to the flesh."

Easy and fun? No! Sometimes I want to keep eating. However, because of the indwelling Christ and His power, I don't *have* to. With God's help, I will eat less, I will lose weight, and I will learn to eat more wisely. (And no doubt I'll enjoy the food even more too.)

Father, thank You for giving me Your power—and thank You for giving me the power of choice. With Your help, God, I don't have to let food be the focus of my life. And I pray You'll help everyone who struggles in this area. Through Christ's name, amen.

Truth's Double-Edged Sword

Have I therefore become your enemy because I tell you the truth? (Galatians 4:16, *NKJV*).

Scripture: Galatians 4:8-20
Song: "Truehearted, Wholehearted"

Telling someone the truth is quite a double-edged sword. For example, the truth "God loves you the way you are" can bring comfort and encouragement to a young person in middle school who struggles daily with his image and self-esteem. On the other hand, if someone hears the truth "You're selfish and rude!" she may get angry, be offended, and shut out the person who was bold enough to be so honest.

In today's Scripture passage, the apostle Paul dished out some hard-hitting truths—even to the point of letting people know he feared that he had labored for them in vain. And Paul knew his candid honesty would do more than ruffle a few feathers. He bluntly asked: "Have I therefore become your enemy because I tell you the truth?"

But he spoke out of love. He was concerned about believers who, after having known God's grace, had turned back to living a life based on rules that would enslave them.

I know from experience that the truth can hurt. However, though it's not easy to hear, I'm thankful when someone who loves me tells it like it is.

Almighty and most merciful God, I know the truth can hurt. But please help me to be thankful and know Your love when Your people speak to me honestly. Please help me to be thankful and see the love someone has for me in telling me a painful truth. I pray this prayer in the name of Jesus, my merciful Savior and Lord. Amen.

The Message of the Cross

The message of the cross is foolishness to those who are perishing, but to us who are being saved it is the power of God (1 Corinthians 1:18).

Scripture: 1 Corinthians 1:18-25
Song: "Near the Cross"

I noticed five different crosses as I went about doing my errands one morning—two affixed to church buildings and three adorning the necks of people. I also thought about the woman's response on a radio talk show as to whether or not she wore cross jewelry. "Well, actually I have several crosses that I wear," she said, "but none have Jesus on them. Jesus isn't still on the cross, you know, or in the grave either."

No, Jesus isn't in the grave, but is now sitting in a place of honor by the throne of God (see Hebrews 12:2). He went through a lot to get there, of course; yet He did this solely on behalf of humanity. And although it is mere foolishness to some, the truth of Jesus' death, burial, and resurrection still remains the source of incomparable power.

According to Paul, those calling the cross "foolishness" are the ones perishing. However, without the cross of Calvary we would all perish, for we would have no hope. Or, as the apostle would later write: "If only for this life we have hope in Christ, we are of all people most to be pitied" (1 Corinthians 15:19).

O God, forgive my foolish ways. I admit I've not always seen the message of the cross as it truly is. It is glorious—and lifesaving! Through Christ, amen.

February 13–19. **Jimmie Oliver Fleming,** of Chester, Virginia, has started a company called T.R.Y., which includes a monthly movie night with her senior neighbors.

Talk It Up!

Love the LORD your God with all your heart and with all your soul and with all your strength (Deuteronomy 6:5).

Scripture: Deuteronomy 6:4-9
Song: "I Love You, Lord"

"This is a very good deal," the cashier said, as I arrived at the register with my two boxes of discounted Christmas cards. "They don't usually mark these down."

"Is that why they disappeared so fast?" I asked.

"Well . . . we did have to make space for Valentine's Day cards."

And even before the Christmas season had ended! Still, early promotion of Valentine's Day was a good idea, I thought, and could also serve as a reminder of God's love, and a reminder to also love Him.

God long ago gave Israel the command proclaimed in our verse, and it certainly applies to all His people today as well. Furthermore, God wants us to write His commandments on our hearts. Why? So we'll be constantly ready to share them. In other words, "Talk it up!"

I know one lady who's famous for saying these words. Yet it isn't just lip service with her. She lives out her philosophy, especially when it comes to her grandchildren. She often brings them to church with her, and my guess is that she "talks up" the Word of God with them along the way. I'm striving to follow that example, and perhaps you are too.

Thank You, **God,** for the love You give to me every day of my life. It feels especially good today on this "Love Day." You are so kind, Lord, it's easy to love You with all my heart, soul, and strength—and I do. Through Jesus, I pray. Amen.

Who Is My Neighbor?

Do not defraud or rob your neighbor (Leviticus 19:13)

Scripture: Leviticus 19:13-18
Song: "Friend of God"

Jesus established in the story of the Good Samaritan that a neighbor isn't just the person who lives next door to you. When I spoke to a new "neighbor" several hundred miles away recently, I wanted to make sure he knew that my intentions hadn't been to defraud the company he worked for.

In an error on my part, I had earlier reported that the paper I'd purchased for my printer, made by this company, was substandard. This neighbor/representative offered to send me two replacement coupons for the printer paper, and I gave him my address.

However, shortly after receiving the coupons and redeeming them, I discovered my error. The paper wasn't substandard after all, but the same quality I'd always purchased. The problem had been caused by the ink cartridge in my printer!

The representative graciously accepted my apology and suggested I share the printer paper with someone else.

I'm sure Jesus would have too, and I've done just that—and was also happy to share this incident and lessons learned from it. I'd made a mistake. But because I'm a friend of God and know of His amazing love for me, I certainly wouldn't have deliberately defrauded or robbed my neighbor!

Lord God, I'm so thankful for Your Word and Your great forgiveness that goes along with it. You're always there for me, whether I do wrong deliberately or in error. I rely on Your presence daily and in all circumstances. In Jesus' name, amen.

Doing Things God's Way

I do not understand what I do. For what I want to do I do not do, but what I hate I do (Romans 7:15).

Scripture: Romans 7:15-24
Song: "There's Peace and Rest in Paradise"

I did it again today, ate food that I shouldn't have eaten. Doing this reminds me of words from a song from my childhood: "Found a peanut. . . . It was rotten. . . . Ate it anyway."

I don't recall ever eating a rotten peanut, but I remember vividly eating peanuts when I shouldn't have. And like in the song, I got a stomachache too. Yet I still continue to do this thing I "hate."

Apparently the apostle Paul had his struggles too. That is, he acknowledged his sin in doing what he shouldn't do. And he knew (as we all eventually learn) that pure willpower isn't the answer. Perhaps we can all identify with this problem in some way. "So I find this law at work," Paul wrote. "Although I want to do good, evil is right there with me" (v. 21).

Temptation will always be right there with us. It's been said that Satan never sleeps, and this is more than just a saying. It is dangerously true. However, we know that Jesus gives us a way out of any temptation—to rely on Him, rest in Him, trust His power to carry us through.

I admit along with Paul that I'm wretched! Yet Jesus will rescue me from this body that is subject to such self-destructive tendencies; hopefully, before I gain too much weight.

Lord, I am weak, and many times I want to ignore Your inner promptings and do things my way. Help me simply to delight myself in Your love. Through Christ, amen.

Check Your Motives

Your boasting is not good. Don't you know that a little yeast leavens the whole batch of dough? (1 Corinthians 5:6).

Scripture: 1 Corinthians 5:1, 2, 6-9
Song: "Humbly I Adore Thee, Verity Unseen"

In the above text, the apostle Paul points out what followers of Christ should already know. Boasting just isn't good. In the case of the Corinthians, they even boasted about their wrongdoing! Yet as Paul asked, "Don't you know that a little yeast leavens the whole batch of dough?" Indeed it does, because a little sin does a whole lot of damage. Or to put it another way, "One bad apple spoils the whole bunch." Yet the Corinthians didn't think they were being immoral.

We see something of this in today's church as well. Though we may forget it now and then, sin is sin. In the particular case of adultery that Paul confronted—in which one of the church members was sleeping with his father's wife—Paul knew that if it wasn't dealt with, destructive consequences would spread much pain in the congregation. And this immoral brother would likely influence others in his ways.

We will always have painful situations to deal with in our churches, but let us constantly check our motives in the way we deal with them. Let love reign as we remember that the goal of any needed confrontation is clear: repentance, full reconciliation, and restored fellowship in love.

Father God, please help me to apply Your infallible Word to every situation in my life. When I sin, prick my conscience until I admit it, and then give me the strength to deal with it according to Your will. In Jesus' name, I pray. Amen.

I Love Bananas!

The fruit of the Spirit is love, joy, peace, forbearance, kindness, goodness, faithfulness, gentleness and self-control. Against such things there is no law (Galatians 5:22, 23).

Scripture: Galatians 5:22-26
Song: "Sweet, Sweet Spirit"

I experienced a crushing blow when I went to my favorite store and found they were out of bananas. And it got worse. When I made a special trip back to the store that afternoon, I saw that the price per pound had been raised by seven cents!

Should I compromise? Should I break the promise I'd made to myself years ago not to pay more than a certain price for my favorite fruit?

Seeing the sweet expression on the young man's face in the produce department made my decision easier. In fact, having gone a couple of days without these delicious treats, I would have paid even more. However, the young man showed me some marked-down bananas, and also explained why they were so economical. "It's oversupply," he said. "First they didn't have any to ship, and now it's too many."

What a wonderful blessing! I was sure that other customers would reap this same benefit. Also I was thankful that I hadn't displayed another attitude that would have been contrary to the fruit of the Spirit. What's more, even though I love bananas, I love God more. And that also means I don't have to say more.

Lord, thank You for providing for me in every instance. I want to follow Your laws always, and bear the fruit that pleases You. And others will see this too and have no question about whom I belong to. Through Christ Jesus I pray. Amen.

Walk This Way!

It is for freedom that Christ has set us free. Stand firm, then, and do not let yourselves be burdened again by a yoke of slavery. . . . Walk by the Spirit, and you will not gratify the desires of the flesh (Galatians 5:1, 16).

Scripture: Galatians 5:1-17
Song: "Walk by the Spirit"

Walking by the Spirit is a lifelong process and is by no means easy. After all, we face a daily battle against a great range of sins, and we're called to resist our purely selfish desires. On the other hand, according to the apostle Paul, it's not so much a battle to fight but a privilege to embrace, a freedom to enjoy.

This was especially important for the Galatian church members to hear. Some teachers among them, who'd been strict followers of the law in their former religion of Judaism, were requiring new Gentile converts to, in a sense, "become Jews first" before they could be Christians. In other words, they'd have to submit to circumcision and other regulations, such as eating the right foods or avoiding certain "work" on the Sabbath.

Paul stood against the whole idea. He stressed that they'd already been justified—declared righteous in God's sight—apart from works of the law. He said, in effect, "Christ has made you free to rely purely on His power, through the indwelling Spirit!"

It's the Holy Spirit who helps us live a holy life. Be free, and obey the Lord out of love alone. When we express ourselves through love, we are walking by the Spirit.

Lord, thank You for setting me free from sin's slavery and opening my eyes to the true freedom that only You can give. Today, I will walk in Your love. In Christ, amen.

A Better Planting

We were . . . buried with him through baptism into death in order that, just as Christ was raised from the dead through the glory of the Father, we too may live a new life (Romans 6:4).

Scripture: Romans 6:1-11
Song: "A New Creature"

At my 99-year-old mother's burial last summer, I continued a tradition I'd started back when my kids were small. It is a final act of respect and acceptance, continued with each family member since their other grandmother's passing back in the 1970s.

After the casket was lowered into the ground, and all but the immediate family had walked away, each of us took a shovelful of dirt and reverently threw it into the grave. I reminded them and myself that this was more than a burial; it was a sowing, a planting of faith—that one day something better will come from this seed. It was also a reminder that we ourselves died to our old life and were buried with Christ in baptism.

Can you imagine my children's horror and disgust if I ever suggested that we go back to the cemetery and dig up their grandparents, just for a short visit? It is such a repulsive thought that we refuse to even imagine it. Is it any less repulsive that we sometimes "resurrect" the old body of sin that we joyfully buried when we surrendered to Christ? How much better to be "dead *to* sin" than to be "dead *in* sin!"

Lord, my sins were put to death on the cross. May I refuse to resurrect them, as You help me to walk in the newness of life for which I was created. In Jesus' name, amen.

February 20–26. **Doc Arnett** has been a career educator and bivocational minister for over 30 years. He and his wife, Randa, live in northeast Kansas and share 21 grandchildren.

Better Ingredients, Better People

The seed on good soil stands for those with a noble and good heart, who hear the word, retain it, and by persevering produce a crop (Luke 8:15).

Scripture: Luke 8:4-15
Song: "Are You Sowing the Seed?"

After several days of leveling, scraping, and shaping, I spent most of another day tilling the area when I was building my croquet lawn. Finally, it was ready to plant.

After sowing a generous mixture of bluegrass, creeping red fescue, and perennial rye grass, I spent another several hours covering the turf with peat moss to hold in moisture and foster germination.

Soon I was elated to see a thick stand of sprouts emerging through the mulch. Within two weeks, a carpet of green covered the area.

Then, after another week . . . *splotches of brown!* Overwatering and hot temperatures had spawned a killing mold that devastated my croquet lawn. I avoided repeating the same mistake with my reseeding. By the end of summer, we were enjoying croquet on the new lawn.

The only way to know the true quality of the "soil" in which we sow the Word of the kingdom is by observing the results. Sometimes something good starts and then fails. But how rewarding to see a good harvest in lives where we have planted or watered the gospel!

Lord, You don't hold me accountable for the seed or the soil, only for the sowing. Help me to sow in faith and trust You for the harvest. In Your holy name, amen.

The Proof of the Planting

You may have had to suffer grief in all kinds of trials. These have come so that the proven genuineness of your faith . . . may result in praise (1 Peter 1:6, 7)

Scripture: 1 Peter 1:3-9
Song: "Refiner's Fire"

Over the past 25 years, Randa and I have buried three parents, one child, and several friends. We lived paycheck-to-paycheck for several years and, for one month in the 1990s, sold our own blood plasma to buy groceries. We've endured the usual familial stress, faced what seemed like insurmountable challenges, and seen the relationship pushed to the breaking point.

Our occasionally cheerful stubbornness and rock-rooted foundations have held firm, though. In fact, I've experienced a degree of love and commitment I never believed possible. Without all those testings, I would still have known that we shared wonderful feelings for each other. But it is only through the trials that the genuine level of our commitment and devotion to each other has emerged.

Most of us would prefer to bypass the difficulties that put our faith to the test. Scuba diving in Hawaii is certainly more fun than sponging vomit out of the carpet. Enjoying the security of a good job is more pleasant than visiting the plasma center. But it is in the heartaches, toils, trials, burdens, and ordeals that our faith is truly demonstrated. Like steel on the anvil, not only is our faith proven by the fire, but it is also made stronger.

Thank You, **Lord,** for the trials You've allowed and, above all, for the grace and faith You supply that sustains me through all of them. In Jesus' name, amen.

Through the Dry Spells

Confess your sins to each other and pray for each other so that you may be healed. The prayer of a righteous person is powerful and effective (James 5:16).

Scripture: James 5:13-20
Song: "When My Love for Christ Grows Weak"

Many years ago, I went through a spiritual dry spell. I'd quit going to church, stopped reading my Bible, and spent almost no time in prayer. I felt wilted, starved and weak emotionally and spiritually. One day, in the midst of a fit of self-pity, I said, "Lord, I just feel so weak!" Whether by imagination or inspiration, I don't know—but I thought I clearly heard God respond, "Of course you're weak; you're not eating anything!"

In spite of my immediate conviction, I had to laugh out loud. One thing for sure: our God has never been shy or reluctant to speak the truth in ways we can understand. I resumed "feeding" on the Word, spending time in prayer, and returned to regular corporate worship. The improvement in my spiritual and emotional well-being was obvious and appreciated.

It seems funny in a way that isn't funny at all: we are usually quick to associate physical weakness with a lack of nourishment and exercise, while ignoring the causes of parallel problems spiritually. No doubt the first step to a new strength is confessing our poor diet to the Lord—and to a trustworthy brother in Christ. Then, let the power of prayer do its work.

Lord, don't let pride or arrogance, ignorance or weakness, keep me from acknowledging my sin to You and others. Help us all, Lord, to stay constant in prayer for one another that we may be healed. Through Christ, amen.

Spare the Vine, Spoil the Vineyard

If your brother or sister sins, go and point out their fault, just between the two of you. If they listen to you, you have won them over (Matthew 18:15).

Scripture: Matthew 18:15-20
Song: "I Am the Vine"

Truth be told, I'm kind of a Will Rogers when it comes to vineyards and such; all I know is what I read in the papers. Or books. I'm confident, though, that there are some similarities between growing grapes and growing corn. If you don't deal with disease in the field or vineyard, you'll quickly face ruin.

Back in 1970, I saw southern corn blight wipe out my entire crop within a couple of weeks. It hit just as the corn was tasseling. What should have been a crop of over 200 bushels an acre yielded less than 40. I made just enough money to pay off the loan I'd borrowed for the planting! Fortunately for me, my entire crop consisted of 16 acres, one acre for each year of my life. It was an FFA project, not my entire livelihood.

Sin, like mold, mildew, fungus, and a host of other bad stuff, can never be treated by indifference. It always gets worse, and it always spreads in viral self-destructiveness. It is not love or respect or courtesy that keeps us silent when we witness the sin of fellow believers. Love for them and for the body of Christ demands that we care enough to confront. And to confront in the deepest humility.

O Lord, have mercy on me, a sinner! And in all humility, I ask for the courage to love and pray for fellow sinners, and even to invite change in them, as You are changing me! By the grace of Christ I pray. Amen.

The Hope of Harvest

Yes, this was written for us, because whoever plows and threshes should be able to do so in the hope of sharing in the harvest (1 Corinthians 9:10).

Scripture: 1 Corinthians 9:3-12
Song: "Bringing in the Sheaves"

It must have been the strangest little tomato garden ever. There was an old cistern in our backyard in Cynthiana, Kentucky. First, I dumped in a pile of broken bricks and stones that had come from tearing out an old porch. Then I hauled in a couple of pickup truckloads of good topsoil and used that for the last three or four feet of fill at the top. I mounded up the dirt a bit and then set out a half-dozen tomato plants. I watered them regularly and applied liquid fertilizer every two weeks.

Boy, did they thrive! I've got a picture of me standing out there, tomato plants towering over my head and loaded up with ripening red globes. My, how we looked forward to enjoying those luscious fruits.

Can you imagine how angry, frustrated, and aggravated I would have been if someone else had taken all those tomatoes? God long ago established that even the ox that treads out the grain should share the fruits of its labor. He has promised us through Christ that we will be richly rewarded for even the slightest of our labors. "If anyone gives even a cup of cold water . . . that person will certainly not lose their reward" (Matthew 10:42)—a reward even better than homegrown tomatoes.

Gracious Heavenly Father, thank You for the promise of harvest, for the rewards of our labors in You. In the name of Jesus, I pray. Amen.

The Reality of Harvest

Let us not become weary in doing good, for at the proper time we will reap a harvest if we do not give up. . . . Let us do good to all people, especially to those who belong to the family of believers (Galatians 6:9, 10).

Scripture: Galatians 5:18–6:10
Song: "You Never Let Go"

One of my colleagues requires his students to give a class report based on an interview with an older adult. Bob stopped by yesterday to tell me about a student who had interviewed me. "He was so impressed with you and talked about how much he enjoyed your class and his conversations with you. You really have influenced that young man."

I then shared briefly with Bob a bit of irony in the situation: I'd come within a hair's breadth of kicking that young man out of my class after the first session last fall! During that disciplinary conversation in my office, he'd argued with me about my class rules and my expectations. "I paid my tuition. I should be able to dress any way I want to and wear whatever I want, as long as it isn't crude or vulgar."

I didn't change my rules, but I did change my mind about expelling him. I decided to exercise patience and see where that would lead. As it turned out, at least according to the young man himself, I'd become a key influence in his life. We never know whether our efforts are going to produce the results for which we hope . . . or not. But we should always do good.

Father, help me never give up on doing good to others. Your Son is the best example for me, so help me follow Him today. I pray in His precious name. Amen.

Like? Love!

This is the message you heard from the beginning: We should love one another (1 John 3:11).

Scripture: 1 John 3:11-17
Song: "Tender Love of Jesus"

You've probably heard many times that as Christians, "we should love one another." However, when we look around our church, we often see people disagreeing and breaking off relationships rather than exploring the depths of God's love in us.

John clearly spells out how we are to live each day. We shouldn't be surprised if the world hates us; that's to be expected. But brothers and sisters in Christ, our actions speak for themselves, proclaiming to that same world whether we truly understand and accept God's love. And John reminds us, in a crystal-clear declaration, "We know that we have passed from death to life, because we love each other" (v. 14).

Our response to others' needs—our willingness to share, to show compassion, even to lay down our lives for another Christian—that's how we "walk the talk." Even when acting in God's love seems unpopular, we need to let His love support our relationships in the church. Even when we know we can't do it in our own strength—even when we know we'd never be able to "like" a particular brother or sister—we can depend on God to love them through us, in His name.

O eternal Lord God, let Your love flow through me to others. I can't generate Your love; I can only convey it. Fill me to overflowing today, through Christ my Lord. Amen.

February 27, 28. **Carol McLean** writes from Venice, Florida, where she does marketing consulting for the Christian book publishing industry. She and her husband, Gary, have twin adult sons.

How Far?

Anyone who loves me will obey my teaching (John 14:23).

Scripture: John 14:18-24
Song: "Where He Leads I'll Follow"

If you look in your wallet or purse, you'll probably find some ID cards that prove you are who you say you are. But what if today you needed proof that you love Jesus, that you belong to the family of God? Here Jesus gives His disciples—present and future—the evidence that identifies them to His Father. "Anyone who loves me will obey my teaching."

The original disciples who followed Jesus knew His teachings well. Now their Lord revealed how each one could prove his or her identity in Him: obedience to His teachings.

So how can you and I today prove that we love Jesus? We show the same proof of identity—we walk each day in obedience to His Word. Problem is, we will never do this perfectly, and our motives will always be tinged with self-interest.

I love how writer Frederick Buechner put it in *The Magnificent Defeat*: "The voice that we hear over our shoulders never says, 'First be sure that your motives are pure and selfless and then follow me.' If it did, then we could none of us follow. So when later on the voice says, 'Take up your cross and follow me,' at least part of what is meant by 'cross' is our realization that we are seldom any less than nine parts fake. Yet our feet can insist on answering him anyway, and on we go, step after step, mile after mile. How far? How far?"

Lord, I'm an imperfect disciple, but my heart is open to Your transforming power. Work in me for the upgrading of Your reputation in my world today. In Christ, amen.

My Prayer Notes

_____
_____
_____
_____
_____
_____
_____
_____
_____
_____
_____
_____
_____
_____
_____
_____
_____
_____
_____
_____
_____
_____
_____
_____

My Prayer Notes

_____

_____

_____

_____

_____

_____

_____

_____

_____

_____

_____

_____

_____

_____

_____

_____

_____

_____

_____

_____

_____

_____

_____

_____

My Prayer Notes

_____
_____
_____
_____
_____
_____
_____
_____
_____
_____
_____
_____
_____
_____
_____
_____
_____
_____
_____
_____
_____
_____
_____
_____

DEVOTIONS®

► **MARCH**

If anyone acknowledges that Jesus is the Son of God,
God lives in them and they in God. And so we know
and rely on the love God has for us.

—*1 John 4:15, 16*

Gary Wilde, Editor | Margaret K. Williams, Project Editor

Photo © iStock | Thinkstock®

DEVOTIONS® is published quarterly by Standard Publishing, Cincinnati, Ohio, www.standardpub.com. Copyright © 2015 by Standard Publishing. All rights reserved. Topics based on the Home Daily Bible Readings, International Sunday School Lessons. Copyright © 2013 by the Committee on the Uniform Series. Printed in the U.S.A. All Scripture quotations, unless otherwise indicated are taken from the *HOLY BIBLE, NEW INTERNATIONAL VERSION®. NIV®.* Copyright © 1973, 1978, 1984, 2011 by Biblica, Inc.® Used by permission of Zondervan. All rights reserved worldwide. Scripture quotations marked (*KJV*) are taken from the *King James Version,* public domain. *Holy Bible, New Living Translation (NLT),* Copyright © 1996, 2004, 2007, 2013. Tyndale House Publishers. *New American Standard Bible (NASB),* Copyright © The Lockman Foundation, 1960, 1962, 1963, 1968, 1971, 1972, 1973, 1975, 1977, 1995. *The Living Bible (TLB),* Copyright © 1971 by Tyndale House Publishers, Wheaton, IL.

God's Assistants

If our heart condemn us, God is greater than our heart, and knoweth all things (1 John 3:20, *KJV*).

Scripture: 1 John 3:18-24
Song: "It's Me, O Lord"

Christianity flourishes around the world. But with this magnitude comes also a multitude of denominations, sects, and branches, each claiming to have the keys to right doctrine. And many of these groups, at times throughout history, have tried to force their particular theological views on others who may oppose them.

These "holy wars," which vary in magnitude, can be as small and simple as family feuds among the pews of the same church, or vast and violent literal wars that have sometimes boiled up between Catholics and Protestants in centuries past. But what is at the heart of these battles? Could it be that we sometimes forget that each individual heart must be led by God, even before the legitimate help that can come from any holy assistants?

Our leaders, our elders, and deacons are important to the church. But each of us has a heart, a mind, and a spirit for God to lead as well. Ultimately we will only be held accountable for our own actions, our own Christian life, and the quality of its fruit. This is a liberating thing too—to place others in the hand of God and allow their own hearts, led by Him, to condemn them or approve them.

Dear Lord, today help me to cease passing judgment on my fellow believers and to allow You—and You alone—to lead their hearts as You lead mine. In Christ, amen.

March 1–5. **Sarah Reeves** is a freelance author and single, homeschooling mother of four. She has been writing devotions and other Christian materials for almost 15 years.

Even If They Do Not Hear

They are of the world: therefore speak they of the world, and the world heareth them (1 John 4:5, *KJV*).

Scripture: 1 John 4:1-6
Song: "Have You Not Known? Have You Not Heard?"

It can sometimes be daunting to behold the religions of the world. Many seem to have no problem attracting millions into their fold. Those involved in Christian evangelism, or church visitation programs, can sometimes feel discouraged when it seems that few are willing to hear the gospel message of grace offered from a heart of love.

The truth is, Christianity has never been a popular religion. From the beginning as Christianity spread across the Roman Empire, persecution against Christians violently erupted.

Of course, our Christian walk and our service aren't primarily about numbers. It isn't about quantity but quality. Our message is the proclamation of unmerited forgiveness through the cross of Christ. For the few who will receive that message with grateful hearts and follow with us our crucified and risen Lord, the joy of salvation will compel them to tell others.

Are you feeling discouraged this morning about those who seem not to hear? Renew your commitment to sharing the gospel with someone in your world, even if they appear unresponsive. Your commission is to share the gracious message, and it is God's job to bring fruit from the effort.

Dear Lord, please help me to remember that it is not my job to convert souls, but rather it is my mission consistently to share Your love and mercy, even with those who would rather listen to the world. I trust You to work in me today! In Jesus' name I pray. Amen.

That Horrible H-Word

If a man say, I love God, and hateth his brother, he is a liar: for he that loveth not his brother whom he hath seen, how can he love God whom he hath not seen? (1 John 4:20, *KJV*).

Scripture: 1 John 4:20–5:5
Song: "This Is My Commandment"

Many of us have memories of a parent or grandparent scolding us if we should ever slip up and say, "I *hate* him!"

"Hate is a strong word. We should love everyone, even if we don't love their ways," our wise elders would say. Hatred is indeed a strong word, and an even stronger emotion, which when left unchecked can wreak havoc on the spirit of all concerned.

In fact, hatred has the strange power to affect the one doing the hating more than the one who is hated. If we harbor such hatred, it tends to develop a deep-seated bitterness in our soul, something very difficult to root out. It's like a mistreated dog whose master teaches him for years to attack others. But then one day the dog turns upon this same master and attacks him.

And there's this, too: If we Christians harbor hatred in our hearts, the Bible calls us liars. Love for God and hatred for His children cannot dwell in the same heart.

Have you held on to hatred for someone who hurt you, perhaps even years ago? You will never know true peace, and the true love of God flowing through your life, as long as you hang on to this most toxic emotion.

Dear Lord, purge my heart of any hatred or bitterness for past hurts. Help me forgive and move on so that I can grow in Your grace, beginning this very moment. I pray in the name of Christ, my forgiving Savior. Amen.

Can Christians Be Depressed?

He brought me up also out of an horrible pit, out of the miry clay, and set my feet upon a rock, and established my goings (Psalm 40:2, *KJV*).

Scripture: Psalm 40:1-10
Song: "Holy Ghost, Dispel Our Sadness"

When I was a young child, our family heard that a preacher we knew had committed suicide. His family, his church, and the many churches he ministered in during his years in evangelism were devastated: *How could it have happened?* Over the next few weeks, it came out that he'd been depressed but had refused help: What would his fellow Christians think of him?

There is a stigma in Christian circles about depression. Does it not show a lack of faith, question God's power, and detract from His glory?

Yet depression is real. Many great saints in the Bible (and down through the centuries) dealt with it, including the psalmist who claims that at one time he was in a "horrible pit" (v. 2). Christians who suffer this particular "thorn in the flesh" (2 Corinthians 12:7) need not face it alone. We have a constantly present God who walks with us, even through the darkest valleys. That same God has put resources out there to help us deal with depression.

If you are clinically depressed or know someone who is, remember that good counselors are ready to help His children deal with their pain and anger. Stuffing it will cause depression; honest revelation brings healing.

Father, give me compassion for those dealing with depression. They need encouragement to meet this difficulty, even as I need others to support me through my own challenges. Lord, have mercy. In Christ, amen.

Nothing to Fear

There is no fear in love; but perfect love casteth out fear: because fear hath torment. He that feareth is not made perfect in love (1 John 4:18, *KJV*).

Scripture: 1 John 4:7-19
Song: "Oh, How I Love Jesus"

Divorce rates in the last several years have skyrocketed, even among Christians. As church leaders scramble to offer effective family counseling services and significant support for couples and parents, the numbers continue to rise with discouraging consistency. Why, in this era of almost limitless abundance, have married couples found it so hard to stay together?

The ability to love and establish secure and intimate relationships is very much rooted in our own confidence and self-worth. Often men and women who aren't secure about their own selves will do things subconsciously to sabotage a relationship.

Fear comes wrapped up in their love. Fear that they are not good enough. Fear that they will not be loved in return. Fear that eventually they will get hurt—so it's better to be the one who lashes out first rather than the one who gets lashed at.

Fearless love doesn't consider itself at all. Fearless love puts its partner first and places the rest in God's hands. Whether you are married or not, please join me in this: Let it be our mission to offer fearless love amidst every one of our relationships, starting this very day.

O God of grace and glory, please help me today to offer a fearless love to my spouse, children, parents, siblings, family, and friends. Help me remember that fearless love puts self last, and that this is the kind of love that You showed all of us. In the holy name of Jesus, my Lord and Savior, I pray. Amen.

Heart—at the Heart!

The tax collector . . . beat his breast and said, "God, have mercy on me, a sinner" (Luke 18:13).

Scripture: Luke 18:9-14
Song: "Mercy Is Boundless and Free"

During a Bible study series focused on following Christ, one man kept expressing disappointment in himself. He wished we had church more than once a week to strengthen his faith for the workaday world. Jeff did what the rest of us did— worshipped regularly, studied the Scriptures—but still felt he fell far short of what God expected of him. Like the tax collector, Jeff may be closer to God's heart than the rest of us do-gooders.

Yes, it's good to worship, to learn, to read our Bibles and pray. But such practices must grow out of a love for God and a desire to please Him. Our heart lies at the heart of the matter! A heart sensitive to sin forms the foundation of a relationship with God. Jeff showed us that kind of heart.

If, like certain Pharisees, we pride ourselves on our personal goodness, we miss the mark. All of us disappoint our Lord. Even if we aren't committing adultery, we may entertain lustful thoughts. Even though we fast and tithe, we may fail to open our hearts and our wallets to those in need. God is honored when, like the tax collector—and Jeff—we recognize God's perfect holiness and admit our own need for mercy.

Father God, forgive the wrong things I've done and the right things I've failed to do. You have rescued and redeemed me. Thank You, through Christ my Lord. Amen.

March 6–12. **Shirley Brosius** is an author from Millersburg, Pennsylvania, and a member of Friends of the Heart, three women who lead women's retreats.

Your Credentials, Please

We are made right with God by placing our faith in Jesus Christ. And this is true for everyone who believes, no matter who we are (Romans 3:22, *NLT*).

Scripture: Romans 3:21-31
Song: "My Faith Has Found a Resting Place"

As a newspaper correspondent, I once interviewed a man who frequently served as a White House consultant. His secretary expressed disappointment when he realized the newspaper had sent me, a part-time reporter, to interview this very important man. Yet because of my newspaper credentials, the secretary ushered me into the man's office.

Because of the Son's credentials, I will one day be ushered into the presence of the Father. When that time comes, it won't matter how impressive my credentials are as a Christian. I may have worshipped and worked and won souls for Christ; I may have tithed and taught and used talents for God. All those good works won't earn me a place in Heaven. We are permitted to enter Heaven's gates only because our Savior's atoning work on the cross opened them for us. All glory to Him!

When I left the newspaper interview, that very important man, who had shaken the hands of five presidents, kissed my hand; I felt special and honored. Imagine the joy that will tingle from our heads to our toes when we enter Heaven, and the Lord himself embraces us.

O God, Creator of Heaven and earth, I do not have an important job. My name is not well known, so I am thankful that earthly credentials mean nothing to You. I do thank You that I am known and loved by Christ, my Savior. In the name of the Father and of the Son and of the Holy Spirit, I pray. Amen.

Forever Friends

So now we can rejoice in our wonderful new relationship with God because our Lord Jesus Christ has made us friends of God (Romans 5:11, *NLT*).

Scripture: Romans 5:6-11
Song: "What a Friend We Have in Jesus"

You've probably heard someone say, "With friends like that, who needs enemies?" We say that when a friend surprises us by doing something that's not in our best interest, something hurtful to us. We expect unkind treatment from an enemy, but not from a friend.

However, we are equally surprised when an enemy blesses us. Yet that is exactly what God did. Even though we were His enemies because of our sins, He showed us the utmost love and respect by coming to earth to die—the incarnate Son taking the punishment for our sins. God showed us that the best way to get rid of enemies is to turn them into friends. We might say, "With enemies like that, who needs friends?"

Since God treated us so well, even when we were at enmity with Him, imagine how well He will treat us now that He calls us friends. We need not fear death itself. God would not separate himself from His friends, and by Christ's resurrection from the dead, we know that someday we too shall survive even the death experience. Regardless of circumstances, friends of God can walk in peace knowing God walks with them.

Heavenly Father, thank You for the friend I have in Jesus. My earthly friends may disappoint me; even my beloved family at times lets me down. But I know I can count on You to support me until I walk into eternity. Call me to thankfulness throughout this day for Your loving presence and support. In Jesus' name, amen.

Like Daffodils, We Shall Bloom

Christ has been raised from the dead. He is the first of a great harvest of all who have died (1 Corinthians 15:20, *NLT*).

Scripture: 1 Corinthians 15:12-25
Song: "He Lives"

Our daughter turned 40 on April 1, but we didn't sing Happy Birthday, light candles, or cut a cake. Most years we observe the day by placing a bouquet of daffodils on her grave. This year, wintry weather prohibited even that. The daffodils were just then poking up from freshly thawed ground.

But even though Christy Marie is not with us, we should sing Happy Birthday, cut a cake, and light candles on her special day. The promise of the resurrection assures us that, although she died as a baby, we will see her again.

The daffodil symbolizes resurrection, for its bulb lies underground, cold and dormant through the winter. In fact, the name *narcissus*, a variety of daffodil, comes from a Greek word meaning "deep sleep" or "numbness."

Yet that bulb holds a spark of life. When touched by warm temperatures and spring rains, it comes to life and blooms in all its brilliant glory. Clumps of blossoms nod in the springtime breeze, assuring us that all is not lost. So in Christ, we will rise again and bloom with those who have gone before us. The promise of the daffodil offers hope and healing to all who have lost loved ones.

Almighty and everlasting God, thank You for overcoming death. Thank You for the hope of eternal life, made sure by the resurrection of Your Son, Jesus. In the holy name of my Lord and Savior, I pray. Amen.

Struck by the Power of God

Now all glory to God, who is able, through his mighty power at work within us, to accomplish infinitely more than we might ask or think (Ephesians 3:20, *NLT*).

Scripture: Ephesians 3:14-21
Song: "Christ Liveth in Me"

We see the power of God demonstrated in Christ's resurrection. However, we may forget that same power works through us as we go about our daily lives: working, parenting, ministering, and even having fun. That power heals broken bodies—whether through a miraculous jolt or the slow and steady influence of nature, doctors, and medicine. That power restores broken lives—whether through a conversion experience or the slow and steady influence of the Holy Spirit. And that power flows through us to touch others as the incarnate hands of Christ.

We ourselves may feel weak and inadequate for what God calls us to do—whether to go to an unreached tribe or an unreached neighbor. But if we take a step in the right direction, we find God walks with us and acts through us. Our weakness is our strength because we realize the power flows from God rather than from our own ingenuity.

May we never underestimate God's power. Through us He can accomplish much more than we might ask or think. He can heal marriages, quench addictions, and restore families. His Spirit gives us strength to face life's challenges as we confidently wait for that day when we will see Him face to face.

Heavenly Father, I will someday fall at the feet of Your Son in awe of His mighty power. But for today, I will trust You with each challenge and every difficulty, confident that Your power will see me through. In Jesus' name, amen.

All Join Hands

There is one body and one Spirit, just as you were called to one hope when you were called (Ephesians 4:4).

Scripture: Ephesians 4:1-6
Song: "Blest Be the Tie That Binds"

Churches in our town sometimes join together for special services—a summer night of praise on a cool riverbank or a fall night of thanksgiving in a warm church. Our local ministers also coordinate a fund to help people who can't pay heating bills or cover other essential needs. We worship and work together because we realize there's more that unites us than divides us.

Our services range from structured traditional to spontaneous contemporary. Some worshippers enjoy singing hymns to organ music while others lift voices to lyrics posted above a praise band. However, we all agree on basic Christian beliefs.

God values community, for He sets us in families where we learn to give and take. There we learn to overlook faults and work out differences. He then sets families in communities, where we learn to support one another on a larger scale. Our society works best when we put others' welfare ahead of our own.

The body of Christ is also a family and bears witness to God's grace as we function harmoniously. Like sour notes in a concert, we taint our witness if we fuss and argue over nonessentials. What better way to witness to an unbelieving world than to work together within and among our congregations to put Christ's goodness and love on display?

Father, keep me in my humble place within the body of Christ. May I never think that my way is the only way to do things. Rather, help me respect and work beside my brothers and sisters in Christ in unity. In His name, amen.

Lots of Love

Because of his great love for us, God, who is rich in mercy, made us alive with Christ even when we were dead in transgressions—it is by grace you have been saved (Ephesians 2:4, 5).

Scripture: Ephesians 2:1-10
Song: "Great Is Thy Faithfulness"

My father was quite reserved when it came to expressing love for us kids. He didn't hug or kiss us or say, "I love you." In fact, I walked lightly around him; I didn't want to upset him by being a bad girl. Yet, in spite of his stern demeanor, I never once doubted my father's love for me. He faithfully provided for the needs of our family. And occasionally, when he returned from a trip, he brought me a gift. That made me feel very special.

Sometimes God seems like my father. When circumstances are pleasant, it's like getting a hug, but when circumstances challenge me, I may wonder if I've upset Him by being a bad girl. At such times, when I don't sense God's love, I wonder if He has turned His back on me.

However, I know in my heart that God loves me unconditionally —like every good father does. Scripture assures me that even when we misbehaved, God loved us so much that He sent Christ to offer atonement on our behalf. Now He sees me as a good girl— perfect in Christ. The grace He offers us to survive every situation in life reminds me of those special gifts my father brought me.

Father, thank You for Your grace. Thank You for loving me, even when I am unlovely, and perhaps even unlikable. May I never doubt that love and seek to pass it on to others who may need just such a touch of Your grace. In Jesus' name, amen.

The Best Seed

You transplanted a vine from Egypt; you drove out the nations and planted it. You cleared the ground for it, and it took root and filled the land (Psalm 80:8, 9).

Scripture: Psalm 80:8-19
Song: "Give of Your Best to the Master"

I love columbine. I have a variety of colors and types planted in my garden, for which the ground was meticulously prepared. Columbine is a flower that reseeds itself, and each year I wait for the new seedlings to show their colors.

One year, a seed sent up a bushy columbine, threatening the choice varieties. I also noticed weaker plants, their beauty diminished. To ignore these robust intruders would hurt my garden. Only the finest examples of each plant could be allowed to reseed, in order to restore the color and health of the whole bed.

Some flowers deteriorate with age and lack of nourishment. Weaker plants produce poor seed and won't put forth healthy, vibrant blooms. If the best is not replanted, the bed dies.

Similarly, the best is given back to God for Him to restore and multiply the fruit. As God renews the bed, I wonder if I am giving God my best seed. Do I hoard the best and give Him the leftovers? Thankfully, the Lord is in the restoration business. He restores my life and relationship with Him, but He needs healthy seed of repentance and trust.

Dear Heavenly Father, You had a plan, but I have been a part of its degradation. By Your Holy Spirit, revive me, that I may never turn back. You alone can restore me and save me. Through Christ I pray. Amen.

March 13–19. **Barbara Durnil** is a retired medical worker and freelance writer in southern Idaho. Listening to God and writing for Him is her joy and passion.

A Perfect Rose

Since God receives glory because of the Son, he will give his own glory to the Son . . . So now I am giving you a new commandment: Love each other. Just as I have loved you, you should love each other (John 13:32, 34, *NLT*).

Scripture: John 13:31-35
Song: "Let the Beauty of Jesus Be Seen in Me"

The house next door was abandoned, the garden's roses badly neglected. I decided to help those flowers. Gathering pruners, insecticide, and fungicide, I started the process. I entered a tangle of dead wood, leaves sticky with aphids, and a covering of mildew and black spot. Bushes meant to bring beauty were instead ugly and contagious.

I cut, sprayed, and decontaminated; and in the center, I found something miraculous. I found God's glory among the decay—a perfect rose. It was vibrant and strong, kissed by a radiant pearl blush. God shined from the wreckage. He designed the rose, after all, and the bush received His glory and returned it back.

Though I exist in a world of decay and disease, I am sure God doesn't want me to settle in and dwell comfortably in that state, but to reveal the glory He gives me. That is a different world, a different kingdom. If He gives me the glory of His indwelling Spirit, then I must give the best back to Him and refuse to become entangled in the dead wood around me.

And how will that look? It will look like love.

God of glory, Your divine love rests on me when I accept Your ways. The light from that love glorifies You when it is manifested in me. Help me convey Your love in all circumstances, that the world may see You amidst its decay. In Jesus' name, amen.

Suckers of the Past

So prepare your minds for action and exercise self-control. . . . So you must live as God's obedient children. Don't slip back into your old ways of living to satisfy your own desires. You didn't know any better then. But now you must be holy in everything you do (1 Peter 1:13-15, *NLT*).

Scripture: 1 Peter 1:13-21
Song: "Yield Not to Temptation"

A groan of frustration leaves my lips. There is another one, straight and tall and ugly! It destroys the symmetry and texture of the contorted filbert tree by my front door. Limbs, called suckers, begin their growth near the ground, hidden from view under the corkscrew branches. When they emerge, they grow straight up, with plain flat leaves, and tower above the twisted silhouette of the tree. I must crawl to the base, find the source, and cut it close to the trunk.

I too must watch for suckers in my life. They revert and grow as I once was—and how I must guard against them! Like an un-attended child, my mind explores my surroundings and absorbs sights and sounds from the world. Without discipline, it gets the rest of me into trouble. I need to be alert and exercise self-control (lest I get sucker-punched by sin).

Cutting the wild branches changes my behavior. I rise above the skirmish. Trusting God becomes my focus, and the suckers don't take hold. I am revived, my hedge is strong, and I am restored to Him once again.

Creator God, You made me a new creation when I found You. But now, to keep the suckers of my old desires from interfering with what You want me to be, I must be grounded in You. Keep me close, precious Savior, I pray. In Your name, amen.

Obedience Makes the Difference

I ask that we love one another. And this is love: that we walk in obedience to his commands. As you have heard from the beginning, his command is that you walk in love (2 John 5, 6).

Scripture: 2 John 4-11
Song: "Love Lifted Me"

My family tree has a branch that crosses mine and rubs me when the wind blows. It has injured my bark. This branch is atheist and foreign to the tree. It is grafted in and grows in an illogical direction, struggling with health and productivity.

For many years I labored to love this individual. I strengthened my emotions before contact and failed miserably before the winds of circumstances calmed. How can I love, when the object of my love rejects totally the Son whom I love so much?

Then I came to a fuller understanding of Jesus' love. His is a kind of love that goes deeper than mere sentiment; it is an unconditional seeking of the other's good. So I set my mind on loving in His way—a fully giving way—rather than focusing on the discomfort of my raw feelings.

And things changed. My love changed to obedience, and obedience became love. Now that was a lot easier!

Today I find I love this individual and hurt when there is pain, failure, and disappointment in that life. My heart breaks for that one. I pray that God's glory may cause bark to connect both branches and heal the injury.

Father, loving is not new; however, obedience changes the means and outcome. Loving is being obedient to You, Lord, something I want dearly. Thank You for giving me the power to obey, for You make all things possible. In Jesus' name, amen.

One Block at a Time

Now in Christ Jesus you who once were far away have been brought near by the blood of Christ. For he himself is our peace (Ephesians 2:13, 14).

Scripture: Ephesians 2:11-22
Song: "They'll Know We Are Christians by Our Love"

Imagine a community garden that was a disaster. It was large enough for all, but included the north end and the south end of the block—and that was the problem. Individuals were assigned their area to plant how they wanted. The south end planted straight, single vegetable rows, while the north end planted squares and intermixed plants. Joe planted banana squash next to Marilyn's delicate beans, and Max planted corn on the south side of Bernie's sun-loving tomatoes. Some hoed the weeds, while others sprayed. But some let the bugs dine and did nothing.

They needed a master gardener to take the barriers down. If they called in the Master, He would judge everyone to be at fault and offer the solution: reconciliation, not more rules. Hostility would disappear, walls would come down, and the people would change from combatants to fellow gardeners.

There could be peace in the garden for those who have accepted the Master's gift. Gone are the laws of gardening; gone are the separate mind-sets. What remains is one neighborhood without strangers. Their unity encourages others who struggle with faith. They know that restoration can grow, one block at a time.

Blessed Lord God, help me live by the reconciliation You provided at the cross. I am part of Your body, so help me see the unity, not separation. In the holy name of Jesus, I pray. Amen.

Perfect Love

God is love. Whoever lives in love lives in God, and God in them (1 John 4:16).

Scripture: 1 John 4:16-19
Song: "Jesus, Thy Boundless Love to Me"

I grew up in, on, around, and under that tree. You might say that tree helped raise me. I dearly loved that tree. Then lightning struck and it fell; its trunk shattered. My heart died a little.

As much as I loved that tree, my love was shallow and immature until I had my first child, and then my heart exploded. The extent of my love was unimaginable, but that was not perfect love. I fiercely protected my baby for fear of harm. I clung to him and guarded his safety, but that was not perfect love either.

As a child, I loved Jesus and thought not of fear. However, this was not perfect love. For as I grew, so did the world around me, and I learned fear.

God is love, so these experiences were tastes of God, but not perfect. I discovered that love is much more than happy memories, emotions, protection, or sentiment. It has more to do with perfect trust. In other words, can I trust that love comes to my life from God's life, an eternal life imparted to me at baptism?

God first gave me love, and then He completed it. Do I fear worldly things at times? Yes, I do. I never, however, fear God's love will fail me, nor do I fear my security in Him. For God is love in me.

God of love, when I see the news of the Middle East, it frightens me. But only for a brief moment, because I am secure in Your love. There is no fear in perfect love. Thank You for my peace today. In Christ, amen.

Joy in the Wind

You are already clean because of the word I have spoken to you. Remain in me, as I also remain in you. No branch can bear fruit by itself (John 15:3, 4).

Scripture: John 15:1-17
Song: "Joyful, Joyful, We Adore Thee"

My neighbor has a weeping willow tree in his yard. Its benefit is tranquil beauty, shade, and rustling coolness. On a hot day, a lounge chair and a glass of lemonade complete the scene. However, when the wind is brisk, some branches detach themselves and fall to the ground. They soon die and leave annoying brown sticks to be burned. No longer is it cool and green, no longer hanging in a canopy over the chair. Torn from the life-giving trunk, those once-living branches no longer give glory to God.

The sticks on the ground could be parts of my life, if I decide my ways are better than the Lord's ways, and I let the wind blow me where it will. Connection to the life-giver is crucial. It means I remain in His love, which means I seek to please Him.

The branches of that beautiful tree sway peacefully and sometimes joyfully in the breezes, but the ones that are green and healthy are those that stay connected. Weeping willow branches don't grow stiff and hard through stark obedience; they float and play with the wind, following the life of the trunk. What a joy it is to love as God loves us, producing fruit and giving almighty God the glory!

My Heavenly Father, You are my trunk and my sustenance. Remaining in You brings life to me and glory to You. The human in me may want to blow off and try my own strength, but that leaves only a growing deadness within me. I will remain and sing Your glories for all to hear. Through Christ, amen.

The Warning Alarms

Blow the trumpet in Zion; sound the alarm on my holy hill. Let all who live in the land tremble, for the day of the LORD is coming. It is close at hand (Joel 2:1).

Scripture: Joel 2:1-11
Song: "Christ Is Coming! Lift Your Eyes!"

We lived on the shore of Lake Erie, and every spring a plague of mayflies attacked. They emerged from the lake after two years of hatching and swarmed by the thousands to the lights on cars, streetlights, and buildings. Parking lots were so covered that snow-plows had to sweep their dead bodies into piles.

The long-winged flies do not bite and only live for 72 hours, but they stain clothing and smell like dead fish. They turn the beautiful landscapes, statues, and flowerbeds into dirty looking eyesores. Pavements become slippery from the dead insects, but while they're alive they sometimes appear on radar screens as a moderate storm! A warning alarm over television and radio alerts various states that the mayflies have hatched.

Alarms usually warn us of a possible danger like tornadoes, hurricanes, or in some places, a bomb threat. Sometimes they sound as an all clear signal.

God sends us silent alarms in our hearts. What am I being warned to watch for? Do I heed and listen to the warning bells that go off in my life? Do I listen to the voice of the Holy Spirit?

Dear Heavenly Father, I want to be alert and work in Your kingdom with a joyful heart. Let me be alert to Your warnings in my spirit. I pray through Jesus' name. Amen.

March 20–26. **Beverly LaHote Schwind** has written five books, contributed stories in *Chicken Soup for the Soul*, and writes a monthly newspaper column called *Patches of Life*.

He Answers

Blow a trumpet in Zion, consecrate a fast, proclaim a solemn assembly (Joel 2:15, *NASB*).

Scripture: Joel 2:15-17
Song: "Precious Lord"

Our minister called the congregation to a fasting and prayer vigil for Kenny, who was well known in our congregation. He was a builder who made many improvements to our building. He was also a leader and teacher among us. Kenny faced open-heart surgery, and his chances of surviving were not good. The doctors told him they would do all they could, but the rest was in God's hands. (And Kenny wanted it to be in God's hands.)

Church members responded to the words of their minister and quickly filled the time slots for continuous praying. He would receive our prayers, 24/7, as we all waited to hear how the surgery went.

Kenny survived the surgery and gave all the glory to God while thanking the people for their faithful support. He regained his strength and witnessed to God's goodness among the people in our community as he returned to his work. God answered our prayers for Kenny, and we became stronger prayer warriors as a result.

The Lord told Solomon that if His people would humble themselves and pray, He would forgive their sin and heal their land (see 2 Chronicles 7:14). God hears the prayers of His people, whether He answers with a no, yes, or wait.

Dear Father, I pray for our country and the leadership that is guiding us. I pray that they will hear Your voice in the choices they make. I pray that Your Holy Spirit will guide them. Through Christ the Lord. Amen.

Lost Years Given Back

I will make up to you for the years that the swarming locust has eaten, the creeping locust, the stripping locust and the gnawing locust (Joel 2:25, *NASB*).

Scripture: Joel 2:20-17
Song: "We Shall Behold Him"

My Uncle Elmer lived a life of darkness, drunkenness, and nightmares after his years in the military. He seemed to be wasting away with no hope for his alcohol addiction. Yet a new life blossomed in him.

We never knew what happened to bring about that drastic change in his life. Late one night, he was brought home so drunk that he couldn't even walk, and his friends left him lying in his front yard. When he woke up hours later, everything was different somehow. He cleaned up his physical appearance, got his finances in order, and never drank again.

He later married his childhood friend and became active in the church. He and his wife took meals to the needy, prayed for the sick, and taught a class. He was known as Happy Elmer because he smiled so much. The years of dark thoughts and depression were healed. Elmer's knowledge of the Scriptures caused many to think he'd gone to seminary.

Over the years, I asked him several times, "What happened on the lawn that night? Did you have a vision?" He only smiled. But we both knew the Lord alone had restored Elmer's lost years. Thanks be to God!

Father God, I thank You for being a God of restoration. I praise You for the Holy Spirit who instills in me an understanding of Your Word in spite of my lack of knowledge. Fill me with gratitude for Your daily mercies. In Jesus' name, amen.

A Familiar Word

It shall be that everyone who calls on the name of the Lord will be saved (Acts 2:21, *NASB*).

Scripture: Acts 2:14-21
Song: "Mighty to Save"

The endorsements on the back cover or inside of a book encourage me to read it. If a respected teacher or one of my favorite authors comments about the book, I am apt to purchase it. My selection many times depends on comments from other readers. I may quote a portion of the book in teaching a class.

In the Bible, God's servants often quoted from past prophets and leaders. Those who came before us can bring clarity to the Scriptures and help their descendants interpret contemporary circumstances. God spoke to the biblical prophets and to the church fathers, and it behooves us to listen to them.

Peter wanted to give creditability to the message he delivered to the crowd, as they tried to understand how these simple men spoke in many different languages. He did it by quoting the prophet Joel, who said, centuries earlier, that everything now unfolding before them would indeed take place. Through the credibility of Joel, Peter was able to explain to the people what was happening. Thankfully, he knew the words of the prophet.

When I read my Bible, I draw closer to God, and His words become familiar to me. I am able to lean on Him and not my own understanding. His Word speaks life.

Thank You, Father, for the words of Peter and Joel as they remind us clearly that everyone who calls upon Your name will be saved. I praise You for saving me through Your Son, Jesus, and His precious sacrifice of atonement. In His name, amen.

Not Slow, but Patient

The LORD is not slow about His promise, as some count slowness, but is patient toward you, not wishing for any to perish but for all to come to repentance (2 Peter 3:9, *NASB*).

Scripture: 2 Peter 3:1-10
Song: "Standing on the Promises"

The band bus was ready to leave for the high-school football game in the next town. I was supposed to be on the bus, but an accident on my route had the road blocked for several miles. This was before the days of cell phones, and I remember being frantic that I would miss the bus.

The other band members were anxious to get on the way, encouraging the driver to get going. However, this driver was a patient man (he had to be to drive teenagers to ball games). When I arrived at the school and saw the bus still there, I rejoiced. The driver hadn't wanted anyone left behind. I thanked him as I stepped into the bus . . . and the band members cheered.

The Lord has promised His return, but we don't have any idea when it will be. Meanwhile, while we wait, there is kingdom work to do as we share the gospel with those who silently despair of this life.

There is so much to do! Seekers need to be welcomed into our lives; the poor need to be loved and helped; the new believers need to be mentored. . . . God is not slow but patient. He waits.

My dear Father in Heaven, thank You for being so patient with me and loving me so deeply. Help me be patient and understanding with everyone in my world of relationships. I want others to know You and call upon Your name too. In the name of Jesus, Lord and Savior of all, I pray. Amen.

Creation Displays Hope

I will gather all nations and bring them down to the Valley of Jehoshaphat. There I will put them on trial (Joel 3:1, 2).

Scripture: Joel 3:1-3, 18-21
Song: "For the Beauty of the Earth"

The winter brought a record ice storm that tore down trees and utility poles, leaving people cold in their homes for a week. The trees around our home grew heavy, and branches fell to the ground. Looking like a war zone, our area was declared a state of emergency by the government. Things looked bleak.

When spring finally arrived and the land became warm with the rays of the sun, good things began to happen. Bulbs broke through the ground, and moss on the rocks turned green. The birds sang, building their nests anew as God's creation displayed hope and life. The land was transformed from bleak to beauty before our very eyes.

Our spirits lifted amidst all of this new, blossoming life. We once again knew we would have crops and vegetation. But now these things were much more precious to us; we so appreciated what had been lost but now was graciously restored.

Joel reminds his people and us that the Lord will allow evil to prevail in the world for a limited time, but then judgment will surely come. In a sense, all of us will face the trial he proclaims. For even in the New Testament we read: "For we must all appear before the judgment seat of Christ, so that each of us may receive what is due us" (2 Corinthians 5:10).

Almighty Lord, when things look bleak, You give us hope. You restore and bring life to the earth and provide for our needs. Thank You for Your merciful love, great judge of the world! Through Christ, amen.

No Matter Their Past

"Let your remorse tear at your hearts and not your garments." Return to the Lord your God, for he is gracious and merciful. He is not easily angered (Joel 2:13, *TLB*).

Scripture: Joel 2:12, 13, 18, 19, 28-32
Song: "Return, O Wanderer, Return"

Tamara walked into class wearing her Jesus T-shirt and carrying a Bible. She was in my class at the rehab center and soon would be going home for a visit. She was eager to see her husband and little boy. Yet, for various reasons, her other family members weren't happy about her coming home. "I'm wearing this shirt home," she commented, and sat down.

"Why?" I asked

"Because it's my favorite."

"How will your family members feel about it?"

"Well, they know I wouldn't have worn this before!"

The Jesus shirt was her statement of belief—and a profound statement about her Savior's ability to transform a life.

When Tamara returned from her visit, she tearfully told how her love for her hurtful, non-believing family members had poured forth. One cousin asked her about knowing Jesus. Tamara didn't wear her Jesus shirt but shared her Jesus heart. It brought results.

Joel reminds the people that God wants to bless them as they return to Him. He tells them that all who call upon the name of the Lord will be saved (see Joel 2:32). No matter their past.

Heavenly Father, let my actions speak more loudly to glorify You than any lettering I could put on a shirt or business sign. Fill my heart with love and compassion for others, so they will want to know You personally. In Jesus' name I pray. Amen.

Be Our Eyes

Moses said, "Please do not leave us. You know where we should camp in the wilderness, and you can be our eyes. If you come with us, we will share with you whatever good things the Lord gives us" (Numbers 10:31, 32).

Scripture: Numbers 10:29-36
Song: "Guide Me, O Thou Great Jehovah"

Despite successful surgery on his brain tumor decades ago when he was only 8, Tyler has been left with numerous limitations. Because of his poor vision and sense of balance, he needs an assistance dog wherever he goes. His present canine companion, Tucker, serves as a good set of eyes and keeps Ty from falling.

It's not all work and no play for Tucker. His master shares treats, trips to ball games and concerts, and even an occasional vacation trip with the big golden retriever. Tucker gets good food, veterinary care, and a comfortable bed. In the summer he has his own sunglasses and a raft to float around in the pool with Tyler. He watches Tyler and watches *out* for him.

The Israelites needed the eyes and experience of Moses' brother-in-law as they came to the wilderness. Like Tucker for Tyler—and Hobab for the Israelites—the Lord can see the way ahead and take us through unfamiliar territory. But unlike Moses and Tyler, we can't make any provision for God. He is our vision, our guide, and our life source for everything.

Lord, guide me in Your wisdom. Help me to rest in the assurance that You dwell in me. I know there is nowhere I can go where You haven't already gone. Through Christ, amen.

March 27–31. **Katherine Douglas**, of Swanton, Ohio, says you'll be reading a lot about sheep this week. But the closest she's come to sheep is walking by the sheep barn at the local county fair.

One Man's Meat

I will tend them in a good pasture . . . There they will lie down in good grazing land, and there they will feed in a rich pasture on the mountains of Israel (Ezekiel 34:14).

Scripture: Ezekiel 34:11-16
Song: "Break Thou the Bread of Life"

If it's edible, my niece probably cannot eat it. She's allergic to dairy products, wheat products, and peanuts to name a few of her no-nos. Sometimes the presence of certain foods in the same room can trigger anaphylaxis, so she's seen the point of an EpiPen® more than once. She's known as a "frequent flyer" in a number of hospital emergency rooms. Even food labels can't always be trusted. As a result, Candace takes great care in her meal preparation and food selections.

Likewise, livestock farmers have to be careful that the right animal gets the right supplements. A number of foods necessary for the diet of some livestock pose a deadly threat to sheep. The mineral, copper, which makes for a healthy coat in cows, poisons sheep. Without the farmer's careful oversight, a sheep can die from something which causes another animal to thrive.

God promised to provide Israel "good grazing land and . . . rich pasture." Jesus is our source of living water and the bread of life (see John 4:10; 6:35.) Our spiritual nutritional needs are met in Him. No wonder the shepherd David declared, "Taste and see that the Lord is good" (Psalm 34:8).

I pray, Lord God, that I won't hunger or thirst for the things of this life that can poison my relationship with You or others. I know Your words are health and life. Keep me from this world's spiritual junk food that I may live as a healthy, growing child in Your family. In the name of Jesus, my Savior, I pray. Amen.

What Makes a Good King?

I will raise up for David a righteous Branch, a King who will reign wisely and do what is just (Jeremiah 23:5).

Scripture: Jeremiah 23:1-8
Song: "King of Kings"

Today I searched the Internet for the names of history's greatest kings. First I Googled *good kings of history*. The first name on some websites? Adolf Hitler. Clearly, my definition of a good king differs somewhat from the cyberspace gurus. So I tried *greatest kings of history*. Some of a dozen or so that appeared included Alexander the Great, Genghis Khan, Akbar, and Frederick II of Prussia. As I read of their reigns, their conquests, their deeds, and what each may best be remembered for, words like *intimidation*, *brutality*, and *oppression* appeared. None of those words describe the king in Jeremiah 23.

This king, "a righteous Branch" in today's Bible reading, has a much more impressive and appealing biographical sketch. Wise, righteous, just, and merciful describe this ruler. Although Jeremiah preceded both of our king's comings, we stand between the two.

Christ, who gave us His righteousness and took our sin, will come again to establish everlasting righteousness. No longer will human beings be making names for themselves by conquest, intimidation, or oppression. "The Lord will be king over the whole earth. On that day there will be one Lord, and his name the only name" (Zechariah 14:9).

Holy Lord, You alone are king over all. I ask that You give our government leaders wisdom in their goals and decisions. I pray that they would be men and women who govern justly, fairly, and wisely. Through Christ the Lord of all. Amen.

Our Good Shepherd

I am the good shepherd. The good shepherd lays down his life for the sheep (John 10:11).

Scripture: John 10:11-18
Song: "Savior, Like a Shepherd Lead Us"

A local rancher was at home when his barn caught fire. He risked his life to save his horses. Neighbors helped him as he tried to evacuate them, but he alone went into the smoke and flames because they were his horses. He wasn't able to save them all, and to this day he wears the scars of his attempted rescues.

We read every day of common people doing the uncommon thing: risking their lives for others—a pet, their livestock, or another human being. How noble!

Would I do the same in their situations? I don't know, but I do know one thing: Jesus Christ did so much more for me and you as our good shepherd. He did more than just risk His life to save us; He laid His life down.

Five times in our reading today we see that the Lord loves us so much that He purposely laid down His life to secure our salvation. He went beyond putting himself in harm's way. He did more than take a chance. Lovingly, determinedly, He set out to save us from sin by the only way it could be done: willingly laying down his life. What a shepherd! What a Savior!

Thank You, Lord Jesus, for Your incarnation and eternal sacrifice to redeem me from my sin and selfishness. Thank You that, before I even was aware of You, You loved me with an everlasting love. Help me, Holy Spirit, to follow my king and shepherd in obedience today. In the name of the Father and of the Son and of the Holy Spirit, I pray. Amen.

Great and Good Shepherd

Now may the God of peace, who through the blood of the eternal covenant brought back from the dead our Lord Jesus, that great Shepherd of the sheep, equip you with everything good for doing his will (Hebrews 13:20, 21).

Scripture: Hebrews 13:17, 20, 21
Song: "Gentle Shepherd"

Craig Rogers, a shepherd in the state of Virginia, loves what he does. He takes great pride in caring for his sheep. He says, "shepherding requires more hands-on work than most livestock farming," yet he never tires of it. He admits to spending more time than he should to watch a new lamb come into the world.

He knows by experience that his sheep depend on him for everything: food, lodging, pasture, protection, and health care. Apart from him and his shepherding dog, his sheep are susceptible to both predators and environmental dangers. For this shepherd, his vocation brings "personal satisfaction with few equals." He sounds like a really good shepherd, doesn't he?

We read in our Scripture yesterday that Jesus is the good shepherd. Today in Hebrews we see He is the "great Shepherd." Throughout His years of ministry among men and women, the Lord Jesus delighted in His sheep, just as Craig Rogers delights in his. God the Father brought the great shepherd back from the dead. Jesus Christ continues today as our great and good shepherd.

Dear Heavenly Father, today I will be tempted to walk independently of You. I want to commit my day to You right now. Give me contentment in what I do—or in what I can no longer do. Help me to model Your Son in teaching or working with others. In His precious name I pray. Amen.

DEVOTIONS®

► **APRIL**

The LORD is my shepherd . . . he leads me . . . . He guides me
. . . you are with me . . . your goodness and love will follow
me . . . I will dwell in the house of the LORD forever.

—*Psalm 23*

Gary Wilde, Editor | Margaret K. Williams, Project Editor

Photo © iStock | Thinkstock®

DEVOTIONS® is published quarterly by Standard Publishing, Cincinnati, Ohio, www.standardpub.com. Copyright © 2015 by Standard Publishing. All rights reserved. Topics based on the Home Daily Bible Readings, International Sunday School Lessons. Copyright © 2013 by the Committee on the Uniform Series. Printed in the U.S.A. All Scripture quotations, unless otherwise indicated, are taken from the *HOLY BIBLE, NEW INTERNATIONAL VERSION®. NIV®.* Copyright © 1973, 1978, 1984, 2011 by Biblica, Inc.® Used by permission of Zondervan. All rights reserved worldwide. Scripture quotations marked (KJV) are taken from the King James Version, public domain. Scripture quotations marked (NKJV) are taken from the New King James Version®. Copyright © 1982 by Thomas Nelson, Inc. Used by permission. All rights reserved.

Safety in Numbers

Be alert and of sober mind. Your enemy the devil prowls around like a roaring lion looking for someone to devour (1 Peter 5:8).

Scripture: 1 Peter 5:1-11
Song: "Bring Them In"

On the televised nature programs, a lion, a cougar, or a jackal rushes at a herd, quickly creating panic. If one animal separates from the rest, the predator has won. For the attacker, separation is the key: isolate vulnerable prey from other robust members of the flock. The young, the old, or the wounded become the prime targets. Even if matched one for one, the disadvantaged hunted seldom escapes the hunter.

In the church, unity is the key: we need one another in the flock. In an increasingly dangerous world, fellow believers provide us with encouragement, support, and help. As caring as our shepherd—our minister—may be, he is one person. Without the care and ministry of the other sheep in our congregation, we're at high risk for enemy attack.

Who could you encourage today? It may be as simple as making a telephone call or sending an e-mail that says, "I'm praying for you this very moment." Whatever it is, be ready to protect a fellow Christian from physical isolation and spiritual discouragement.

Father, make me alert to the needs of the members in my church family. Help me to go beyond a handshake or a smile and get involved with the difficulties that come to each life. I pray in Jesus' name. Amen.

April 1, 2. **Katherine Douglas** of Swanton, Ohio, says you'll be reading a lot about sheep this week. But the closest she's come to sheep is walking by the sheep barn at the local county fair.

The Spirit's Sulphur

You prepare a table before me in the presence of my enemies. You anoint my head with oil; my cup overflows (Psalm 23:5).

Scripture: Psalm 23
Song: "Come, Holy Spirit"

Summertime brings insects by the hoards. For sheep around the world, the list of pesky pests is long. According to author and former shepherd, Phillip Keller, sheep are victimized by warble flies, heel flies, deerflies, nose flies, botflies, mosquitoes, and a host of other winged warriors. Today's western shepherds use commercial sprays to fight the pests, but for centuries home remedies did the trick—various combinations of linseed oil, tar, and sulphur.

In Keller's book, *A Shepherd Looks at Psalm 23*, we read that once the anointing oil is applied, "an incredible transformation" occurs among the suffering sheep. No longer agitated, they grow quiet and content. Keller likens it to the work of the Holy Spirit in our lives. With the anointing balm of our comforter, the Holy Spirit, we get relief from the distractions and irritations of life.

I can't will myself to relax when my husband's Alzheimer's disease gives us both a really bad day, like it has today. I call out again for peace and comfort—and it only comes from the anointing hand of my shepherd, the Lord Jesus.

O gracious Father, I need Your nurturing today. I'm troubled in mind and spirit, and You alone can get me through the pain and uncertainty that I feel. Fill me to overflowing with the compassion of Your Son and the joy of Your salvation. In the name of Jesus, who lives and reigns with You and the Holy Spirit. Amen.

Fading Condemnation

For God did not send his Son into the world to condemn the world, but to save the world through him (John 3:17).

Scripture: John 3:17-21
Song: "Pass Me Not, O Gentle Savior"

None of us has a perfect life at the moment, nor do we have a perfect past. If we allow the power of our past to control our future, we will never move forward. But here's the real problem: Even though I know I'm forgiven and free of my past life, will I hold someone else's past against them instead of sharing the saving grace of Jesus with them?

Sometimes we hold others accountable when what they truly need is to be held—simply to be held in all compassion.

No matter who we are or what we have done, we can be free. We can experience life in a whole new way. We can move beyound our past when we boldly declare we will live by the truth of His Word and not the shame of our failures.

The past has stolen enough of our days. Enough is enough. We can't start a new chapter in life if we keep rereading the last one. It will cost us a little bit of courage, but we can do it. After all, our Savior, Jesus, specializes in second chances. He is the restorer of hope, the giver of joy, and the provider of eternal life. When we turn our eyes upon Him, condemnation fades away.

Merciful Father, I am struggling with past sins today. I know they are forgiven through the cross of my Savior, but their guilt still pesters my heart. Take the guilt and replace it with gratitude. I trust You to do it! Soon may I know only Your mercy, Your healing power, and Your grace. In Jesus' name, amen.

April 3–9. **Tammy Whitehurst** is a motivational Christian speaker and writer who travels and shares the joy of Jesus with small and large audiences. She lives in White Oak, Texas.

Recalculate!

Do not love the world or anything in the world. If anyone loves the world, love for the Father is not in them (1 John 2:15).

Scripture: 1 John 2:15-17
Song: "Jesus, Lover of My Soul"

It's easy to let our lives drift off course, because it rarely happens overnight. Slowly but surely it happens . . . and then we wake up one day and find ourselves in a dry, dark desert. We chose a little detour, but it led to a broad highway taking us far from the lighted path.

Mistakes were made. Life happened. We bought things we thought would satisfy our soul. But they only opened us to an even deeper desire.

Will we let that desire lead us to its source? If not, today we will miss the peace that surpasses all understanding, a heavenly kind of inner quiet the world cannot give us. For we have finally come to know that the world can't make us rich.

True richness comes from knowing the one who owns it all. And it has nothing to do with the circumstances. Even amidst a daily chaos, where life may not unfold as we expected, with Jesus it can be more than we ever imagined.

When I hear: "Do not love the world," I'm nudged to take a quick exit from the fast lane I'm traveling in order to get back in the faith lane.

Is it time for a U-turn? As my GPS says, "Recalculating."

Lord, I need help choosing between the things of this world and the truth in Your Word. I have allowed my natural desires to cloud my vision of Your surpassing peace. Help me to hear Your voice within every longing. In Your name, amen.

Face Down Meets Face Up

"No one ever spoke the way this man does," the guards replied (John 7:46).

Scripture: John 7:45-52
Song: "In the Garden"

We go through tough times—that is the life we live. As Jesus put it to His disciples: "In this world you will have trouble" (John 16:33a). Thus we know that becoming a Christian doesn't make the tough times go away. However, we do have Jesus to lean on and to walk with us through the difficult times.

Jesus' words fill us with hope when we are hopeless because He loves us even when we hurt too much to love back. He cares when we couldn't care less, and He holds us in His vision, even when we aren't looking for Him.

Yes, His words soothe our souls and calm us down. When we listen, hopeless meets hope; facedown meets faceup. Spiritually dry meets living water pouring over us.

If you are walking through a difficult time, do not forget that Jesus is holding out His hand for you to grasp. Hold His hand and let Him carry You through this time. His words will fill You with hope in the brighter days ahead and with joy as You remember Your identity in Him: a beloved child of the king.

His words are the promises we so desperately need to hear. There is another side to troubles, and Jesus spoke of this as well: "But take heart! I have overcome the world" (John 16:33b).

Lord Jesus Christ, I need to hear from You this very day. I need Your words to fill me up, to give me wisdom and courage, to help me walk forward in joy and peace. Only You can uphold me this way, and I trust You to do it. In Your holy name, amen.

Complainer or Conqueror?

They spoke against God and against Moses, and said, "Why have you brought us up out of Egypt to die in the wilderness? There is no bread! There is no water! And we detest this miserable food!" (Numbers 21:5).

Scripture: Numbers 21:4-9
Song: "Come, Thou Fount of Every Blessing"

I've noticed that people tend to fall into two categories: conquerors or complainers. As a result, our words can make us a drain or a fountain. Are we refreshing those around us or draining those who come near us? Think about this for a second. People are either delighted to see us coming or overjoyed to see us leaving.

What overall effect do you have? Swirling in complaints, we thrust others away. But a positive spirit is so attractive!

And what damage a complaining spirit can do! Surely even the great Moses became discouraged with the constant haranguing of the people in the desert. It is a serious thing to put obstacles in the way of God's chosen leaders.

There comes a point in everyone's life when we must decide to shift gears. Shift into high gear and get out of low gear. The bottom line is we will never get to where we want to be by complaining about where we are today. If we are running this race with endurance, we look beyond the problem and pursue the goal. It's an attitude shift that's absolutely essential. In the name of Jesus we can be conquerors.

O Father in Heaven, help me to see everything today as a blessing from Your hand—You can use the difficulties for good and even redeem the evil. Please forgive me when I have not been grateful. Through Christ I pray. Amen.

Will You Be a Faith Keeper?

Later, Joseph of Arimathea asked Pilate for the body of Jesus. Now Joseph was a disciple of Jesus, but secretly because he feared the Jewish leaders (John 19:38).

Scripture: John 19:38-42
Song: "At the Cross"

There are all kinds of keepers in this world.

The Scorekeeper: makes sure to let us know we didn't win. They point out the losers.

The Bookkeeper: writes down everything we owe and never forgets anything or forgives anyone.

The Housekeeper: keeps everything dusted, picked up, and perfect in the house; no time for play, for laughter—for anything—until the house is spotless.

The Peacekeeper: tries to control the situation, smoothing things over, and never rocking the boat.

And finally, there is the Promise keeper: Jesus! Actually, He's both the promise maker and promise keeper. His word never returns void, and He always restores, refreshes, and renews. What He says will happen, will happen.

Joseph of Arimathea apparently feared a public identification with Jesus. And it was, indeed, risky. Why claim allegiance to a prosecuted and executed criminal?

Is it any less risky today? Yet this same Jesus is alive and invites our allegiance, moment by moment. His promises never fail.

Dear God, I want to trust and obey my risen Lord. I want to be a stronger faith keeper. Help me to look to the one who conquered even the grave, that I might overcome the fear of my world's disapproval. In the name of Jesus I pray. Amen.

The Good, the Bad, and the Ugly

Speak evil of no man . . . For we ourselves also were sometimes foolish, disobedient, deceived, serving divers lusts and pleasures, living in malice and envy, hateful, and hating one another (Titus 3:2, 3, *KJV*).

Scripture: Titus 3:1-7
Song: "Amazing Grace"

Satan knows our name and calls us by our sin. God knows our sin and calls us by our name—a blessed difference!

The Point: It's not what we have been called, it is what we answer to that counts. Those names we were called through seething teeth do not define who we are unless we let them.

According to Titus, we must speak evil of no one. After all, he told those church members that they could once legitimately be called sinners—disobedient, living by their own desires, "hating one another."

But now we, like they, have been adopted into the kingdom family and are now called children of God. That name voids and erases all the other epithets ever maliciously hurled our way, past or present. But that is only part of the process; we must ask others to forgive us for our wrongdoings as well.

The next time you hear the enemy inviting you to look at your past failures and sins, listen for God saying to you, "Look at my Son." For "the kindness and love of God our Saviour toward man appeared" (v. 4, *KJV*), and that has made all the difference.

Dear Lord God, thank You for Your grace that made me, through the washing of regeneration, a new creation. I want to live today in a way that glorifies only You, my Creator and Father. In Jesus' name I pray. Amen.

What's Love Got to Do with It?

God so loved the world that he gave his one and only Son, that whoever believes in him shall not perish but have eternal life (John 3:16).

Scripture: John 3:1-16
Song: "All the Sacrifice Is Ended"

Some people say the best things in life are the people we love, the places we've seen, and the memories we've made along the way. It's true, isn't it? But underneath it all is the greatest thing: That we have an eternal Savior. This life is best when it's unending life in Him.

When we consider how valuable people are and how amazing God is to His people, we begin to desire to have a heart like His. Clearly, in light of the cross, God's heart is a giving heart. Can we be giving like that? Could we love others that much?

Even the thoroughly secular philosopher Georges Bataille was able to say something quite profound and beautiful about sacrifice: "Sacrifice is nothing other than the production of sacred things." Think about it. When we pour ourselves out in love for others, if affects them for the good and makes them into something better. If it lifts their eyes to Heaven, it has the chance to bring them into Christ's sacred family.

More and more, I want to see people through the eyes of Jesus—to see them as so valuable and worthy of love that even the Lord of the universe would sacrifice himself on their behalf. So, what sacrifice will I too consider?

Heavenly Father, I believe that You gave Jesus to save me from my sins. I confess that I cannot fully understand that love, but I thank You and praise You with all of my heart. I pray in His precious, holy name. Amen.

Professional Proof

When they came to Jesus and found that he was already dead, they did not break his legs (John 19:33).

Scripture: John 19:31-37
Song: "My Faith Has Found a Resting Place"

During the last few months of my grandmother's life, whenever her nurses thought death might be near, they let us know. I remember rushing to the hospital one night, expecting the worst. But shortly after we arrived, Gram sat up, laughed and joked with us, and ate dinner. This happened a few times, and we were always happy to see her revive.

But early one Sunday morning, the doctor said Gram had only hours to live, and we hurried to her side. She lay still and unresponsive as we visited quietly. We prayed. We read the Bible to her and she died.

The transformation from life to death happened in an instant, just as it did when Jesus died. When the soldiers came to Jesus, ready to break His legs in an effort to speed His death, they realized He had already died. These soldiers, trained to carry out crucifixions, were skilled in causing death, familiar with the transformation that takes place in a body after a person has died. And so these enemies of Jesus, by acknowledging Christ's death, refute the belief, held even today by some people, that Jesus didn't really die on the cross. Christ's executioners provide firsthand evidence that Jesus physically died for our sin.

Dear Lord, I'm so glad I never have to doubt the fact that You died to take the punishment for my sin. I praise You for rising and ascending too. In Your name, amen.

April 10–16. **Kathy Hardee** writes from her home in Illinois. She enjoys telling people about her great God and spending time with her husband and family, which includes seven grandchildren.

The Truth, Our Confidence

If we receive the witness of men, the witness of God is greater; for this is the witness of God which He has testified of His Son (1 John 5:9, *NKJV*).

Scripture: 1 John 5:6-12
Song: "Tell Me the Story of Jesus"

I served as one of 12 jurors on a murder trial. Several young people had partied all night and then beat a girl to death, throwing her bludgeoned body into a ditch alongside a country road. A jogger, who passed by with her curious golden retriever, found the body a few days later.

The prosecuting attorney presented mostly circumstantial evidence. However, the defendant wrote a confession that caused the jury to vote guilty, unanimously, after only a few minutes of deliberation. She gave details about that horrible night. She expressed how she felt and what she thought as she watched her former friend being beaten to death.

The thin, young, blonde defendant looked vulnerable and innocent. However, her own testimony proved her guilt.

God understands the need for a true witness and certain testimony. And that's what He has provided for us in His Word. With God as our witness, we can trust that Jesus is the Christ, the Messiah sent from God to save His people from their sins.

May we live every day confident that God's testimony is true: "And this is the testimony: that God has given us eternal life, and this life is in his Son" (v. 11).

Dear God, thank You for giving me Your Word, the Bible. Help me to live in light of the truths You have given. And thank You for the most important truth of all, that I have eternal life through Jesus Christ, Your Son. In Jesus' name I pray, amen.

Our Joy in Christ

The Lord is near to those who have a broken heart, and saves such as have a contrite spirit (Psalm 34:18, *NKJV*).

Scripture: Psalm 34:15-20
Song: "The Broken Heart"

During my late teens and early twenties, I strayed from God. But I didn't just inadvertently wander off; I deliberately walked away. Everything I'd been told not to do, I did. This went on for about four years.

But then the day came when I wanted the joy of God back in my life. I longed for His pleasure. I missed the closeness we once shared. So I began reading my Bible again, and praying.

But it brought me no happiness. In my mind, I knew Jesus had died for me, and that God had forgiven me, but my heart disagreed. I didn't feel forgiven, only remorseful. Perhaps you can relate?

Today's Scripture gives us hope. It proclaims the wonderful truth that God is near those who have a broken heart over their sin. In fact, did you know God enjoys living with people who acknowledge the depths of their sinfulness (see Isaiah 57:15)? And He is pleased with those who depend solely on Christ's shed blood for the forgiveness of their sin.

Lingering sadness over our past sins may always be with us. But instead of overwhelming us, we can allow it to draw us nearer to this one who died in our place, who paid for our sin.

God, My Father, thank You for offering Your Son as a sacrifice for my sin. I will praise You every day— and for all of eternity—for taking the punishment I deserved. May my joy always be in You! Through Christ's precious name, amen.

All Fulfilled

"Let's not tear it," they said to one another. "Let's decide by lot who will get it." This happened that the scripture might be fulfilled (John 19:24).

Scripture: John 19:23-25
Song: "No One Ever Cared for Me like Jesus"

A group of students came to class prepared to take a test. The teacher told them to read the instructions carefully before they answered the questions. When the bell rang, the teacher collected the papers.

It turned out that every student who handed in a blank test received an A+. Those who answered questions, even correctly, received a failing grade. Why? At the end of the long paragraph of boring instructions were these words: "Do not answer the following questions. Sign your test, and then turn it in at the end of class."

That day the importance of reading and following instructions was permanently etched upon those students' minds.

Jesus knew the importance of following instructions too. He knew Scripture well. So He knew exactly what needed to be done to save His people from their sins. Therefore, nothing about the cross surprised Him. Everything Jesus did, everything He said (or didn't say) was according to God's plan. If just one Old Testament prophecy about the Messiah had not been fulfilled, we would still be in our sins, and Christ would have died for nothing.

Lord Christ, I'm overwhelmed with gratitude that You voluntarily laid down Your life for me. You were aware of the horrors You would suffer, yet You willingly accepted that suffering for me. I praise Your name. Amen.

We Are Family

When Jesus therefore saw His mother, and the disciple whom He loved standing by, He said to His mother, "Woman, behold your son!" (John 19:26, *NKJV*).

Scripture: John 19:26, 27
Song: "The Bond of Love"

Eric, Andi, Valerie, and Amy are the same age as my children. I feel a similar responsibility towards them as I do toward my own kids. I want to encourage, advise, help, and guide them. I'm thrilled with their successes and saddened by their hurts.

I've known Arlene for less than a year. I love her. She reminds me of my grandma.

Carole is my mentor, friend, and adviser. Her encouragement and guidance are instrumental in my walk with Christ.

Mary, Becky, Sue, and Bonnie are like sisters. Karen is like a twin sister. What she feels, I feel. What happens to her seems to happen to me—even though we live 650 miles apart. Steve and John are like brothers to me. We all, as Christians, are family.

Jesus demonstrated the significance of our spiritual family ties on the cross, when He said to Mary, "Behold your son!" and when He said to John, "Behold your mother!"

John wasn't Mary's son; James was. So were Joses, Simon, and Judas (see Matthew 13:55 *NKJV*). But Jesus chose John to care for His mother. From that hour on, John took Mary into his home.

O Father, may we show this same kind of care and concern for those in Your family, the church. Thank You for welcoming me into this blessed fellowship, and please help me to grow in love for every one of my spiritual siblings. In Jesus' name, amen.

Go Ahead—Jump!

Peter arose and ran to the tomb (Luke 24:12, *NKJV*).

Scripture: Luke 24:1-12
Song: "Father of Everlasting Grace"

A few weeks after my son's wedding, I hurt my new daughter-in-law's feelings. When I found out that I'd offended her, I was deeply troubled, not knowing what to do. So I wrote Chrissy an e-mail and begged her to forgive me.

I sent the e-mail, and then checked my in-box every five minutes, hoping our relationship would be restored. When she returned her e-mail with precious words of forgiveness, I jumped for joy.

It's hard to imagine the sorrow Peter must have felt after he denied Jesus three times on the night before His crucifixion. How he must have regretted saying he never knew His master. The Bible tells us Peter wept bitterly (see Luke 22:54-62).

Later, when Peter heard the tomb of Jesus was empty, he ran to see for himself. Possibly he hoped Jesus had risen from the grave, as He said He would, and maybe he longed for the opportunity to say, "I'm sorry."

When we sin, we too can run to Christ. The empty tomb is proof that God accepted Jesus' sacrifice for our sins. Therefore, if we confess our sins, God will forgive us (see 1 John 1:9). Thanks to Jesus. (Doesn't that make you want to jump for joy?)

Father God, I praise You for the forgiveness You offer through the shed blood of Your Son, my Savior, Jesus Christ. I trust solely in the work He did on the cross for me, and I'll forever sing His praises. Worthy is the Lamb, in the name of the Father and of the Son and of the Holy Spirit. Amen.

Life After Life

Praise be to the God and Father of our Lord Jesus Christ! In his great mercy he has given us new birth into a living hope through the resurrection of Jesus Christ from the dead (1 Peter 1:3).

Scripture: John 20:1-10; 1 Peter 1:3-5, 8, 9
Song: "Victory in My Soul"

During the months before my father died, I usually ended our visits with prayer. We both needed to know that God was near, as Dad's health was failing fast.

When the hospice nurse said Dad had only a couple of days to live, I begged God to let me be with him when he died. I wanted to say good-bye with a prayer, one last time. All day on Friday, Dad's condition stayed the same. But on Saturday evening his breathing changed, and I knew it was time to pray.

I began my prayer with Psalm 23. When I finished and opened my eyes, Dad was gone. He had quietly and peacefully taken his last breath. "That was perfect," my brother said.

And it really was perfect. Not because he died peacefully and free from pain, but because Jesus conquered death for His children. Dad closed his eyes here, but he opened them in Heaven.

The gospel is good news because Jesus rose from the grave—the Father accepted His sacrifice for our sin. For those who love and believe in Him, death is swallowed up in victory. Thanks be to God, who gives us everlasting life through Christ our Lord.

Father in Heaven, please open my eyes to the glories of spending eternity with You. Remind me of Your triumph over death. You are the only true and living God, the Lord of glory. I praise Your holy name, through Christ. Amen.

Share Your Spiritual Gifts

I long to see you so that I may impart to you some spiritual gift to make you strong—that is, that you and I may be mutually encouraged by each other's faith (Romans 1:11, 12).

Scripture: Romans 1:1-15
Song: "Give Me a Heart Like Thine"

Every Sunday people walk into church with serious needs. The single mom hopes for enough money to pay the rent. A father fears he will lose his job. A teenager argues with his parents all the way to church because he wants more privileges. They all come to this gathering looking for help.

The apostle Paul had never been to Rome and didn't know the believers in the church there, which was probably started by Jewish Christians after the Day of Pentecost. Yet he wanted to give them a gift, something to help them become stronger believers. So he wrote the church members a letter.

In this epistle the apostle emphasizes that God's righteousness is a free gift for Jews and Gentiles alike. And it is received by faith. It is a glorious message for present-day believers as well.

For example, suppose we came to church every Sunday intent on strengthening the faith of our fellow-worshippers? It wouldn't take much—a smile, a hug, a listening ear, an invitation to lunch, a promise to pray.

You have spiritual gifts. Share them with friends in Christ.

Dear God, many of my friends are discouraged. Others live with despair every day. I look forward to opportunities to share with them the joy You can give. In the holy name of Jesus, my Lord and Savior, I pray. Amen.

April 17–23. **Jewell Johnson** lives in Arizona with her husband, LeRoy. They are parents to six children and grandparents to nine. Besides writing, Jewell enjoys reading, walking, and quilting.

Peace in Suffering

We also glory in our sufferings, because we know that suffering produces perseverance; perseverance, character; and character, hope. And hope does not put us to shame, because God's love has been poured out into our hearts (Romans 5:3-5).

Scripture: Romans 5:1-5
Song: "Wonderful Peace"

Our daughter was ill with eating disorders for 13 years, a time when my faith wavered. Some days I believed our prayers for her healing would be effective. Other times, my faith bottomed out. Yet, through the prayers of Christians, she recovered.

So when our grandson had an accident that resulted in a spinal cord injury, I remembered that past blessing and prayed fervent prayers for him. I know now that, in His time and in His way, God always responds to our suffering-induced pleadings.

Suffering was the norm for the believers Paul addressed. Roman Christians were besieged by doubts, financial and physical needs, and persecutions. Yet Paul encouraged them to glory in tribulations because of what these difficulties could accomplish in them—things like perseverance, character, and hope.

Is it any different for us today? Problems consume this world system, and God allows them for a time. If you are overwhelmed by a situation and can't see a way out, recall His promised presence. By faith, take His hand and walk with Him through the tough times. He will use the situation to grow You.

O Father, help me to see my difficulties today as opportunities to develop greater endurance and a deeper faith in Your power. And thank You for Your enduring peace. It can flow within any difficulty, assuring me of Christ's presence. Through Him, amen.

The Power of One

For as by one man's disobedience many were made sinners, so by the obedience of one shall many be made righteous (Romans 5:19, *KJV*).

Scripture: Romans 5:18-21
Song: "Speak, My Lord"

In 1603 Dr. John Reynolds envisioned a new translation of the Bible. Though colleagues opposed the project, he appealed to King James, who liked the idea. The king appointed 54 Bible scholars from all parts of Great Britain to translate the Hebrew, Greek, and Aramaic into English. In 1611, the *King James Bible* was made available to English-speaking people.

We might say that one man, John Reynolds, received a heavenly calling and obeyed. The results were astounding. Today we continue to enjoy the fruit of Dr. Reynolds's idea whenever we read the *King James Version* of the Bible.

The one man whom Paul proclaimed made a universal difference for good over evil. Through one man's disobedience, the sin of Adam, the human race was devastated. But Jesus, obedient to God's plan, delivered us from Adam's curse, bringing light and life to all who believe.

A parent speaking positive words can change a child's life. An employer offering affirming words can keep a discouraged employee going. One person consistently praying for a friend can bring him to Christ. Never underestimate the power of one to bring good to many.

Dear Jesus, thank You for becoming the second Adam, the one who successfully faced temptation and sin—and defeated it forever on behalf of us all. I am so grateful for the forgiveness of sins I now enjoy. In Your precious name I pray. Amen.

Men and Nature Rejoice

We ourselves, who have the firstfruits of the Spirit, groan inwardly as we wait eagerly for our adoption to sonship, the redemption of our bodies (Romans 8:23).

Scripture: Romans 8:18-25
Song: "Jesus Is Coming Again"

One spring I planted petunias in pots on our patio. As I watered and fertilized them, they rewarded me with bountiful blooms. But one morning when I looked outside, dirt was scattered on the cement, and not a flower remained. The explanation? Wild pigs roaming the area had made a trip through our yard in the night, eaten the flowers, and uprooted the plants.

God created a perfect environment for people and nature. The curse of sin affected both, however. For example, we humans become tired. Our bodies suffer diseases, and we groan as we wait for our complete redemption—freedom from the limitations of this body.

Nature, too, suffered from the fall. Plants are attacked by weeds, worms, and . . . wild pigs. These groan too, waiting for restoration to a perfect state.

The new heavens and new earth will change everything (see 2 Peter 3:12, 13). Nature will be redeemed and recreated. Believers will receive glorified bodies like Jesus' resurrected body. And the great thing for us today: To assure us of the glories ahead, God gave us the Holy Spirit as a living guarantee that better things are coming for all creation.

Almighty and Everlasting God, I can't fathom what a resurrected body will be like, but by faith I look forward to a body like Yours. And the reality of a new earth is a heavenly thought! All glory to You, through Christ my Lord. Amen.

The Prayer Helper

The Spirit helps us in our weakness. We do not know what we ought to pray for, but the Spirit himself intercedes for us through wordless groans (Romans 8:26).

Scripture: Romans 8:26-30
Song: "Day by Day"

When I began a new job in a new company, I wanted to know what their benefit package included. What kind of health insurance did the company offer? How many vacation days would I receive? How many sick days? Benefits are important on a job.

In our walk with God, we enjoy many benefits. We receive help in every area of our lives, even help to pray, through the intercession of the Holy Spirit on our behalf.

Why would the Spirit intercede for us? Perhaps it's because, in many cases, we simply don't know how we should pray. At other times, we're so overwhelmed by the problems we face that we forget to pray at all. Then there are occasions when our faith is at a low, and we can hardly bring ourselves to believe that God could change the situation.

Thus we have a helper in prayer. For each need, the Holy Spirit knows the perfect will of God, and He appeals to the Father on behalf of these needs. At other times He will show us what to pray for. In some instances, He prays for us.

Bottom line: Let us never be intimidated by the enormity of our needs. Call out to God. The Holy Spirit is with you, and He will intercede for you and through you.

Lord, I long to be effective in prayer. Give me courage to reach out in faith, cooperating with the Spirit to pray—and to do—Your will. Through Christ, amen.

Suffering to Bear His Name

Five times I received from the Jews the forty lashes minus one. Three times I was beaten with rods, once I was pelted with stones, three times I was shipwrecked, I spent a night and a day in the open sea (2 Corinthians 11:24, 25).

Scripture: 2 Corinthians 11:21-27
Song: "Must Jesus Bear the Cross Alone?"

Rosalind Bell-Smith attended art school intent on pursuing a career in that field. Then she met Jonathan Goforth, who planned to spend his life on the mission field. When Jonathan proposed to Rosalind, he made her promise she'd always put God's work first.

In China, Jonathan's passion for evangelism led him to journey into the country's interior. Knowing the diseases that lurked inland, Rosalind hesitated to take her young children there. But with Jonathan's assurances of God's sovereignty, Rosalind and the children went nevertheless. But the price was high: she buried 5 of her 11 children in Chinese soil.

The apostle Paul also suffered much to preach the gospel—daily mental anguish for the churches he had founded, constant distress over the false teachers who never stopped defaming his character, and unbelievable physical tortures.

Though most of us won't suffer as Rosalind Goforth or the apostle Paul, all Christians need to arm themselves with their overall approach to life: If need be, I am willing to share in the sufferings of Jesus in order to bear His name (see 1 Peter 4:13).

Dear Heavenly Father, work in my life until I thoroughly love and embrace Your perfect will with joy in my heart. Help me to see it as an honor to share in Your Son's sufferings. I pray in His holy name. Amen.

Unfathomable Love

Christ Jesus who died—more than that, who was raised to life—is at the right hand of God and is also interceding for us (Romans 8:34).

Scripture: Romans 5:6-11; 8:31-39
Song: "Holy Trinity, Thanks and Praise to Thee"

I have a friend who has faithfully prayed for our family for over 30 years. When two of our grandsons had accidents and suffered spinal cord injuries, she prayed. She prays for the safety of our sons who have seizures. When I was laid low with a fractured pelvis, she prayed for me until I was on my feet.

I am so thankful that Arlene carries our family to God's throne every day. But someone else prays for me and my family too. It is Jesus. And according to our Scripture today, He also intercedes for you.

Jesus gave His life for us, acquitting us of sin, and then left this earth. However, He has not left us; His Spirit dwells in us. Though Jesus lives in Heaven, day by day through His ministry of intercession, we experience God's presence.

Because Jesus prays for us, we receive merciful help with our needs. Because He intercedes, we have God's help to overcome daily temptations. As Jesus prays at God's right hand, we receive strength when we are weak.

You need not fail or become discouraged no matter what the trial. At this very minute, Christ Jesus, the risen Son of God, is pleading your case at His Father's right hand.

O Jesus, thank You for praying for me at the right hand of the Father. I can't comprehend the mystery of the holy Trinity, but I rejoice in the loving presence of the Father, Son, and Holy Spirit. How I appreciate Your eternal care and love. Amen.

Do You See What I See?

Blessed are your eyes because they see, and your ears because they hear (Matthew 13:16).

Scripture: Matthew 13:10-17
Song: "Face to Face"

A team of three men and two women, equipped with bolts, pitons, ropes, and pins, ascend a rugged mountain peak. Inch by inch, hook by hook, they creep, securing their anchors in crannies. Hours of straining, slipping, and pulling result in the thrill of a lifetime—the peace and beauty found at the summit.

My excitement grows with theirs as I watch the videos with great interest, wonder, and a bit of envy. How I wish I could see the world from that perspective, hear the rush of the wind, feel the warmth of the sun, smell the freshness of the air. Though my imagination works overtime, it can never simulate the marvel of standing on a mountaintop and gazing at the world below. Only the ones who endure the climb realize the splendor of the view.

Similarly, only those who believe and trust in Jesus know the fullness of His love, mercy, and grace. We hear Him speak of the promise of resurrected life in the formation of cherry blossoms. We see His power in the waves crashing on rocky shores. We smell His presence in the air after a storm. We taste His goodness in the familiar words of a friend. We are blessed—so fortunate—because of our affiliation with Jesus.

Dear Lord, nothing can match the richness, the splendor, the peace, or the beauty I've found in You. You alone are worthy to be praised, and I offer You my whole life. In the name of Jesus, Lord and Savior of all, I pray. Amen.

April 24–30. **Brenda K. Hendricks** enjoys writing and painting for children of all ages. She lives in Freeburg, Pennsylvania, with her husband and her high-spirited Airedale, Hunter.

The Sin of Neglect

You have not strengthened the weak or healed the sick or bound up the injured. You have not brought back the strays or searched for the lost. You have ruled them harshly and brutally (Ezekiel 34:4).

Scripture: Ezekiel 34:1-10
Song: "Rescue the Perishing"

Little children scavenging through garbage dumps in search of anything edible filled my husband with compassion while he did a military tour in El Salvador. In charge of the kitchen on an army base there, he received orders to dispose of boxes of canned foods that the U.S. government deemed outdated.

What a dilemma! He wanted to give the discarded victuals to the locals. But the authorities said: no handouts. So he instructed his committee, within earshot of the civilian helpers, to take the boxes to the dump with specific directions concerning their placement . . . on the other side of the fence. The next morning, not one of the boxes remained in the dump site.

It seems criminal to throw away perfectly good food in the midst of a poverty-stricken country, doesn't it? Yet, we live in a spiritually poverty-stricken nation and do little to feed the deprived souls around us. I wonder if our indifference would change if we could see souls as we see physical bodies. Would we be surprised at the malnourished state of many churchgoers? We may even be shocked at our own deprivation.

Heavenly Father, today I face a stark truth: I need more of Your Son, more of Your Word, more prayer, more tender care for others. I have neglected my responsibilities in tending to Your sheep. Forgive me, Lord, and motivate me to use the resources You supply for ministry to others. In Jesus' name, amen.

Childlike . . . or Just Childish?

Truly I tell you, unless you change and become like little children, you will never enter the kingdom of heaven (Matthew 18:3).

Scripture: Matthew 18:1-5, 10-14
Song: "Gracious Spirit, Dwell with Me"

My 6-year-old granddaughter, Sydney Rose, adores me. She says she wants to be just like me when she grows up. That'll probably change as she matures, but for now I'm elated by her words. Mostly she admires my creativity and sits for hours attempting to copy my drawings.

Despite her admiration, Sydney can become angry when I don't let her have her own way. She tells me I'm mean and that we're not friends any more. "Go away," she says before storming to her room and refusing to look at me, much less talk to me.

I leave her there to sulk. Eventually, usually just a few minutes later, she returns to the living room with a book, a game, or drawing paper and crayons, the twinkle restored in her eyes.

How quickly children forgive and move on!

Perhaps that's one part of the childlike attributes Jesus wants us to cultivate. Of course, acceptance of authority, the willingness to believe, and the desire to please our Father all play into Jesus' command to become like little children. But maybe, just maybe, the component we lack the most as adults is our willingness to forgive and move on. We are to be childlike . . . not childish.

Dear Lord, develop within me those childlike characteristics that please You, especially the willingness to forgive and move on, as I welcome Your children, both young and old. In Jesus' name I pray. Amen.

Keep Watch Like Good Shepherds

Keep watch over yourselves and all the flock of which the Holy Spirit has made you overseers. Be shepherds of the church of God, which he bought with his own blood (Acts 20:28).

Scripture: Acts 20:25-28
Song: "Reach Out and Touch"

Stress often accompanies running errands the night before vacation. One such occasion packed more of a wallop than my family and I had ever experienced. We stopped to fill the gas tank. A young man at the pump across from us stepped out of his car, placed the nozzle into his tank, and lit up a cigarette.

My husband, a head taller than the other man, grabbed the fellow by the front of his shirt, swiped the cigarette from his mouth, and stomped it out, all in a heartbeat. Gene said, "You can blow yourself up at your own convenience. But you will not blow up my family."

He let go of the man, who stumbled to regain his balance. My daughters and I, gaping in disbelief, stared at the big man we knew and loved. We'd never seen that side of him in action.

Gene's familiar, gentle, lamb-like spirit had turned into a roaring lion in the face of danger. He escalated from self-preservation to preservation of those he loved.

Similarly, God expects mature Christians to watch over weaker believers. He expects church leaders to protect the members. And in every case He calls us to put our own interests aside.

Heavenly Father, thank You for those church elders who protect and care for me. Help me, in turn, to show the shepherd's love to those for whom You have made me an overseer. In Jesus' name, amen.

Love: an Action Word

Again Jesus said, "Simon son of John, do you love me?" He answered, "Yes, Lord, you know that I love you." Jesus said, "Take care of my sheep" (John 21:16).

Scripture: John 21:15-19
Song: "Make Me a Servant"

I love coffee. I love this book. I love my job. I love your hair style. I love . . .

I loathe that we've overused the word *love* to the point of exhausting its meaning! We've become so accustomed to saying we love everything, from the apps on our phones to our favorite zucchini casserole, that we repeat the phrase to one another with as much meaningless intent. Many people have told me they love me. Few, however, have followed their words with actions, proving their affection. You see, *love* is an action word.

Call me sensitive, but when I'm excluded from activities by those who claim to love me, I don't feel loved. I feel rejected, hurt, and let down. Shamefully, I may retaliate. Instead of treating them the way I want to be treated, the way that shows love, I hold out on them, as well.

Apparently, mindless expressions date back a couple millennia. Peter swore he loved Jesus. He swore he'd follow Jesus to the death. When the opportunity arose for Peter to back up those words with action, he swore he had never known Jesus. Later, on a beautiful lakeshore, Jesus commanded Peter to prove his love by telling others about his risen Lord.

Dear Heavenly Father, Your Word reminds me that my words—too easily spoken—lose their meaning without actions to back them up. Today, help me walk the talk. In the name of Christ I pray. Amen.

Me Swooning . . . Seriously?

Jesus said, "You have now seen him; in fact, he is the one speaking with you." Then the man said, "Lord, I believe," and he worshiped him (John 9:37, 38).

Scripture: John 9:35-41
Song: "When We See Christ"

I'm not one to swoon over celebrities. At least, I never thought I was until the day I met my all-time favorite author. While others in our party spoke to him, I sat at the other end of the table eating my salad and chatting with those around me.

Eventually, he politely excused himself but paused at the empty chair directly across from me, asking whether he could join my friends and me. I responded, not with a polite smile, but with a giddy schoolgirl grin. We talked about my writing goals as well as his. He gave me some solid advice, sending my swoon-ometer over the top, much to my chagrin.

Nevertheless, the excitement soon wore off, and life returned to normal, unlike the blind man's encounter with Jesus. That day, the beggar received physical sight. But when Jesus heard that the Pharisees rejected the blind man, Jesus looked for him, which resulted in a gift even greater than physical sight—the man received spiritual insight.

Likewise, Jesus seeks us, introduces himself to us, and offers spiritual insight—sometimes through the words of others, sometimes through His written Word—so that we too may freely worship Him.

Precious Lord, because You sought me, I have received spiritual sight, and I worship You. Because You walk with me, I can sing Your praises even in the face of rejection and heartache. Thank You, in Christ's name. Amen.

Happy Recognition

The gatekeeper opens the gate for him, and the sheep listen to his voice. He calls his own sheep by name and leads them out (John 10:3).

Scripture: John 10:1-15
Song: "The Lord Is My Shepherd"

I stand in front of the elementary school along with dozens of other parents, grandparents, and guardians, waiting for the little lambs to frolic through the gates. Finally, the doors swing open. The gatekeeper-like teacher stands guard.

The first kindergartner spies her caregiver, slaps the teacher's hand, and darts to her guardian. All the children repeat the process. None of them speaks to an unknown adult. They don't even look at anyone other than the person waiting for them. They're too excited to see the smile on a well-known face, to go home, to play, to have a snack in familiar surroundings.

The guardians seem just as elated to reunite with their little lambs. Hands clasp. Chatter fills the air. Together they walk to vehicles, climb in, buckle up, and head home.

Later that evening, I replay the scene in my mind. What joy fills our souls when we reunite with our loved ones. Small children, and even babies, recognize to whom they belong and are often distressed when cradled in the arms of a stranger.

Likewise, we as Christians recognize our Lord's voice and follow Him wherever He leads. We shy away from foreign doctrines, not out of fear, but because we know to whom we belong.

Savior, keep me in Your tender care, for I am Yours. Fill me with love today for the others who are Yours as well. In Your precious name I pray. Amen.

My Prayer Notes

DEVOTIONS®

▶ **MAY**

The Lord is good, a refuge in times of trouble.
He cares for those who trust in him,

—*Nahum 1:7*

Gary Wilde, Editor | Margaret K. Williams, Project Editor

Photo © iStock | Thinkstock®

DEVOTIONS® is published quarterly by Standard Publishing, Cincinnati, Ohio, www.standardpub.com. Copyright © 2015 by Standard Publishing. All rights reserved. Topics based on the Home Daily Bible Readings, International Sunday School Lessons. Copyright © 2013 by the Committee on the Uniform Series. Printed in the U.S.A. All Scripture quotations, unless otherwise indicated are taken from the *HOLY BIBLE, NEW INTERNATIONAL VERSION*®. *NIV*®. Copyright © 1973, 1978, 1984, 2011 by Biblica, Inc.® Used by permission of Zondervan. All rights reserved worldwide. Scripture quotations marked *(NKJV)* are taken from the *New King James Version*®. Copyright © 1982 by Thomas Nelson, Inc. Used by permission. All rights reserved. Scripture quotations marked *(NLT)* are taken from the Holy Bible, *New Living Translation*. Copyright © 1996, 2004, 2007, 2013 by Tyndale House Foundation. Used by permission of Tyndale House Publishers, Inc., Carol Stream, Illinois 60188. All rights reserved.

Getting to Know Him

You have searched me, Lord, and you know me (Psalm 139:1).

Scripture: Psalm 139:1-6
Song: "Search Me, O God"

We were classmates throughout our years at Cobbs Creek Elementary. Also attending the same church, we pleaded each week to be allowed to go home together for the afternoon. Over the years Danny and I came to know pretty much everything there was to know about each other. But that's how best friendships evolve, isn't it?

Granted, in this age of social media, "friendships" may constitute nothing more than a request followed by an acceptance. Two clicks. Done. Nonetheless, those deepest relationships remain rooted in a process of times spent together over an extended period. As regards the most important relationship of all, however, one party has quite the head start.

Imagine someone knowing everything, literally everything, about you before you even knew His name. Don't stop there. Consider also that this same individual desires nothing more than to be your best friend, in spite of all that knowledge. And did I mention that He happens to be perfect . . . divinely so?

The psalmist found such truth "too lofty . . . to attain" (v. 6). No doubt. And yet, all that's required is for us to strive to get to know Him half as well as He already knows us.

O Lord, I desire to grow closer to You. May I remain open to all that You would have me experience while awaiting an eternity in Your presence. In Christ, amen.

May 1–7. **Robert L. Stephens,** a retiree, loves spending time with family, freelance writing, and public speaking. He and his wife, Linda, who live in Glen Allen, Virginia, travel frequently.

Side By Side

Where can I go from your Spirit? Where can I flee from your presence? (Psalm 139:7).

Scripture: Psalm 139:7-12
Song: "Lord, as to Thy Dear Cross We Flee"

It remains a favorite photograph. Taken in the backyard, it shows me standing with my father atop a bulldozer. I can't recall the project, but I'll never forget the thrill of being allowed to help. I was always happiest when by his side. I'm sure he felt the same . . . most of the time.

I have another Father. I wish I could claim always to have desired His presence too. I cannot. Many times I felt I didn't deserve being there. Awash in worldliness, ill feelings toward another—failing after failing—sent me into seclusion. I lacked the psalmist's understanding: There's no hiding from God.

Pop was a patient man. The infrequency with which he lovingly let me know he needed to tackle something solo attests to it. I understood. We had a special relationship that was as strong as ever at the time of his death in 2001. As to my heavenly Father, I now cherish His omnipresence, whether I'm walking in the light or stumbling again into the darkness.

My father's love had human limitations. As for our Lord, though we will continue to falter, His faithfulness endures. He walks by our side not just most of the time but eternally. Praise God!

Gracious Father, for Your steadfast presence in my life I offer thanksgiving and praise. Though I falter repeatedly, may I ever cling to Your hand as tightly as You do to mine. Guide my steps as we walk side by side toward paradise. I pray this prayer in the name of Jesus, my Savior and Lord. Amen.

Now Hear This!

The voice of the Lord is over the waters; the God of glory thunders . . . over the mighty waters (Psalm 29:3).

Scripture: Psalm 29:1-9
Song: "Softly and Tenderly"

It's called a boatswain's pipe or bosun's whistle. Historically, the pipe was used to inform a ship's crew whenever verbal communication couldn't be heard over the sound of the sea or storm. When I served in the navy, the whistle usually preceded a message delivered over the public address system. It instructed, in effect, "Now hear this."

David's description of our Lord's voice leaves no doubt: we won't need to be tipped off that a message is forthcoming. God speaks; God is heard. Rending gigantic trees, shaking the desert—hard to imagine anyone missing it. Yet ironically, the loudest message I've ever gotten from God came as a whisper.

Years removed from a youth spent amid a loving church congregation, I gradually transformed myself into a solitary believer. Surely I could give thanks to God on the golf course or elsewhere just as well as from a pew! And then, "Come home." Again, "Come home." Whispered, yet clearly heard above all my life's static. Over time resisting ceased to be an option.

Whether powerfully or softly, God speaks in the way that ensures we hear. And then, in a demonstration of amazing faith, He leaves the response to us. Shhh-h-h. Did you hear that?

Precious Lord, noise of the world threatens to drown out what I most need to hear. Yet You continually get Your message through. Grant me not only the ability to hear, Lord, but wisdom to know how best to respond. In Jesus' name, amen.

An Amazing Response

Do not be afraid; you will not be put to shame. Do not fear disgrace; you will not be humiliated (Isaiah 54:4).

Scripture: Isaiah 54:1-10
Song: "Shouting His Praise"

As a child, I remember (once!) trying to be last in line. Yet my time to speak to the minister soon arrived. He stood outside the church door exchanging pleasantries with departing members. But there was nothing pleasant about what I needed to do.

My mother, a choir member, had allowed me to sit unattended during worship . . . provided my chosen location offered a direct line of sight. When our eyes met at the end of the service, I immediately regretted my inattentive behavior. And having been told I should apologize only heightened my distress.

As God's child, I'm continuously within my Father's field of vision. I can't see His face, yet I sometimes shudder thinking how often it too may reflect disappointment. Simply pondering the question evokes regrets. Until, that is, I recall the lessons I learned on the front steps of my church so many years ago.

The minister's pat on the back following my apology filled me with determination to behave better, and Mom's expression as she watched reassured me she would always love me.

Humankind's behavior falls woefully short of what our Father desires. But He simply calls us to start again. In fact, His response to our repentance is incomprehensible—mercy, grace, and unshakable love. All for saying, "I'm sorry." Amazing!

Father, help me think less of myself as I renew my joy in Your promise to love me unconditionally. All honor and glory I give to You. Through Christ my Lord I pray. Amen.

An Odd Yet Divine Combination

The LORD is slow to anger but great in power; the LORD will not leave the guilty unpunished (Nahum 1:3).

Scripture: Nahum 1:1-8
Song: "Holy, Holy, Holy!"

My geometry teacher was small in stature, had a wonderfully contagious laugh, and was undoubtedly the school's most popular teacher. This seemingly belied another well-known trait—his ability to scare the daylights out of you.

Beloved yet potentially terrifying seems an odd combination doesn't it? You should know that he always allowed ample time for things to resolve themselves before choosing to act. Writing on the chalkboard, he would ignore disruptive behavior behind him for a time. How long? No one knew. That's what was scary.

Nahum knew the Lord's desire that His children behave properly, living according to His will. He also recognized the potential outcome for those whose sinful nature persistently won out, thus his foretelling of the destruction of Nineveh. Fifty years later, patience exhausted, the Lord did as Nahum prophesied.

I don't recall much about my teacher's words, once compelled to restore order. I do distinctly recall and admire his unwavering determination to give us every chance, more than deserved, to be our best. Nothing, however, compares to the manner in which our Lord reigns—unflinchingly intolerant of sin, yet ceaselessly merciful toward us sinners striving to be our best. What a blessed irony.

I desire, **Father,** to live by Your will, yet in brokenness I sin. I pledge this day—in Your strength, not mine—to continue toward becoming what You'd have me be. All the while, I ask in Jesus' name, for Your unmerited grace. Amen.

Our Father Knows Best

But Jonah ran away from the Lord (Jonah 1:3).

Scripture: Jonah 1:1-6
Song: "Father, We Thank Thee"

Bud had enough. Parental attempts to persuade him to do what they felt best led him to make a weighty decision. He moved out. So began an episode of *Father Knows Best*, a popular 1950s television series. In a scenario repeated throughout the ages, attempts to control another's actions culminated in rebellion. Though this particular example had been scripted, Jonah may have thought it a form of reality TV.

Reacting to a much higher authority, and without explanation, Jonah fled his Creator. Perhaps like Bud, he was driven by a seemingly inherent human desire to control one's own life. Whenever guidance from another, even someone respected and loved, runs contrary to a deeply held personal preference, bad things can happen.

Of far more importance than any possible similarities in the two situations, however, is one key difference. In spite of wanting only the best for their children, parents sometimes get it wrong. Granted, Bud came home . . . but only after Dad heeded a friend's sage advice to alter his strategy.

Our heavenly Father requires no such assist. Remarkably, the choice to either follow or reject His guidance remains ours. So, pondering our options we, like Jonah, do well to remind ourselves—our Father always knows best.

You illumine my path, **Lord,** one step at a time. Yet, despite believing that You alone know what's best, I often choose another direction. Give me the courage to set aside self-will and simply step into Your light. In Christ, amen.

What Do You Need?

Now the LORD **provided a huge fish to swallow Jonah** (Jonah 1:17).

Scripture: Jonah 1:7-17
Song: "God Will Take Care of You"

Forgive my boasting, but I had it at an early age: the ability to know just what I needed. Unfortunately, not everyone agreed. Plead as I might (and did), my mother simply couldn't fathom that my future hinged on having a first baseman's mitt or a Red Ryder BB gun or . . . Oh, the frustration I routinely encountered when attempting unsuccessfully to bring her around to my way of thinking!

Jonah's discernment of what was best had apparently expanded to include not just his needs but those of others as well. When confronted with a contrary opinion regarding how best to deal with Nineveh, he did what I never even contemplated. He ran. Now adrift on a raging sea, Jonah may have feared the rift between himself and his Father had become irreparable.

Over time I actually got my baseball glove and air rifle. Ironically, however, it's all those other things my parents provided—unconditional love included—that consistently evoke my fondest memories and garner my eternal gratitude.

I can't know Jonah's thoughts as he convinced others to throw him overboard. I have no question, however, about what he ultimately came to realize: God always provides—even when what's needed is . . . a huge fish.

The longer I live, **Father,** the more I realize how little I know, and yet my journey, like that of Jonah, has instilled within me an unshakable certainty. You not only know exactly what I need but are steadfast in ensuring I have it. Praise You, in Christ. Amen.

Heavenly Benefactor

What shall I render to the LORD for all His benefits toward me? (Psalm 116:12, *NKJV*).

Scripture: Psalm 116:1-14
Song: "Trusting Jesus"

In the film *Daddy Long Legs*, Fred Astaire played the part of a mysterious benefactor, Jervis Pendleton. The recipient was Leslie Caron, who played Julie Andre. All through her life as an orphan, Julie's benefactor remained a secret.

How different for the Christian who knows God as the great benefactor. The trouble is, we are all too blind to the benefits showered on us by our benefactor. Yet who of us can possibly fathom the depths of the word *benefactor* when it comes to God? Impossible, of course. The main thing is for us to take time to pause on a regular basis and think about the gracious goodness of our God and all His gifts to us each day.

Words fail us. We try to describe God, and we find no word is adequate. The only way left for us is simply to worship the Lord and thank Him for all He has done. When we seem to come to the end of that list (if we ever do), we can then switch gears in the spirit of this old proverb: "If you cannot be grateful for what you have received, then be thankful for what you have been spared."

O Gracious God in Heaven, please keep reminding me of all Your benefits, for sometimes I fail to acknowledge them as I should. I do wish to tell You how grateful I am—and to say that I'm determined this day to serve You with renewed effort. In the holy name of Jesus, my Lord and Savior, I pray. Amen.

May 8–14. **David Nicholas**, a minister and writer, lives in New South Wales, Australia, and has written for *Devotions* several times over the years.

Endless Collectors

Who has preceded Me, that I shall pay him? Everything under heaven is Mine (Job 41:11, *NKJV*).

Scripture: Job 41:1-11
Song: "I Serve a Risen Savior"

What collectors we are. Vance Packard wrote *The Wastemakers* in 1960, telling us about modern American society and the quantity of goods our culture collects. The book speaks of what one reviewer described as "force feeding," which leads people into buying things that are wasteful. Certain television programs reveal the horrors of hoarding, showing how some disturbed people collect and collect and collect. Even the normal among us gather to ourselves endless objects.

Yet everything belongs to God; we came into the world with nothing, and we'll leave it with nothing—regardless of what we may collect along the way. The trouble is, by collecting what Packard calls waste, we begin to think we are owners when we are only keepers, stewards for God of all He loans us.

Job couldn't offer God anything, of course, and God didn't owe Job anything. We must always remember Job had previously demanded a hearing and vindication from God. However, who was Job to argue with God? He owned nothing.

We are all, in a sense, paupers on this earth and never in a place where we can argue with God. However, when we recognize that Christ is in us—and we are in Him by God's grace—we are never truly poor.

Father, remind me today of my riches in Christ and the inheritance awaiting me at the end of days. You are so generous that I can only repay You with a thankful heart—and with my life as a living sacrifice in Your kingdom work. In Jesus' name, amen.

Our Biggest Need

It will be a sign and witness to the Lord Almighty in the land of Egypt. When they cry out to the Lord because of their oppressors, he will send them a savior and defender, and he will rescue them (Isaiah 19:20).

Scripture: Isaiah 19:19-22
Song: "At Calvary"

If asked, we could come up with a large list of what we think we need. Sadly, we tend to confuse our wants with our needs. The biggest failure of humans is that we overlook our biggest need, the need of a Savior, one who delivers us from sin.

Egypt is in crisis, and God chides Pharaoh's advisers for leading people astray. Judgment will come, but that is not the end of the story, for God will apply grace. A Savior sent from God will arrive.

So often leaders lead us astray. Even as the Egyptians were promised a savior, we also have a Savior in Jesus who is mighty to keep us. Mighty to save. May we ask God to keep on reminding us that our greatest need is for a Savior—and constantly thank Him for coming, incarnate, to fill the need.

John Calvin states a clear warning, perfectly applicable to our Scripture today: "No man is excluded from calling upon God, the gate of salvation is set open unto all men: neither is there any other thing which keepeth us back from entering in, save only our own unbelief."

Dear Lord, please grant me a better memory so that I do not forget all You have done and can do. I am blessed by a salvation that I could never attain on my own, nor can I maintain it in my own strength. All my trust relies on You! In Jesus' name, amen.

Sure Answers

Do not hide Your face from Your servant, for I am in trouble; hear me speedily (Psalm 69:17, *NKJV*).

Scripture: Psalm 69:13-18
Song: "Near to the Heart of God"

Somewhere I read of a Scottish mother who was worried about feeding her children. Her barrel of flour was empty. One of her children said, "Mither, what are you greetin (weeping) aboot? Dinna God hear ye scrapin o' the bottom o' the barrel?" Yes, God surely hears and God surely answers.

The psalmist wanted deliverance from his enemies. It's a reasonable desire; after all, God understood what he faced. In the same way our mighty God is well aware of our needs and the troubles we face.

Nevertheless, the psalmist felt in great danger of sinking into deep water. His enemies swirled with hatred, and "deep waters" (vv. 2, 14) threatened to sweep him away. However, God could not refuse the call of His servant.

The Lord still hears and answers all who trust in Him. Sometimes He answers Yes, sometimes No, and sometimes Wait. So keep praying, even the desperate prayers like those of the psalm writer, even when your heart can hardly find the words. As John Bunyan, famous for writing the *The Pilgrim's Progress,* once said: "In prayer it is better to have a heart without words than words without a heart."

Almighty and Merciful God, please strengthen my belief as I face my daily troubles. I especially want to rely on Your listening ear when I pray. You hear every plea of my heart, spoken and unspoken. May I trust more and more Your great love for every one of Your children. In the name of Jesus I pray. Amen.

The Truly Great One

The men of Nineveh will rise up in the judgment with this generation and condemn it, for they repented at the preaching of Jonah; and indeed a greater than Jonah is here (Luke 11:32, *NKJV*).

Scripture: Luke 11:29-32
Song: "I Walk with the King"

Muhammad Ali, born Cassius Clay, Jr., is known for saying, "I am the greatest." He is welcome to think in this way, and he was certainly a stellar boxing champ—floating like a butterfly, stinging like a bee.

But Christians know there is a far greater champion—the Lord Jesus Christ. As the apostle Paul wrote regarding the Lord's bout with evil: "Having disarmed principalities and powers, He made a public spectacle of them, triumphing over them in it" (Colossians 2:15, *NKJV*).

Our passage tells us of Jonah to make a point: Even though Jesus was greater by far than the reluctant prophet, at least his hearers responded to the message. Yet His people refused the preaching of Jesus. They wanted signs and wonders more than the salvation He offered. How quickly we miss the mark when we think about God, forgetting that Jesus is truly the greatest.

True faith comes not by special proofs but as a result of God's clear call to repentance. It is a matter, ultimately, not of the mind but of the will.

O Eternal Lord God, may I never forget that You are the greatest by whom all things are created, and in whom all things consist. Having come from Heaven, Your Son is the most dynamic person to ever walk this earth. In this I can have full and complete confidence. In His name. Amen.

Endless Contract

**"Lo, I am with you always, even to the end of the age."
Amen** (Matthew 28:20, *NKJV*).

Scripture: Matthew 28:16-20
Song: "O Jesus, I Have Promised"

What a wonderful passage for today's reading! We are all familiar with the words, "Till death do us part" in the traditional wedding ceremony. God wants us to remember that when we are in Christ there is no end—no departing—unlike marriage contracts which end at death. The promise in this heavenly contract is simple: the continuing presence of Jesus. Forever.

Jesus wouldn't just be a memory for His disciples. Rather, He will always be present with them, right through thick and thin, even to the end of this world and beyond.

It's true that we can sometimes be lonely. But as the great Christian statesman Dag Hammarskjold once said: "What makes loneliness an anguish is not that I have no one to share my burden, but this: I have only my own burden to bear." The point being that Jesus' church is being built, and the Lord has promised His indwelling presence to each member—that we may take up each other's burdens in a community of mutual encouragement and growth (see Galatians 6:2).

God has promised to be with us in Jesus. Always with us. No good-byes. We can say He is in me and I am in Him. All of us are a part of one another, never to be separated.

Loving God, I rejoice in the fellowship and unity I have with my brothers and sisters in Christ, also members of His body with me. Keep me ready to share their burdens as I share mine. In the name of Jesus, amen.

Letters Alive

Jonah prayed to the Lord his God from the fish's belly. And he said: "I cried out to the Lord because of my affliction, and He answered me" (Jonah 2:1, 2, *NKJV*).

Scripture: Jonah 2
Song: "Faith Is the Victory"

We would be amazed if we knew exactly how many letters miss their mark. For instance, in 2008 approximately 90 million undelivered items ended up in the United States Postal Services Dead Letter Office. The senders were evidently confident their missives would reach their destination. *Wrong!*

How different with Jonah when he prayed. He knew his prayers would reach their destination, for they were correctly addressed to God. No surprise here, for God doesn't have a dead letter office.

Jonah didn't pray to some idol made with hands but to the living God—the most high God of Israel—the one in whose image he had been made. Jonah prayed. God acted, rescuing him from the horrors of the deep.

Similarly, we too can be sure that when we pray to the God and Father of our Lord Jesus Christ, our prayers will be heard, and they will be answered—as God sees fit, in His way, and in His time. But let us pray, as much as possible, with sincere motives. Thus we'll avoid the definition offered by quipster Robert Brault: "The object of most prayers is to wangle an advance on good intentions."

Dear Heavenly Father, I am grateful to know that You hear my prayers. I trust You to work Your will through the answers You give, even when I don't fully understand Your plan. In Christ I pray. Amen.

God Calls, God Equips

Do not say, "I am too young." You must go to everyone I send you to and say whatever I command you (Jeremiah 1:7).

Scripture: Jeremiah 1:4-10
Song: "Follow On"

A year after college, Teddy had found work, but not what he believed he was called to do. Finally, he set his sights on a new opportunity. He had completed the interviews and submitted samples of his work. Now, he waited for a phone call, hoping and praying to hear, "You got the job!" Ironically, when the call came, the employer had to convince him it was for real: "We really do want you to come and work for us."

Jeremiah was a young man when he got the call from God. He couldn't believe God was asking him to preach judgment and truth to God's people. "I do not know how to speak; I am too young" (v. 6) Jeremiah said. But God repeated the call several times, using words like *command* (v. 7) and *appoint* (v. 10). God also reassured Jeremiah that He would be with him (see v. 19), giving the young prophet the words to speak.

We can learn from Jeremiah's experience. When God persistently calls us to a task or repeatedly offers us an opportunity, it's important to say, "Yes, Lord." No excuses. We too can be certain: He'll give us the words, the wisdom, and the will to do what He calls us to do.

Lord God, give me wisdom to recognize when You are calling me to serve You, and give me courage and the will to do what You call me to do. In the name of Jesus, Lord and Savior of all, I pray. Amen.

May 15–21. **Randall Murphree** is editor of *American Family Association Journal* in Tupelo, Mississippi. He enjoys travel, reading Christian fiction, and writing—especially daily devotions.

Blessed U-Turn

Tell the people: This is what the LORD Almighty says: "Return to me," declares the LORD Almighty, "and I will return to you," says the LORD Almighty (Zechariah 1:3).

Scripture: Zechariah 1:1-6
Song: "Jesus Paid It All"

Wabush, a remote Canadian town, was once totally isolated before a single road was built, entrance and exit all in one. If you go there, the only way out is to turn around. Author Brian Weatherdon says, "Each of us, by birth, arrives in a town called Sin. As in Wabush, there is only one way out. But in order to take that road, one must first turn around. That complete about-face is what the Bible calls repentance, and without it, there's no way out of town."

In Zechariah's time, God's people had recently returned from Babylonian captivity, but they had not returned spiritually. Their relationship to God was still unstable at best, rebellious at worst. Zechariah's challenge was to make them see that each one must reestablish a personal relationship with the Lord.

Clearly, the Israelites' choice of direction was a serious issue—God even refers to the evil ways and the evil deeds that their forebears had practiced. He warns them not to keep going in that direction, but to turn back to Him.

When we're on a path of rebellion or we're living a sinful lifestyle, make that U-turn in order to walk closely again with God. Only then can we enjoy true fellowship with Him.

Father God, I pray that I will be eager to obey You whenever You call me to turn around and make my way back to You. In the name of Your Son, my Savior, I pray. Amen.

Found, and God Rejoices

"Rejoice with me; I have found my lost coin." In the same way, I tell you, there is rejoicing in the presence of the angels of God over one sinner who repents (Luke 15:9, 10).

Scripture: Luke 15:8-10
Song: "Rejoice, the Lord Is King!"

At an estimated value of $250 million, the Kruger millions disappeared in 1890 in South Africa. The Boers, Dutch descendants in the nation, were determined to hide their wealth from the British, whom they expected would soon capture their capital city in the Second Anglo-Boer War. The gold treasure has never been found.

The mystery of the missing Kruger millions is one of many lost treasure stories one can read about in history. It's hard to imagine how such an amount could be lost forever. On the other hand, most of us can identify with the poor woman in the Luke 15 parable when she lost one coin. A Jewish woman in New Testament times customarily saved up 10 coins, and she often wore them as a necklace or headdress, symbolizing that she was a married woman. To lose one coin was a serious problem.

We understand her much better than we understand the Kruger treasure—every dollar counted. So no wonder she called her friends to rejoice when she found the coin. It is like that for God. How precious every single person is to our heavenly Father! If one goes astray, He will always call other believers to rejoice when the lost one returns to the fold.

Father God, help me to remember how beloved I am in Your sight and to know that You rejoice when I repent and turn back to You. May You grow in me the same fruit of mercy, by Your Holy Spirit. In Jesus' name, amen.

Let Us Lead!

I tell you that it will be more bearable for Sodom on the day of judgment than for you (Matthew 11:24).

Scripture: Matthew 11:20-24
Song: "Come, Ye Sinners, Poor and Needy"

When we look at the world's spiritual state today, we may wonder how long God will put up with the way we treat Him, reject His love, and ignore His principles for right living. The issues of abortion and euthanasia, pornography and sexual promiscuity, drugs and other substance abuse, marriage and divorce, are bringing our culture close to moral chaos. Are we not in danger of God's judgment?

In the Old Testament, Jehovah destroyed cities and their inhabitants—Sodom and Gomorrah for example—because of their rejection of His righteousness. In the New Testament, we find Jesus denouncing three cities—Chorazin, Bethsaida, and Capernaum—because they have rejected Him.

Ironically, these cities were in northern Galilee, the place Jesus chose as the center of His ministry, where He performed more of His miracles than in any other area. Yet they rejected Him and suffered a heavy hand of judgment.

Is there a lesson here for our day? Doesn't our own nation need to fall on its knees, repent of personal and corporate sins, and return to living by the Creator's moral law? It begins when His people, the church, lead the way.

Dear Father in Heaven, I ask Your forgiveness for every way I've failed to be Your representative in a world that is in desperate need of Your love and Your salvation. Make me an instrument to draw others to You. I pray this prayer in the name of Jesus, my merciful Savior and Lord. Amen.

Repentance Leads to Grace

However, I consider my life worth nothing to me; my only aim is to finish the race and complete the task the Lord Jesus has given me—the task of testifying to the good news of God's grace (Acts 20:24).

Scripture: Acts 20:18-24
Song: "Repent, the Kingdom Draweth Nigh"

Author Kent Crockett tells the story of a little boy who prayed, "Dear Jesus, I'm so sorry I made such a mess in my room today." The lad paused, then added, "But I sure had fun doing it." We smile, but aren't we adults too often willing to apologize to God for whatever sin we've committed, while remaining reluctant to turn from it?

In today's Scripture, Paul teaches us that repentance resides at the heart of the Christian walk. The great apostle has just said good-bye to the elders in the church at Ephesus, knowing he will likely never see them again. He remembers serving with them in humility, and he recalls trials and tears.

Then he moves on to remind them of the need for repentance and faith in Christ. Repentance won't be merely a one-time occurrence, but an ongoing attitude to be practiced throughout the journey of spiritual growth. Paul then tells them he's headed next to Jerusalem, where he expects affliction and persecution. But finally, he ends the passage by coming back to the grace of God.

Merciful God, thank You for Your grace, Your unconditional and unmerited favor, poured out upon my life and for your loving, abiding presence each day. Help me live in an attitude of humility and repentance so that my life always reflects Your grace. Through Christ I pray. Amen.

Life for All

When they heard this, they had no further objections and praised God, saying, "So then, even to Gentiles God has granted repentance that leads to life" (Acts 11:18).

Scripture: Acts 11:11-18
Song: "Wonderful Words of Life"

"I could, as a free man, look across the bay toward the Eastern Shore where I was born a slave," said Frederick Douglass. A runaway slave, Douglass (1818–1895) rose to prominence as a social reformer and leader during the turbulent years of the abolitionist movement in the U.S. To compare slavery and freedom to Gentile and Jew is not a perfect parallel, but Douglass, looking across the bay to where he was born a slave, certainly harkens back to an Old Testament scene. I imagine God's people looking back across the Red Sea to Egypt, the land where they had been slaves.

The New Testament writers preach salvation for all people—Jew and Gentile alike. Though Jehovah may have once seemed to the Hebrews to be a local deity, it was now clear to the world: the Lord God was, indeed, granting to the Gentiles too the repentance that leads to life. No longer would any person ever have to wonder if he or she has access to the kingdom of God.

Many early Jewish converts to Christianity still saw Gentiles as enemies and didn't believe they should be allowed in the church. But God's schedule had clearly reached the time when He wanted all to know: you are welcome to walk with me.

Dear Father, help me to remember that Your salvation by grace through faith in Jesus is available to all, even to my "enemies"—and You want no one to perish. In the holy name of Jesus I pray. Amen.

Run or Repent?

In my distress I called to the LORD, and he answered me (Jonah 2:2).

Scripture: Jonah 2
Song: "Rise, My Soul, to Watch and Pray"

Some choices you make might not always be the right choice. But you always have the option to change your mind and turn around. It's never too late to reconsider your decisions.

Jonah learned that lesson, but only after trying to run from God. But we shouldn't be too hard on Jonah. His story seems to be the story of most of us at some point in our lives. God calls us to a task, but we argue with Him because He wants us to do good for someone we don't like. He persists in calling, and we try to run away—as if we think we can escape the Almighty.

When Jonah finally turned around and agreed to warn the citizens of Ninevah, he didn't do it very well. Thus he continued to bring misfortune and troubles on himself. Even after God had brought the people of Ninevah to repentance under the prophet's preaching, Jonah still wasn't happy.

The story of Jonah should give us hope for our world today, a world that seems to be running as fast as it can run from God. But Ninevah repented and was saved from God's wrath and judgment. We can be encouraged to know that if God's people follow His plan, there is still hope for a lost world.

Heavenly Father, I confess that I sometimes run from Your callings when I think they'll be unpleasant. Help me to welcome Your call on my life so that Your love can be seen in me. In Christ my Lord, amen.

Simultaneous Love and Justice

The LORD, the compassionate and gracious God . . . Yet he does not leave the guilty unpunished (Exodus 34:6, 7).

Scripture: Exodus 34:4-9
Song: "What Wondrous Love Is This?"

Only God can be simultaneously loving and just. We humans tend to view him one way or the other: either God saves everyone, or none of us will make it. The complete story is that we can honor our maker as "the compassionate and gracious God" and also believe that He is just, that He will "not leave the guilty unpunished."

At first this seems to be a dilemma, but the larger picture is the good news itself. God must punish sin, and "all have sinned" (Romans 3:23). But our gracious God punished our sins in Christ. Jesus stepped into the human drama by visiting this fallen planet as the perfect combination of full humanity and full deity. He proved God's love by willingly taking my punishment while also satisfying God's justice. It is a message so unusual—so unlike ordinary religion—that it can be embraced only by faith.

Trying to understand God without Jesus, I may grasp only God's wrath toward me. But when I view God through the lens of Jesus, I am assured of my salvation because someone did for me what I could never do for myself.

Father, I know that worship is the only appropriate response to Your eternal plan to save me. I can say with Moses, "Forgive our wickedness and our sin, and take us as your inheritance" (v. 9). Thank You for Your perfect nature, which can show Your hatred of sin and yet love me as a sinner because of the death of Jesus. In His name, amen.

May 22–28. **Bob Mize,** who has written for Devotions in the past, is a minister, chaplain, and freelance writer who lives in Lubbock, Texas.

Redemption Ready

The Lord replied, "I have forgiven them, as you asked" (Numbers 14:20).

Scripture: Numbers 14:10, 11, 17-20
Song: "Father of Mercies"

Clyde Thompson's life story reads like a movie script. His biography, *The Meanest Man in Texas,* tells how Clyde was "diverted by the devil" beginning at age 19. It was then that he was charged with murder and became the youngest man in Texas' history to be placed on death row. After two attempted prison breaks, he was considered incorrigible and placed in solitary confinement for 11 years.

His daddy was a preacher to the Native Americans in the Oklahoma Territory, but Clyde rejected his dad's religion—until, out of desperation in solitary confinement, he requested a New Testament. Any other request would be denied.

I heard his testimony many times, how he began reading the Bible with one purpose: to prove it wrong. "But it proved me wrong," he would say. Not only did his commitment to Christ mean an about-face, but he was eventually given a full pardon and restoration of citizenship. He then married, adopted an Indian daughter, and spent the rest of his life restoring ex-offenders from the same prison that had been his home for 38 years.

Sometimes it takes a long time for God to get a person's attention, but then the Lord doesn't view time like we do. Continue to pray for anyone who seems beyond redemption. They aren't.

Lord, You are so patient with me, and I thank You for never giving up on any human being. I pray for those outside of Christ, for my awareness of them, and for the opportunity to share Jesus as Savior. In His name, amen.

You Didn't Desert Them

In your great mercy you did not abandon them to die in the wilderness (Nehemiah 9:19, *NLT*).

Scripture: Nehemiah 9:16-21
Song: "Immortal Love, Forever Full"

Forty years is a long time to wander aimlessly through life. For four decades the Israelites didn't listen to God and forgot what little they did hear. They were, for the most part, rather stubborn pilgrims—two generations of complaining and committing awful blasphemies.

A detached reader of the Israelites' story would think God had every right to banish them, or even destroy them. Instead, as the historian Nehemiah spoke to God, "In your great mercy you did not abandon them to die in the wilderness." Do you wonder how God views our world today, how He can possibly put up with us any longer?

Is it any different with my friends and family? On a personal level, I sometimes cry out, "Lord, how many times have I plugged my ears and forgotten Your promises? I am ashamed to think how much You have sustained me, in spite of my ingratitude. You have continued to feed me, give me drink, clothe me, give me health, and guide me day and night."

Today I am so thankful that Scripture promises, "Even though God has the right to show his anger and his power, he is very patient with those on whom his anger falls, who are destined for destruction" (Romans 9:22, *NLT*).

Father of mercies, let me see more clearly and understand more deeply the amazing grace that You have for me. May I share it with someone today who needs to know true love. In Jesus' name, amen.

Just Dust—Recreated!

As a father has compassion on his children, so the Lord has compassion on those who fear him; for he knows how we are formed (Psalm 103:13, 14).

Scripture: Psalm 103:1-14
Song: "There Is a Balm in Gilead"

"Then the Lord God formed man from the dust of the ground and breathed into his nostrils the breath of life, and the man became a living being" (Genesis 2:7). The biblical account of my origin is amazing. Still more impressive is that God has not forgotten the material from which He made me . . . dust!

While I am "fearfully and wonderfully made" (Psalm 139:14), I am of this earth, from dust to dust. God has made me a little lower than the heavenly beings, crowned me with glory and honor, yet He understands my fatigue and doubt. Yes, He created me ruler over the works of His hands and put everything under my feet—flocks, herds, beasts, fish, and birds—yet He knows when I feel defeated, tempted, and worried. Though I was perfectly knit together in my mother's womb (see v. 13), He makes note of my fear and vulnerability.

Yes, God understands my physical and emotional limits. But He has also given me the peace of solitude, the refreshment of prayer, and the oblivion of sleep. When no human seems to understand, God does, and still He loves me profoundly. I am awe-struck by creation, but eternally grateful for my recreation.

You know me better than I know myself, **O Lord.** May I flee to You for physical, emotional, and spiritual rest each day. Help me realize that You often seek to meet my needs through the fellowship of other believers. May I, in turn, be ready to minister Your encouragement wherever I find the need. Through Christ I pray. Amen.

In Distress

Listen closely to my prayer, O LORD; hear my urgent cry. I will call to you whenever I'm in trouble, and you will answer me (Psalm 86:6, 7, *NLT*).

Scripture: Psalm 86:1-7
Song: "When My Love to God Grows Weak"

I once read that the shortest prayer is *"Help!"* It certainly summarizes all the Bible references to "calling on the name of the Lord" (Acts 22:16, *NLT*). Ever since I called to God for salvation I have continued to cry *Help.* When I feel guilty calling on Him, He puts me at ease. After all, James 1:5, 6 promises, "If you need wisdom, ask our generous God, and he will give it to you. He will not rebuke you for asking. But when you ask him, be sure that your faith is in God alone."

It is OK to call on the Lord at any time, but especially in a crisis. I think of the thief on the cross. I've never been that desperate or procrastinated for that long. But I share his motivation: I desperately need an answer. In other words, Jesus isn't interested in the shape I am in when I cry out, just that I do it.

"On 9/11 we ran for cover," wrote Max Lucado. "On 9/12 we ran to God. . . . Ironic. Osama Bin Laden intended to bring America to her knees, and he did—we prayed. What does this say about us? At least this much: we are a spiritual people. For all our talk about secularism, self-reliance and self-sufficiency, where do we turn in turbulence? We turn to God."

My Creator, thank You for hearing me and never tiring of blessing me. I know You won't always respond in the way I want or expect. Help me to believe, though, that Your ways are always for my good. Through Christ my Lord I pray. Amen.

In God We Trust

Teach me your way, Lord, that I may rely on your faithfulness; give me an undivided heart, that I may fear your name (Psalm 86:11).

Scripture: Psalm 86:8-13
Song: "Only in Thee"

The motto "In God We Trust" has been on all American currency since 1956. While secularists want it removed, do believers live it?

Answer this: What is impossible for me to do without God's help? In those areas I admit my sufficiency comes from Him. How much of my life, though, is lived without depending upon God? If my accomplishments come from my own mental acumen or physical exertion or sheer willpower and self-talk, then my trust is in self.

After all, if I can answer my own prayer requests, it is not prayer. If I can forgive my own sins, it is not confession and divine grace. If I require answers to every question in life and beyond, it is not faith. If I can win others to Christ by my own wit, elocution, logic, or persuasion, it is not evangelism, and certainly not dependence upon God in prayer.

Self-sufficiency has always been the downfall of humans. The tower of Babel is still being built and some world leaders still sound like Nebuchadnezzar: "Is not this the great Babylon I have built . . . by my mighty power and for the glory of my majesty?" (Daniel 4:30). Lord, have mercy!

You are the only God, Creator, Holy Spirit, and Provider. May I truly put my trust in You, not just in word but in practical deeds. I pray this prayer through the power of my Lord and Savior, Jesus. Amen.

Angry! Really?

Should I not have concern for the great city of Nineveh?
(Jonah 4:11).

Scripture: Jonah 4
Song: "Is Thy Heart Right with God?"

Jonah's selfishness and self-pity led him to depression. It makes me go to the mirror and ask myself: "Do I have a low-grade anger at God, or even overt bitterness and cynicism?"

Why was Jonah angry? Perhaps he was embarrassed that his warnings were overridden by God's mercy. Or maybe he hated Assyrians so much that he wished their destruction more than their repentance. Or could it be that his nationalism urged God to obliterate the Assyrians as a victory for Israel?

Again, I ask myself the tough questions this prophet raises for my own heart. Have I ever doubted that God would accept some nations or people that I despise? Is the Lord trying to convict me of a secret prejudice? a stubborn heart? a self-will that is quick to tell God rather than ask Him? Is God trying to show me that my depression may be an ingrown, unresolved anger?

I can see that it's easy for me to be a Jonah. But even more so, I affirm these things about Jonah's God: (1) He is not willing that any should perish (see Matthew 18:14), but that everyone should repent; (2) He loves all nations and every person in them. That is why we are called to pray for them and share Christ with them. (3) He loves all children, those "who cannot tell their right hand from their left" (Jonah 4:11).

Jehovah, I do not deserve Your grace. Remind me throughout the day that I would be no better than the most evil were it not for my Lord and Savior. Amen.

The Times Are Changing . . . Really?

"I brought you up out of Egypt and led you into the land I swore to give to your ancestors" (Judges 2:1).

Scripture: Judges 2:1-5
Song: "This Is My Father's World"

In the early 1960s I worked at a title company in Muncie, Indiana, as a typist and "Girl Friday." I pounded out property descriptions—long and complicated legal descriptions of farmland—onto deeds, mortgages, or lease documents.

The record-keeping of the 1960s is obsolete. Our typewriters were big, clunky manuals, with tangly metal keys. Daily I would walk across the street to the courthouse to do title search. The legal description and the history of every parcel of land in the county were housed there, in huge, heavy books.

Today's title companies use twenty-first century word processing, along with twenty-first century cloud storage. What a world! Technology has completely changed everything about title work.

Everything, that is, except property descriptions. When God transferred title to the promised land to Abraham's descendants—He defined the boundaries of the land by rivers. Today, every property surveyed is still measured from certain fixed boundaries—rivers, streams, shorelines, sometimes even trees. Legal descriptions of Indiana farmland are still worded much like descriptions of land written up in the Old Testament, thousands of years ago.

God and Father, thank You for teaching me to remember Your ways of doing things and saying things. May I be ready to follow Your lead today. Through Christ, amen.

May 29–31. **Anne Collins** is a homemaker and a teacher living in Venice, Florida. Her loves are faith, family, friends, fitness, flowers, fabrics, and writing!

What About Our Descendants?

After that whole generation had been gathered to their ancestors, another generation grew up who knew neither the Lord nor what he had done for Israel (Judges 2:10).

Scripture: Judges 2:6-10
Song: "Find Us Faithful"

Our grandson had become discouraged and dropped out of his college nursing program. I think one of his classes proved quite difficult for him—maybe it was chemistry, or perhaps human anatomy. I prayed for an opportunity to speak with him.

Soon I was able to tell him how much faith I have in him, in his strength and good judgment. I reminded him that the nursing field has great need for people of his caliber and temperament. I shared that I believe in prayer, and that I knew his faith and mine in Christ would help him make a good decision. "And Jake, to me it's obvious you have a passion for nursing."

"Thank you, Grandma," he said. "I guess I didn't know that." I don't know what he'll do. But I do believe he'll remember what I said.

I feel pretty vulnerable when I try to talk with grandkids about Christ. (I feel anxiety now, just writing about this feeling!) But I believe it is a grandparent's responsibility to share, especially with young people, the things we know to be true. Our next generation needs to hear our wisdom—about our fears, our beliefs, and our common connection to Christ Jesus.

Thank You, God, for Jesus. Protect and guide us, for I fear that another generation could grow up knowing neither the Lord nor what He has done. Teach us how to be the bridge, so that Your presence may go with our children, our grandchildren, our great-grandchildren. In Jesus' precious name, amen.

When Will We Ever Learn?

When the judge died, the people returned to ways even more corrupt than those of their ancestors (Judges 2:19).

Scripture: Judges 2:16-23
Song: "Teach Me, My God and King"

Seeking to understand the panorama and people of world history can be like contemplating the cosmos. It is so complex, so vast. Where does the history of God's people fit in? The book of Judges depicts heroes, victory, defeat, sin, redemption, chaos. Can any saga be more representative of the whole history of human passions?

The Israelites experienced long periods of peace and loyalty to God, especially when a God-fearing leader was in charge. But when good leaders died, generations of people often returned to idol worship, betrayal, wars, and intrigue. In short, moral confusion would reign once again.

God allowed them to learn from their mistakes, though. The people were tested, and many suffered. But the Lord's covenant remained unbreakable, though not yet fully realized.

Isn't Judges one of many templates presented in the Bible that remind us that today we are indeed active participants in the panorama of world history? Today's world news, alarmingly, reads like Judges, but on a larger scale. God's revelation continues. "Whatever is has already been, and what will be has been before; and God will call the past to account" (Ecclesiastes 3:15).

Almighty God, as I stand within Your vast collection of worlds-within-galaxies, I am amazed that I too am Your creation. Although broken and weak, I am indeed part of all of it. You are king of all. Praise to You, through Christ my Lord. Amen.

DEVOTIONS®

▶ **June**

The LORD is my strength and my defense. . . . He is my God, and I will praise him, . . . and I will exalt him.

—*Exodus 15:2*

Gary Wilde, Editor | Margaret K. Williams, Project Editor | Photo © iStock | Thinkstock®

DEVOTIONS® is published quarterly by Standard Publishing, Cincinnati, Ohio, www.standardpub.com. Copyright © 2016 by Standard Publishing. All rights reserved. Topics based on the Home Daily Bible Readings, International Sunday School Lessons. Copyright © 2013 by the Committee on the Uniform Series. Printed in the U.S.A. All Scripture quotations, unless otherwise indicated, are taken from the HOLY BIBLE, NEW INTERNATIONAL VERSION®. NIV®. Copyright © 1973, 1978, 1984, 2011 by Biblica, Inc.® Used by permission of Zondervan. All rights reserved worldwide. Scripture quotations marked (*KJV*) are taken from the *King James Version*. *New American Standard Bible* (*NASB*), Copyright © The Lockman Foundation, 1960, 1962, 1963, 1968, 1971, 1972, 1973, 1975, 1977, 1995. *The New King James Version* (*NKJV*). Copyright © 1982 by Thomas Nelson, Inc. *The Revised Standard Version of the Bible* (*RSV*), copyrighted 1946, 1952, 1971, 1973.

Joshua Fit the Battle . . . with Help

By faith the prostitute Rahab, because she welcomed the spies, was not killed with those who were disobedient (Hebrews 11:31).

Scripture: Hebrews 11:29-40
Song: "Savior"

Welcome Rahab, a Canaanite woman, a linen maker, a prostitute, an idol-worshipper. She lives in Jericho.

The people of Jericho live in fear. God has commanded Joshua to destroy the city and all its inhabitants. But ahead of the siege, two of Joshua's spies sneak into Jericho, and they ask for shelter in Rahab's house.

Rahab decides to treat the spies kindly. As her heart flies out to her beloved family, she begins to want to be kind. She will help the spies, but asks in return: "Will you spare my family?"

Isn't this a wonderful conversion? She aligns herself with God's purpose and begins to speak of her new trust in the Lord: "For the Lord your God is God in heaven above and on the earth below" (Joshua 2:11).

Rahab hides the spies and could have been accused of treason. Instead, she and her family are rescued. She is treated kindly in return for her own kindness. She becomes a woman of dignity and faith, her mind and heart transformed by the power of God's grace.

Dear Father, thank You for Your transforming grace. May I too become a woman of dignity and faith, discerning Your will and determining, daily, to carry it out. I pray in the precious name of Jesus. Amen.

June 1–4. **Anne Collins** is a homemaker and a teacher living in Venice, Florida. Her loves are faith, family, friends, fitness, flowers, fabrics, and . . . writing.

Look Up and Worship

Hear this, you kings! Listen, you rulers! I, even I, will sing to the Lord; I will praise the Lord, the God of Israel, in song (Judges 5:3).

Scripture: Judges 5:1-5
Song: "Praise to the Lord, the Almighty"

Judy slips outdoors at first light to welcome the sunrise. We bicycle, through silence, stopping at a park bench for our catch-up visit, before the busyness of the day begins.

But Sam and I love to bicycle in mid-afternoon. Here in Florida the sky is huge mounds of puffy cumulus clouds—white towers, drifting through the bluest blue. A sunbeam shining through a hole in the clouds is a stairway to Heaven. We search for those cloud pictures. "See that dog over there leaping!" "Look over there—two kids in a bathtub!" "Ohhhh look, look at that castle!"

Denise and Caroline are my sunset friends. We stand above the beach to watch the sun slowly, silently, slip into the Gulf waters. We are surrounded by colors I can't even name—pastels and vibrant colors. The colors reflect in the water. A gentle breeze kicks up. The earth turns softly, and no two sunsets are ever the same.

I watch the moon rise from my front yard. I steal out into dark-before-dawn to simply stand in awe and amazement—to watch, to be still, and to be comforted as our tiny "blue marble in space" swims and swirls through the cosmos. In the midst of His marvelous creation, I will praise the Lord.

Thank You, God, for the heavens that proclaim Your glory. Thank You for the joy Deborah expresses in her victory song! You, and only You, great God, are king! Amen.

List Those Blessings

Most blessed of women be Jael, the wife of Heber the Kenite, most blessed of tent-dwelling women (Judges 5:24).

Scripture: Judges 5:24-27
Song: "Angels Help Us to Adore Him"

It was a glorious morning in early spring. The screen door slapped behind me as I flew outside into sunshine; I leapt with pure delight into fresh grass—dewy, dotted with dozens of dandelions. "YO!" I shouted—to the bluest sky imaginable, "YO!" I was 5-years-old, but even then I knew a joy without bounds.

I still awaken to boundless gratitude, reviewing the years:

Strangers save my life.

Grandma Florence teaches me the love of sewing.

Jesus speaks to me through the Word.

A nurse saves my life.

I receive strength.

Children fill our home with life and music.

Jesus speaks to me through my writing.

My prayer for friends is answered a hundredfold.

Friends bless our home with their presence.

A wise friend and teacher invites me to write again.

Open the doors of your heart—begin calling on occasions when you know for certain that God touches your life. Make a list and add to it. The fact that we have access to these sacred treasures is a miracle in itself, isn't it? Most blessed women and men are we!

O God, my list goes on and on. Thank You for the gift of joy that is ever present, even while I am shaky and broken. Thank You for my heart's remembrance that You are in control, all the time. Through Christ my Redeemer, amen.

These Women Seized the Day!

Now Deborah, a prophet, the wife of Lappidoth, was leading Israel at that time (Judges 4:4).

Scripture: Judges 4:1-10
Song: "All Glory, Laud, and Honor"

I think of gender equality as a recent phenomenon. Women as leaders of nations and armies? Whoa. Time travel back 3,000 years. This is what happened.

Deborah had received instructions directly from God. So she ordered the leader of her army to conduct Israel's campaign against the Canaanites, exactly as the Lord had commanded.

But the general of her army challenged her. "If you don't go with me," (see v. 8) said Barak, "I won't go! Without you, I will not take 10,000 men into battle against the Canaanites."

Deborah agreed, but warned Barak: for his lack of faith, the enemy leader, Sisera, would be delivered not into his hands, but into the hands of a woman.

Then comes another woman, Jael, the brave, clever, tent-woman. She offers her apparent hospitality to Sisera. With milk and a blanket, like a baby, she puts him to sleep—and stabs him to death with a tent peg (see Judges 4:18, 21).

Surprised? Yet God, throughout history, has chosen women to be leaders and victors. Sometimes women, even heroines, prefer to stay out of the limelight. Or their stories are just never recorded; but Deborah's and Jael's stories survive.

Great God, today I'm reminded that Old Testament adventures so often eclipse any modern fiction. Thank You for the strength of women who obeyed and followed You. You bless us with strength when we need it! Through Christ, amen.

Right Time to Shout

Do not give a war cry . . . do not say a word until the day I tell you to shout. Then shout! (Joshua 6:10).

Scripture: Judges 6:1-10
Song: "We've Come This Far by Faith"

Super Bowl XLIX will long be remembered for the Seattle Seahawks' 28–24 loss to New England. Late in the game, Seattle fans had good reason to cheer, as their outstanding team was only one yard and about one minute away from winning its second consecutive Super Bowl victory. But unexpectedly Seattle's coach called for a pass instead of a run, and a Patriot intercepted the pass. End of game! End of Seahawks fans' elated shouting.

Unlike the Seattle football fans, we must not raise a victory shout too soon. In the journey of our spiritual growth, ultimate victory requires patience, perseverance, and persistent faith. The apostle Paul warned: "If you think you are standing firm, be careful that you don't fall!" (1 Corinthians 10:12).

Paul refused to rest. He kept pressing on toward the goal of maturity in Christ. His refusal to give a victory shout prematurely surely contributed to his "victory" at the end of the Christian race. Eventually, he was able to say, confidently: "I have fought the good fight, I have finished the race, I have kept the faith"(2 Timothy 4:7). Wouldn't that be a great epitaph for you and me as well?

Heavenly Father, may I depend on You, not on myself, to cross life's finish line victoriously. Sustain me in forward progress this day and always, through each decision I make today. I pray in Jesus' name. Amen.

June 5–11. Jim Dyet, a former minister and editor, is now retired, living with Gloria, his wife of 59 years, in Colorado Springs. He enjoys freelance writing, golfing, and walking his two dogs.

Golf, Gold, God

Let them know that you, whose name is the Lord—that you alone are the Most High over all the earth (Psalm 83:18).

Scripture: Psalm 83:1-12, 18
Song: "Great Is the Lord"

Spending time in a golf cart with another golfer, or walking with him from the first tee to the 18th green, gives me a fairly good sense of that person's value system. A Christian often turns to a discussion of spiritual matters, which shows he values highly his relationship with the God who loves him.

However, I played once with a golfer whose god seemed to be — gold. During the first nine holes, he talked incessantly about stocks and bonds, a subject that was way over my head. On the 10th hole, he told me he will have saved a million dollars by the end of the year. By the time we reached the 17th hole, he had shared his plans to double his business's bottom line and buy a radio station and a piece of choice real estate property.

As we were leaving the 18th green, he said he was going to go back to the rattlesnake-infested ravine on the 11th hole to find golf balls so he wouldn't have to purchase any. What amazing values!

The experience made me realize once again: Gold is no substitute for God. It cannot satisfy the soul, nor does it have any eternal value. Money isn't inherently evil, but "the love of money is a root of all kinds of evil" (1 Timothy 6:10). Why? Because it can subtly become a replacement god.

Lord God of all Creation, You are the Most High over all the earth. May I value You all the days of my life—on and off the golf course. For You alone are worthy of all my love. In Jesus' name, amen.

The Only Source of Personal Peace

Then Gideon built an altar there to the Lord and named it The Lord is Peace (Judges 6:24, *NASB*).

Scripture: Judges 6:19-24
Song: "Hail the Prince of Peace Eternal"

When news broke in 2014 that comedic actor Robin Williams had hanged himself, shock struck millions of his fans. Williams' death was preceded by severe depression, alcoholism, and addiction to cocaine. Although he had brought laughter to many, apparently Williams had been crying inside for a long time.

Certainly some depression has biological causes. However, in many other cases it results from excessive worry as tensions at home and abroad seem to spiral out of control. It seems that the cost of keeping body and soul together increases monthly, global conflict escalates, terrorism threatens our personal safety, and dangerous new diseases seem to spring up overnight.

So how can we shoo worry from our doorstep and welcome peace into our homes and hearts?

I believe that the Lord is the only source of peace and that He is always near His people. If we take our concerns to Him and leave them with Him—His peace will guard our hearts and minds (see Philippians 4:5-7). Isaiah 26:3 (*NASB*) promises: "The steadfast of mind you will keep in perfect peace, because he trusts in you."

Instead of looking around and being distressed, or even depressed, we can look above and be at rest.

Heavenly Father, I have many reasons to worry today, but one overriding reason to have peace of mind: my life is in Your hands. Though I'll be tempted to take it back, I ask You to carry me through every difficulty. In Jesus' name, amen.

Head East or Is It West?

When he rose early the next morning and squeezed the fleece together, he wrung the dew out of the fleece, a bowlful of water (Judges 6:38, *NKJV*).

Scripture: Judges 6:36-40
Song: "Come, Every Soul by Sin Oppressed"

Allegedly a new resident in a rural area called the county commissioners' office to request the removal of a "Deer Crossing" warning sign. She explained: "Too many deer are being hit by cars out here. I don't think this is a good place for them to be crossing anymore." Obviously, she had misinterpreted the sign.

We ought to be cautious about asking God for a sign in order to know His will. We may end up depending more on our hoped-for signs than on Scripture.

When I was a young minister, a woman told me the Lord had given her a sign in the clouds. She said the sign indicated she should head east to a certain city and evangelize it. I seriously doubted the validity of the sign, not only because the woman had a vivid imagination but because the community she named was located to the west, not the east!

The Bible doesn't supply specific guidance for every situation. If I need to buy a car, I won't find *Toyota* or *Chrysler* anywhere in the Bible. But I will find guidelines for using money wisely. In fact, the Bible abounds in such wisdom. If I consistently apply its principles, I can keep the fleece in storage.

Heavenly Father, please help me follow the counsel Your Word supplies, for "[it] is a lamp to my feet and a light to my path" (Psalm 119:105, *NKJV*). I simply need Your wisdom to apply it during the routines of my day. In Jesus' name, amen.

Take a Stand!

While each man held his position around the camp, all the Midianites ran, crying out as they fled (Judges 7:21).

Scripture: Judges 7:19-23
Song: "Stand Up, Stand Up for Jesus"

Dudley Tyng, a minister in Philadelphia in the mid 1800s, drew large crowds to noonday services at the local YMCA. In a sermon in March of 1958, Tyng said, "I would rather that this right arm were amputated at the trunk than that I should come short of my duty to you in delivering God's message."

The next week while watching a corn thrasher operation, one of his sleeves got caught in the machine. His arm's main artery was severed and a nerve was damaged. Shock and loss of blood took his life on April 19. As Tyng lay dying, he whispered to those at his bedside, "Let us all stand up for Jesus."

The following week, George Duffield, Tyng's friend, coworker, and minister of Temple Presbyterian Church in Philadelphia, preached about standing for the Lord. At the close of his sermon he read a poem inspired by Tyng's final words. Soon the poem was printed and distributed throughout Temple's Sunday school, and eventually it became the much-loved hymn, "Stand Up, Stand Up for Jesus."

Doesn't it seem to you that Christianity is under attack today from secularists and religious extremists? Can we rise to the challenge of Dudley Tyng's dying words: "Let us all stand up for Jesus"?

Dear Heavenly Father, empower me by Your Spirit to stand up for Your Son, Jesus, and to fight the battles before me with the most powerful weapon You've given—love. In the name of our merciful Lord and Savior, amen.

Keeping the Memory Fresh!

The children of Israel did not remember the Lord their God, who had delivered them from the hands of all their enemies on every side (Judges 8:34, *NKJV*).

Scripture: Judges 8:28-35
Song: "I Remember Calvary"

I chuckled at a sign in a gift shop that read, "When the memory goes, forget it." Memory loss is often associated with seniors, but many seniors have sharp memories. They can open old photo albums and identify not only faces but also date, place, and circumstances connected with each photo. As long as you are willing to look and listen, those seniors are willing to point to the photos and tell you all about them.

Of course, it really doesn't matter if you forget some things. Don't beat yourself up if you have forgotten that the Magna Carta was signed in 1215 or that a scalene triangle has no equal sides and no equal angles. However, you should never forget your mother's birthday, your wedding anniversary, or your boss's name. Forget any of those important facts, and you may be in trouble.

It's especially important to remember God's goodness. The psalmist wrote: "Bless the Lord, O my soul, and forget not all his benefits" (Psalm 103:2, *NKJV*). I think a good way to remember past blessings is to take time daily to recall past events in which God met a need and/or encouraged you in some way. That kind of good memory can help keep the heart in tune with God.

May I never forget, Father, how good You have been to me in spite of my many failings. Thank You for who You are and for Your faithfulness in making me more like Your Son. I pray in His precious name. Amen.

Never Alone

The Lord said to him, "Surely I will be with you, and you shall defeat Midian as one man" (Judges 6:16, *NASB*).

Scripture: Judges 6:11-18
Song: "I Must Tell Jesus"

My wife, Gloria, and little children have quite a rapport. Perhaps her friendly smile and white hair attract little kids to her. Recently, while we were waiting in a crowded restaurant's foyer to be seated, Gloria was sitting on a bench, when a 4-year-old girl sat beside her and cuddled up to her. The youngster poured out her troubles to Gloria. "Momma treats me mean. She smokes too much and has to go to the doctor. Grandma is really, really big." Gloria put her arm around the little girl and tried to console her. It seemed she was telling her, "I am right here with you, and I understand."

We never outgrow trouble, and sometimes the trouble seems overwhelming. The world treats us mean. We face health problems, family problems, financial problems, and problems at work. Perhaps the problems seem overwhelming, and we feel the need to tell someone about them.

Thankfully, we can tell our loving heavenly Father all about our troubles. He is right there with us (see Deuteronomy 33:27). And like Gideon, who feared he was no match for the fierce Midianites, we can take comfort in God's promise, "Surely I will be with you."

Lord, You promised to be with me always, and sometimes You come to me through the love and care of Your people, my fellow church members. Help me to rely on Your presence as I face today's challenges. In Jesus' name, amen.

Mighty or Flighty?

Jephthah the Gileadite was a mighty warrior. His father was Gilead; his mother was a prostitute (Judges 11:1).

Scripture: Judges 11:1-3
Song: "What a Mighty God We Serve"

I've received many second chances in life, which I liken to "messing up" and "cleaning up." However, cleaning up in the spiritual sense always requires God's help. Oftentimes these are things I can't run away from. So I ask myself, *am I mighty or flighty?*

If I'm mighty, then I can simply stand on God's Word, knowing He will help me clean up my mess. Of course, I recognize that with many situations in ordinary life, God gives me the freedom to clean up my own mess. (I've made some of those in my kitchen. That is, I've prepared foods even the dog wouldn't eat. And rightfully so, since I don't have a dog!)

I'm not sure if Jephthah had a choice in fleeing from his brothers, but I can identify, because I'm sometimes too weak to stand and fight. I prefer to run instead.

What will it take for me to learn once and for all that God will do my fighting for me, even when I'm on the run? Perhaps today I will take some time to let the blessed lyrics of today's song sink a little deeper into my heart: "What a mighty God we serve. Angels bow before him. Heaven and earth adore him."

Heavenly Father, I'm so thankful to belong to You. Praise You for continually fighting my battles, whether I'm fleeing or standing still. In Jesus' name I pray. Amen.

June 12–18. **Jimmie Oliver Fleming** lives in Chester, Virginia. She still has fond memories of a best pet costume contest she judged last year!

He's the Answer

Then Jephthah sent messengers to the Ammonite king with the question: "What do you have against me that you have attacked my country?" (Judges 11:12).

Scripture: Judges 11:12-18
Song: "Ask What You Will"

Wartime raises many questions, especially for the leaders who must make serious life or death decisions on short notice. And just as there are various kinds of questions, there are also various kinds of wars.

Leadership isn't easy, and sometimes even good leaders look back and ask themselves, "Why did I do that?" or "Why did I say that?" or "Why did I think that?"

When the Ammonite king responded to Jephthah's question, he said that the Israelites had mistreated him and taken his country's land, thus provoking an attack. But Jephthah wouldn't take *that* for an answer and war ensued.

Whatever "that" is, and whatever results or consequences come from "that" in our own lives, the certainty of it is that when we come to the Lord with questions, He has the answers. God alone has the ability to answer all questions, and in all categories.

Our part can be quite difficult: discerning His answers. It requires a dedication to walk closely with our God each day. Then we begin to sense His leading, whether through gentle intuition or the wise words of a trusted friend in Christ.

Dear God, help me continually rely on Your Word for any questions I have and to trust that You are guiding me to the right answers. When I don't fully understand, I thank You for Your leadership in my life. Through Christ Jesus, amen.

Permission Denied!

Then Israel sent messengers to Sihon king of the Amorites, who ruled in Heshbon, and said to him, "Let us pass through your country to our own place" (Judges 11:19).

Scripture: Judges 11:19-22
Song: "The Lord Will Make a Way Somehow"

Today's Scripture brings to mind a 6-year-old neighbor girl's take on asking permission. As I worked in my front yard on that hot day, doing battle with burned out grass as usual, the little girl walked by (going to her friend's house as usual). "You should always ask permission when you want to go on a different street from where you live," she offered. "Even if it's not far away."

"Yes, you should," I agreed, waving to the girl's mother standing at the end of the street watching her daughter.

"Everybody should ask permission," she continued. "And the moon and stars have to ask permission from God their Father too."

"Oh? And why is that?" I asked with genuine curiosity.

"Well, so they'll know what street to shine on!" she exclaimed.

Israel had asked permission to pass through a particular country. The response? Denied! Yet, ultimately, Israel received a greater victory (see vv. 20-22).

Likewise, we face many No's in any given span of months and years. Can we see that some of them may well lead, under the sovereign hand of God, to a very blessed Yes?

Heavenly Creator, I know that You "will make a way." Help me let go of any temptation to despair when I face a permission denied. I trust You to lead through rough waters to a peaceful shore. In Christ, amen.

The Ultimate Judge

Do you not possess what Chemosh your god gives you to possess? So whatever the Lord our God has driven out before us, we will possess it (Judges 11:24, *NASB*).

Scripture: Judges 11:23-28
Song: "What God Has for Me, It Is for Me"

It's been said that there are three sides to every story: yours, mine, and the truth. God, the ultimate judge, always has the right side of the story and acts accordingly.

In our Scripture today, it appears that Jephthah—at least for argument's sake—recognized the king's god named Chemosh. But far more important was Jephthah's previous acknowledgment of the Lord as the most worthy judge between the two nations' points of view. Here, the bottom line for Jephthah seems to be: If God has given land to Israel, then Israel should gratefully receive it.

Hooray for Jephthah! And hooray for me! Indeed, I'm continually learning: What the Lord has given me is mine. May I gratefully receive it and live it out. I'll not only possess it, but use it too.

Because God's gift includes the spirit of forgiveness, I have a wonderful weapon for spiritual warfare. When someone wages a relational battle with me, I need not shrink back into discouragement. Lyrics from our song declare, "What God has for me, it is for me. I know without a doubt, He will bring me out."

O Lord, thank You for keeping me safe during daily conflicts. I know that You always judge rightly each situation, so may I stay close to You, asking and offering forgiveness as You lead me to do so. Through Christ I pray. Amen.

Bad Promise, Sad Result

When he saw her, he tore his clothes . . . "Oh no, my daughter! You have brought me down and I am devastated. I have made a vow to the Lord that I cannot break" (Judges 11:35).

Scripture: Judges 11:34-40
Song: "Lord, I'm Coming Home"

We rightly question Jephthah's tragic vow to the Lord—that he would sacrifice whatever first came from his front door upon his return from victorious battle. What an unwise promise!

Yet in Jephthah's confused mind, his hasty vow couldn't be withdrawn. Sadly, the most mercy the man could offer his only daughter was to grant her two months' leave. The girl wanted to weep for herself—that she would die without ever having married. Thus, she gathered friends to be with her.

Recently I witnessed a birthday celebration at which a young woman sat at a long table with a dozen of her female friends. One of the men in the gathering, who apparently was her father, took pictures of her posing with her friends. As she walked past our table and told us her age, she also mentioned several places from where her friends had traveled to celebrate with her.

That was such a happy gathering of friends, contrasting so sharply with the woeful gathering around the girl in our Bible passage. Very likely, good family decisions over the years led up to a happy birthday celebration. Yet even one ill-advised statement and a misguided sense of honor can ruin the most sacred of relationships.

Heavenly Father, I want to serve You in every way that I possibly can while living here on this earth. Guide my words and actions that they may be wise and produce good fruit. In the precious name of Jesus I pray. Amen.

Due Consideration and Discussion

God, who knows the heart, showed that he accepted them [the Gentiles] by giving the Holy Spirit to them, just as he did to us (Acts 15:8).

Scripture: Acts 15:6-21
Song: "So Glad I'm Here"

The song for this devotional came to mind immediately as I recalled the retirement-celebration remarks of a long-time minister. "I'm very thankful for everyone here tonight," he said. "However, I have to apologize for not remembering people's names anymore. All I know is what's in the Bible, 'Matthew, Mark, Luke, and John.'"

The program chairperson came back to the microphone and echoed agreement. "I think that's true," she said. "Although he acts like he knows even more."

Perhaps we can identify with sometimes *acting* as if we know more than we do! Ever been there?

One thing is certain. God knows all—even the deep inner workings of the human heart. As the Council at Jerusalem considered how the Gentiles were to be incorporated into a mostly Jewish church, some insisted the new converts must be circumcised and obey the law of Moses.

Those hearts couldn't let go of beloved tradition. And perhaps they acted as if they had the final word on truth in the matter. But only God has that word: He is truth. Thankfully, our all-knowing Lord is all-powerful too. Thus His grace won the day.

Lord, I believe. Help me to make Your message of gracious salvation clear in my actions as well as in my words. Lead me to someone today who needs to know Your love through my friendship. I ask this in Jesus' name. Amen.

Now

Jephthah said to them: "Didn't you hate me and drive me from my father's house? Why do you come to me now, when you're in trouble?" (Judges 11:7).

Scripture: Judges 11:4-11
Song: "Come, Now Is the Time to Worship"

Recently I went to a department store and asked for help in the jewelry department. As usual, it took a while for someone to come and assist me. "As usual" means I'm a frequent visitor at this store.

I had vowed privately and publicly never to return to that store again. Yet there I stood. What's more, I had a sign that mentioned eating my words, or "eating crow." The impatient clerk, who was apparently ready for lunch—or perhaps had been on her lunch break when paged to help me—looked at my sign and licked her lips nervously. I smiled and walked away, knowing things would have gone "as usual."

Likewise, things may have gone on as usual for those who sought Jephthah's help . . . if not for their desperate situation. They now needed the business of someone they had once cruelly rejected because of his heritage.

Any kind of discrimination or racism is ugly, whether in ancient days or in our day. Yet a gracious person may, with God's help, find the courage to say: "That was then, this is now. How may I help you?"

Lord, I'm so thankful You will never turn me away due to my background, my heritage, my race, or anything else. It is only my actions that lead me out of close fellowship with You. I need You every day of my life and always will. Thank You for Your unconditional love, through the cross of Christ. Amen.

Message or Messenger?

Why do you ask my name? It is beyond understanding (Judges 13:18).

Scripture: Judges 13:8-18
Song: "His Name Is Wonderful"

He stood atop a bench on SW 4th Street, downtown Portland, near the park. With his Bible open, he preached passionately as people hurried down the sidewalk. Most looked away, not giving him a second thought, but a few had gathered to listen.

I've always liked street preachers, so I stopped and caught the last part of his message. After the man finished, he jumped down from his bench and moved up the street. Maybe he was changing locations to avoid loitering laws. Trying to get his attention, I shouted, "Hey! So what's your name?" He looked over his shoulder and replied, "My name doesn't matter; it's only the message that's important," and off he trotted.

At first, I felt slighted. I only wanted to meet him, possibly invite him to speak to our youth group. After some pondering, I realized the man was right—at least in one way—the message makes the difference, not the preachers' names or who they are.

The angel in today's passage also refused to give his name. It might have distracted from his message. Besides, he didn't need the recognition. Likewise, whenever we share God's Word, let us remember that any acclaim or honor belongs only to Him.

Lord, Your name is truly wonderful. It was Your message of salvation that drew me to You. That is where I found the gift of eternal life. Thank You, in Christ. Amen.

June 19–25. **Charles Earl Harrel** served as a minister for more than 30 years before stepping aside to pursue writing. He enjoys playing 12-string guitar, photography, and teaching from God's Word.

Not Just Experience, but Duty

As the flame blazed up from the altar toward heaven, the angel of the Lord ascended in the flame (Judges 13:20).

Scripture: Judges 13:19-23
Song: "O Worship the King"

Sunday's worship service went longer than normal. Laura, the song leader, looked at me as if asking a question: *Should I stop?* I shook my head, no. I could always shorten my sermon, but I hesitated to end the praise and worship time. Something special was happening.

The first thing I noticed was a yellowish glow around our music team on the platform. The pulpit area glowed as well. Next, the temperature felt like it jumped 15 degrees, yet no one had turned on the heat. Then I saw it, up high, a fog-like mist. The sanctuary looked like a smoke-filled room, but the smoke was coming down, instead of rising up. We all witnessed it.

Throughout the congregation, people started moving toward the altars. Overwhelmed by a sweet, divine presence, they dropped to their knees. Conviction filled their hearts. Tears flowed everywhere.

Sometimes, amazing things do occur during worship. It doesn't mean we will see an angel of the Lord or tongues of fire at the altar. Such outward signs can happen—I know. But the greatest miracles take place inwardly; they transform lives, heal bodies, and redeem souls. Therefore, whenever you worship, simply focus on loving God and leave the rest up to Him.

Most Precious God, You are worthy of all praise. Remind me to start and finish each day in adoration of You, and not to seek an experience but to fulfill my duty to Your greatness. Glory to Your name, through Christ my Lord! Amen.

Why the Long Hair?

During the entire period of their Nazirite vow, no razor may be used on their head. They must be holy until the period of their dedication to the Lord is over; they must let their hair grow long (Number 6:5).

Scripture: Numbers 6:1-8, 13-17
Song: "What Shall I Render?"

"Who do you think you are—Samson?" I never let on, but the constant teasing bothered me. My friends thought it was funny that I had stopped cutting my hair. They didn't understand that I had made a special vow to God.

Old Testament saints occasionally made vows unto God, most having to do with drawing closer to Him. New Testament saints made them too, including the apostle Paul (see Acts 18:18).

As a Christian, I knew I wasn't living under the laws of the old covenant. Still, I decided to undertake a Nazirite vow (or at least commit to the spirit behind it). Knowing that such pledges involved, among other things, not cutting one's hair, I decided to follow that example. Over time, my hair grew to shoulder length.

I never told anyone about my vow, but it involved my desire to write. Ironically, as my hair grew longer, I sensed a new strength in my writing ability. When the 12-month pledge ended, I cut my hair again.

God has given us many ways to dedicate our lives to Him: prayer, study, service, even an occasional vow. But more than all these, God simply desires our steadfast love.

Lord, I have made many pledges over the years, but none is more important than the one to love You with all my heart. May I keep that vow forever. In Jesus' name, amen.

In His Power

The Spirit of the Lord came powerfully upon him so that he tore the lion apart with his bare hands as he might have torn a young goat (Judges 14:6).

Scripture: Judges 14:1-9
Song: "By My Spirit"

With bare hands, they broke handcuffs, tore phone books in half, bent metal rods, and executed other feats of strength. We were watching the Power Team perform at a youth convention. Team members were accomplished athletes who used their physical abilities to encourage youth to strive for higher goals, physically and spiritually. They also integrated the gospel message into the performance and prayed with people afterwards.

Their presentation was inspiring, but I had to remind myself that they were just talented human beings. Their strength and athletic ability came from physical conditioning and practicing certain routines to perfection. Obviously, God had blessed them, but they weren't endowed like Samson. His strength came from the Spirit of the Lord through a supernatural anointing.

When God anoints us today, He does not normally give us superhuman strength to tear things asunder, which might frighten our neighbors! But He does empower us in other ways. He gives us strength to persevere. By His Spirit, we are able to pray without ceasing, overcome doubts, and stand up for our faith. According to the apostle Paul, we can do all these things and more through Christ who strengthens us (see Philippians 4:13).

Almighty God and Father, Your Spirit not only guides me each day but also strengthens my faith. Thank You! In the holy name of Jesus, my Lord and Savior, I pray. Amen.

Attention Grabbers

So he went out and caught three hundred foxes and tied them tail to tail in pairs. He then fastened a torch to every pair of tails, lit the torches and let the foxes loose in the standing grain of the Philistines (Judges 15:4, 5).

Scripture: Judges 15:1-8
Song: "Trust and Obey"

The young red fox lay wounded along the roadside, no doubt hit by a passing car and left to die. My uncle, a naturalist, stopped, carefully scooped up the little fox, and took it home to nurse it back to health. Whenever we visited Uncle Al, he would bring the fox into his house so we could see it. When it was time to go back to its pen, the fox raced about the house, jumped on counters, hid under chairs—anything to avoid being captured and returned to his outside enclosure. Catching him was almost impossible.

I can only imagine the effort it took for Samson to round up three hundred foxes and set their tails aflame. Even with burnt tails, I hope those wily foxes somehow survived. The Philistine fields, however, did not.

God employs unusual methods. Some of His actions are divine judgments in response to sin and idolatry; other incidents draw our attention to His plans and purposes. Moses' burning bush (see Exodus 3) and Balaam's talking donkey (see Numbers 22) are prime examples of the latter. Whether rightful judgments or spiritual attention grabbers, we need to give them prayerful consideration.

Father, I realize that not every circumstance has a spiritual application. And sometimes the Bible in its dedication to stark honesty, just shows us human foibles. So give me discernment when there's something important to learn. In Christ, amen.

Second Chances

Sovereign Lord, remember me. Please, God, strengthen me just once more, and let me with one blow get revenge on the Philistines for my two eyes (Judges 16:28).

Scripture: Judges 16:23-31
Song: "To Be Used of God"

It started during the 1960s as an antiestablishment movement. The hippie lifestyle embraced free love, peace, and personal freedom which sometimes included experimenting with mind-altering drugs. Their "if-it-feels-good-do-it" message influenced Allie in all the wrong ways. Although she had grown up in church, she drifted away from God.

For years, she immersed herself in this new culture, looking for enlightenment. Sadly, she didn't find what she expected. One day after a drug-induced stupor, she fell on her face and called out: "God, if You're still up there, please take me back." God accepted her back with love and forgiveness.

Later, under the supervision of a local church, she opened a Christian halfway house in Fresno County. Feeling comfortable with the familiar surroundings, her hippie friends came in by the scores. Many found a new purpose through Christ.

Allie's request of God wasn't about revenge or payback like Samson's prayer was. She only wanted to make up for wasted time and lost opportunities.

We can lose our way. Although we may forget our purpose, the Lord never does. As the God of second chances, He waits for us to return to Him; He is never more than a prayer away.

Dear God, remember me and give me another chance at faithfulness, not just to love You but to serve You. In the name of Jesus, amen.

The Quickening

The woman gave birth to a boy and named him Samson. He grew and the Lord blessed him, and the Spirit of the Lord began to stir him while he was in Mahaneh Dan, between Zorah and Eshtaol (Judges 13:24, 25).

Scripture: Judges 13:1-7, 24, 25
Song: "Come, O Come, Thou Quickening Spirit"

As a young child, I loved camping. In fact, I still do. My favorite spot was a primitive campground near Old Mammoth on the backside of the Sierra Nevadas. The rugged mountains of this range seemed to rise up through the sky and disappear into the heavens. At night, the stars came out and sparkled like glitter, decorating the horizon in all directions. The immenseness of it all overwhelmed me with awe.

I remember thinking that someone had made this place, purposefully. But who? Did God really exist? And if He did, why didn't He reveal himself? That night, after I climbed into my sleeping bag, He did—not with words but with a warm feeling—a type of quickening from within.

As I grew older, I realized this feeling was the Spirit of the Lord stirring my heart. Long before I received eternal life or became a minister, He had been preparing me for ministry.

God is always pursuing us. Even now, He may be tugging at your spirit, calling you for a special purpose in His kingdom. As Samson discovered, long before He anoints us for any ministry, He stirs our hearts first.

Spirit of the living God, many times I have felt Your presence, calling me, quickening my spirit. Send me forth to do Your bidding. For the Father's glory, I pray, through Christ. Amen.

A Stranger's Heart

You shall not oppress a stranger; you know the heart of a stranger, for you were strangers in the land of Egypt (Exodus 23:9, *RSV*).

Scripture: Exodus 23:1-9
Song: "Come to Us, Beloved Stranger"

How do you say, "May I borrow a cup of sugar?" in Burmese? Nepali? Arabic? Spanish? If you lived in an apartment in Clarkston, Georgia, this could be a common question. Clarkston is an international village a few miles northeast of Atlanta, and *Time* magazine cited it as the most diverse square mile in America. It is home to refugees from almost 150 countries, who speak more than 70 languages.

Many of these refugees have fled their home countries to escape war, persecution, and massacre. In the 1990s, the United Nations and the United States government chose Clarkston as a prime location for displaced refugees. These strangers enjoy the freedoms of America. They also face the same physical, social, and spiritual needs as US citizens. Mission organizations and churches colabor to meet some of these basic needs.

The Israelites had been strangers in another land. They knew the sadness, fear, and loneliness of displacement; they realized that culture and language barriers hinder relationships, making life hard. Their experiences remind me to show compassion and to be a friend to those with needs.

Lord, give me compassion to help, share, empathize, and love others well. Equip and use me to display Your presence and provision. In Jesus' name, amen.

June 26–30. **Vickie Hodges** lives with her husband, Steve, in the mountains of western Colorado. She loves to travel, camp, paint, and engage with people from various cultures.

You're on Fire!

Depart from me, you who are cursed, into the eternal fire prepared for the devil and his angels (Matthew 25:41).

Scripture: Matthew 25:41-46
Song: "Cast Away the Works of Darkness"

Eager to test their new two-person ice fishing tent, Steve and Ron assembled the shelter over the two holes they had bored in the frozen Blue Mesa Reservoir. Inside the dark hut, they ignited the lantern and the propane heater, then rigged their fishing poles. The red glow of the heater's flame warmed the inside of the tent. Insulated with layers of clothing and gloves, the men settled into their camp chairs and into the routine of jigging their baited hooks through the holes.

Fifteen minutes later, Steve yelled, "Fish on!" as he began reeling in the first catch of the day, pitching forward and backward, giving his line tension and slack in cadence with the fish's struggle. But soon Ron noticed Steve had tipped back into the heater. "Steve!" he shouted. "You're on fire!"

"I sure am! This one's really fighting!"

Ron bolted from his chair, grabbed Steve's shoulders, spun him around, and pounded out the blazing jacket with his leather gloves. Because of those layers—and the excitement of the catch—Steve was unaware that he had been literally ablaze.

Sadly, the unrighteous mentioned in today's passage will someday reside in an eternal fire they chose for themselves while on earth. Unlike Steve, they won't be able to claim ignorance of the cause.

Jesus, thank You for being the means of eternal life. "Nothing in my hands I bring; simply to Thy cross I cling" (Rock of Ages). Through Your precious name I pray. Amen.

Take Heed

Consider what you do, for you judge not for man but for the Lord; he is with you in giving judgment (2 Chronicles 19:6, *RSV*).

Scripture: 2 Chronicles 19:4-7
Song: "Fairest Lord Jesus"

What's this? Our domestic water bill arrived in today's mail. It was higher than the previous two months. I called Dayton, the Chief Operator for our local domestic water company. He explained that there were two possibilities.

First, there could be a leak in the underground line from the meter to our house. Second, the meter reader could have made a mistake when checking the usage on the dial. Dayton explained how to open the top cover in the meter pit and flip open the little lid on the meter. The meter gauges include a leak indicator, a sweep hand, and an odometer. When water passes through the meter, all of these gauges move.

A dripping faucet or leak in the line causes a revolution of the indicator. The sweep hand makes one rotation on the dial for every 10 gallons of usage. Finally, the odometer clicks each time 10 gallons pass through the system. Since our leak indicator and sweep hand were motionless and because these are human-read meters, our company concluded there had been a mistake by the meter reader.

Jehoshaphat appointed judges and told them to consider carefully. They were not to make any mistakes, because a lot depended on the correctness of their judgements.

Heavenly Father, it's impossible never to make a mistake. I need Your guidance to help me make correct decisions as often as possible. In Jesus' name, amen.

Relentless!

He told them a parable, to the effect that they ought always to pray and not lose heart (Luke 18:1, *RSV*).

Scripture: Luke 18:1-8
Song: "Prayer Is the Key"

With 45 seconds remaining on the scoreboard, the crowded high school gymnasium erupted. Fans cheered, whistled, clapped, stomped, and screamed. It became clear that the girls' basketball team from Hoxie, Kansas, a tiny dot on the map, would soon win the game.

But this wasn't just an ordinary league competition; it was the playoff game for the state championship. Moreover, a once-in-a-lifetime title was at stake. This squad of girls would soon secure their fourth banner as state basketball champions.

During four brief years of participating in high school sports, their persistence and dedication had netted an unprecedented 95 game winning streak. Over the course of their high school career, these girls learned to work together and play together. They practiced early in the morning before classes began and again later in the day after classes ended. The players disciplined their bodies and minds, learning never to abandon hope. They were relentless.

In Jesus' parable, the widow persevered against all odds. She continued requesting help and never stopped hoping. Like that widow, I am in constant need of help against spiritual forces that try to take me down. I must be relentless in prayer.

O Lord, I'm grateful You hear my requests all the time. Strengthen me so I don't despair and keep infusing Your strength in me to resist every temptation that comes my way. In Your holy name I pray. Amen.

Return of the Rainbow

The word of God spread. The number of disciples in Jerusalem increased rapidly (Acts 6:7).

Scripture: Acts 6:1-7
Song: "A Mighty Fortress Is Our God"

Rainbow trout thrived in Colorado rivers, lakes, and streams until the 1990s. At that time, they nearly disappeared. Myxobolus Cerebralis, the parasite that causes Whirling Disease, killed almost 90 percent of the rainbow trout in Colorado. This disease deforms the spine in young fish, making them unable to swim or to feed properly. But in 2003, biologists began cross-breeding a strain of domesticated rainbow trout found in Germany, the Hofer trout, which resist the deadly parasite.

During the time that the number of rainbow trout had been declining, the aggressive carnivorous brown trout had begun taking over waterways. Biologists realized they had to manage the brown trout before they could reinstate the rainbow trout. Despite challenges, the rainbow has returned to Colorado and now are naturally increasing and thriving.

As the new church grew, Greek widows felt neglected. The busy apostles faced a dilemma: preach the gospel or care for the physically needy? To fix the problem, they chose seven honest, wise men. These disciples began handling the finances and accounting. They also provided for the financial needs of widows and orphans. As the number of disciples increased, so did the spreading of God's Word.

Heavenly Father, I'm often faced with problems that seem to have no remedy. Remind me that Your wise way will cause Your plans to flourish and prosper. Just keep my heart and mind open to Your leading. In Jesus' name, amen.

My Prayer Notes

DEVOTIONS®

▶ **July**

"I am who I am." . . . "This is my name forever, the name you shall call me from generation to generation."

—*Exodus 3:14, 15*

Gary Wilde, Editor | Margaret K. Williams, Project Editor | Photo © iStock | Thinkstock®

DEVOTIONS® is published quarterly by Standard Publishing, Cincinnati, Ohio, www.standardpub.com. Copyright © 2016 by Standard Publishing. All rights reserved. Topics based on the Home Daily Bible Readings, International Sunday School Lessons. Copyright © 2013 by the Committee on the Uniform Series. Printed in the U.S.A. All Scripture quotations, unless otherwise indicated, are taken from the *HOLY BIBLE, NEW INTERNATIONAL VERSION*®. *NIV*®. Copyright © 1973, 1978, 1984, 2011 by Biblica, Inc.® Used by permission of Zondervan. All rights reserved worldwide. Scripture quotations marked (*RSV*) are taken from *The Revised Standard Version of the Bible (RSV)*, copyrighted 1946, 1952, © 1971, 1973.

From the Summit

The Lord called to him [Moses] out of the mountain, saying, "Thus you shall say to the house of Jacob, and tell the people of Israel" (Exodus 19:3, *RSV*).

Scripture: Exodus 19:1-9
Song: "Power for Service"

"We have a 'highball'!" the conductor yelled to the engineer as we left the Manitou & Pikes Peak Cog Railway station. The world's highest cog train was bound for the Pikes Peak summit of 14,115 feet. The nine-mile trip would take a couple of hours and would include a temperature drop of nearly 30 degrees.

In the late 1880s, the owner of the Simmons Mattress Company, Zalman Simmons, rode a mule to the top of the mountain. After the rough ride, he decided to start a company to build this cog railway. Then in 1893, from the crest of Pikes Peak, Katharine Lee Bates wrote the words to "America the Beautiful." Views of the Great Plains, Sangre de Cristo Range, Collegiate Peaks, and traces of old mining towns inspire great thoughts by those who climb, whether by train, footpath, or highway.

God met Moses on Mt. Sinai. He reminded Moses of all He had done for the children of Israel, promising that if they obeyed His covenant He would establish them as a holy nation. Today, from the summit of God's glory and grace, He calls me to himself.

Heavenly Father, You delivered me from the bonds of sin through Jesus Christ, Your Son. Thank You for meeting me in the valleys and summits of my journey of faith every day. I cherish Your promised presence, in His name. Amen.

July 1, 2. **Vickie Hodges** lives with her husband, Steve, in the mountains of western Colorado. She loves to travel, camp, paint, and engage with people from various cultures.

Get Out of Here!

Then the Lord said, "I have seen the affliction of my people who are in Egypt, and have heard their cry because of their taskmasters; I know their sufferings" (Exodus 3:7, *RSV*).

Scripture: Exodus 3:1-12
Song: "We've a Story to Tell to the Nations"

We want you to go away! At the Christian conference I attended a few years ago, several booths provided swag for attendees, but the slogan on the free T-shirts at the missions booth captured me. *We want you to go away?* At first, I laughed, but after the intent sunk in, I decided to talk with a missions representative. One of his statements really got me thinking. He said, "The best way to go *there* is to leave *here.*"

Shortly afterward, our daughters told us they wanted to go on a short-term missions trip with their friends to a country in Asia. My husband and I have always encouraged our kids to be mission-minded by urging them to pray for and give to missionaries, serve in soup kitchens, and collect winter coats for the homeless. But somehow we never thought they might want to travel to dangerous countries in order to help needy people!

Today's verses remind me that God calls all of us to be missionaries. Certainly not everyone will move abroad or even change zip codes. However, it's clear the Lord invites us to help meet human need and to be His representatives wherever we are. When Moses was 80 years old, God told him to be a missionary. And Moses—ultimately—said, "Yes."

Father, even when it's hard, strengthen me to say "Yes" to Your revealed will. Use me to minister to those who are afflicted, oppressed, and suffering. In Christ, amen.

Success in God Alone

As long as he sought the Lord, God gave him success (2 Chronicles 26:5).

Scripture: 2 Chronicles 26:1-10, 15
Song: "In Christ Alone"

John had been exceptionally gifted by God. He loved the Lord and His church, and from an early age, he dedicated his life to preaching the Word. Because of his ability to touch hearts and preach in a powerful way, he became well-known and sought after. He began serving larger churches and was chosen to speak at many meetings and conventions.

But John developed a dangerous pride. For one thing, he became more and more concerned with how people perceived him, rather than how he could lead them closer to God. Success to him meant being recognized for the scholar he was.

John was well-liked and attractive. His downfall came when he gave into a temptation that flattered both his pride and manhood. His marriage and family fell apart, and just as God took away Uzziah's leadership in His nation, He took away John's leadership in Christ's church.

"It won't happen to me," we say. But pride can lead any one of us into a serious breach of faith and fellowship with our Lord. He certainly doesn't want that! As we walk closely with Him, He leads us into the kind of success He has chosen for us: that we enhance His reputation in the world around us.

Father, I want to have the same burning desire to seek You as I did when I first believed. Guard my heart against pride, and keep me a faithful servant. In Christ, amen.

July 3–9. **Janet Mountjoy** and her husband are now retired after working with churches in the Midwest and South for 35 years. She enjoys time with their family, writing, reading, and camping.

Serve and Be Free!

Is not this the kind of fasting I have chosen: to loose the chains of injustice and untie the cords of the yoke, to set the oppressed free and break every yoke? (Isaiah 58:6).

Scripture: Isaiah 58:6-12
Song: "My Task"

When I was 9, Mom made a decision: Lent was coming, and she decided *not* to give up anything. Rather, she would *do* new things—acts that would help others and honor God. She began volunteering at a hospital, started visiting homebound church members, and spent more time with our neighbors.

In her late 70s, when many might retire from service, she heard of a Cambodian refugee family who had just come to the United States. She made arrangements to have them settle in a house next door. Then she and my step dad adopted the family—took them to church and doctors' appointments, helped them learn American ways of banking, shopping, and driving. They became family, and in time that family became Christian.

Mom's Lenten decision never ended; rather, it became her everyday life. In a sense, that initial decision was her personal independence day. It freed her for true servanthood in God's kingdom—a kind of liberty that surpasses all others.

The Lord calls us to set aside a whole lifetime to fight injustice and oppression, to provide for those in need, and to take care of our families. He's promised that when we do these things, our lights will shine, and we will be healed and free.

Father, so many people don't know You. Give me a heart-desire to reach out and help with a self-sacrificial love, as Your servant. I pray that I will honor You. Amen.

I Love This!

The Lord reigns, he is robed in majesty; the Lord is robed in majesty and armed with strength; indeed, the world is established, firm and secure. Your throne was established long ago; you are from all eternity (Psalm 93:1, 2).

Scripture: Psalm 93
Song: "How Great Is Our God"

What an awesome God we serve! And I don't mean "awesome" as in "totally cool." Rather, awesome in that a sense of awe—a holy fear or reverence—should well up in us when we realize just how mighty and transcendent He is. For the seas themselves lift up their voices and clap their waves in praise (v. 3).

But even more amazing than His power is God's love. He loves you and me personally! When I consider that the Creator of the cosmos knows me, loves me, and hears my prayers, I'm dumb-founded, awestruck. I want to cry out, as Peter did to Jesus, "Go away from me, Lord; I am a sinful man!" (Luke 5:8). I don't deserve God's love, but He loves me anyway. He promises He will continue to love me throughout eternity.

My response? To honor Him with my life every day. I want to walk closely with Him and learn to love as He loves. I want to know Him more deeply, as I seek to discern His will. I want to enter into His throne room some day and bow at His feet.

There's no greater blessing than to be known and loved by the Lord of all. To put a new spin on an old song: "Jesus knows me, this I love."

Holy Creator of all, please forgive me when I view You merely as my pal. You are an awesome Lord, mighty and majestic. I bow before You and give You my praise. How thankful I am that You chose to know and love me! Through Christ, amen.

Why Does He Love You?

I want you to know that God's salvation has been sent to the Gentiles, and they will listen (Acts 28:28).

Scripture: Acts 28:23-29
Song: "He Reigns"

When Paul first proclaimed that God's salvation was also for Gentiles, the response was anything but rejoicing. Jealousy emerged, and charges of blasphemy filled the air. Soon Paul was imprisoned, beaten, and stoned for this teaching because the Jews felt any messianic message was only for them, the keepers of long-standing divine promises. But their jealousy became their downfall. The gospel not only then went to the Gentiles, but it was spread by them, far and wide.

How is it for us today? Can we look down on others and feel they're unworthy or incapable of receiving God's grace? I recall some comments that sounded much like some of the religious leaders in Paul's audiences. "Don't waste your time; they'll never listen," or "You're not going to try to study with those people, are you?" or "He's so wrapped up in a sinful lifestyle," or "It's too late for her."

Let us remember today that Jesus came for only one type of person: the one who needs Him. All others, as He often said, already have their reward. In fact, we might say there is only one requirement for salvation: You have to be a sinner. And if He loves you today, it is for one reason alone: You need loving.

Father, I pray for myself and for Your church. Help me to see everyone as You see them: prime candidates for Your love and redemption. Place it on my heart to reach out to those who long for better days and a more hopeful future—the kind of life only You can give. In the name of my gracious Savior I pray. Amen.

Unequally Yoked?

Do not be yoked together with unbelievers. For what do righteousness and wickedness have in common? (2 Corinthians 6:14).

Scripture: 2 Corinthians 6:14–7:1
Song: "O Bride of Christ on High"

Rob and Ashley met and dated in college. They had different church backgrounds, but in the college dating setting, it didn't seem to matter. They simply ignored the fact that their ideas of spousal and parenting roles differed greatly.

But as graduation day drew closer, the couple realized they needed to talk seriously about their future together. They strove to be honest about their expectations for marriage and family, and they considered what their family's spiritual life would be. In spite of their early desire to ignore their differences, they eventually decided to break up.

But what does "unequally yoked" mean in our Bible passage today? It's the general principle that believers and unbelievers are better off not marrying. Beyond the differences that Christian couples may face, there is a much greater gulf of separation between those who do or don't hold to the apostolic faith.

It's as if Paul is saying "a family that prays together, stays together." But if there is no basis for prayer between husband and wife, the foundation for a happy future will be shaky at best. After all, if a yoke ties two together, then pulling in different directions will throw both off balance.

Father, help me to be honest about the friends I make and the situations I enter. Let me take Your gentle warnings seriously and rely on Your wisdom as I form relationships of mutual encouragement in Christian growth. Through Christ my Lord, amen.

Why Holiness?

Since everything will be destroyed in this way, what kind of people ought you to be? You ought to live holy and godly lives as you look forward to the day of God (2 Peter 3:11, 12).

Scripture: 2 Peter 3:11-16
Song: "O to Be Like Thee"

What kind of people ought we to be? What a great question! One way to think of it is: The Lord Jesus has a special purpose for His people before He returns to us as the great judge. He's not calling us to "be good" merely so we won't be "destroyed" on that day. Rather, He wants us to be holy (that is, dedicated to His service), proclaiming His salvation to everyone we can.

Holiness is living a life set apart for God, one that focuses on living and loving and sharing in a way that honors Him. A holy life is our worship.

Tammy has devoted her life to ministering to the homeless. Kathryn took a part-time job in order to be more available to help victims of human trafficking. Ted sold his business and home to pay for school so he can prepare to preach the gospel. Even though her position was high, Georgia lived frugally all of her life, sending her money to help missionaries in Africa. All of these people chose holy lives—not for themselves, but for the sake of others.

Peter's life was not without problems or persecution, nor did it end peacefully. But his soul was free and full of hope. His holy life is still an example to us today, as our lives can be an example to those around us.

Dear Father, I want my life to show what it means to be a child of Yours. Please guard my words, my thoughts, and my actions as I walk with You today. In Christ, amen.

It's an Honor to Be Known

I heard the voice of the Lord saying, "Whom shall I send? And who will go for us?" And I said, "Here am I. Send me!" (Isaiah 6:8).

Scripture: Isaiah 6:1-8
Song: "He Knows My Name"

When I was 10-years-old, we lived in Washington, DC. On Easter weekend, the president hosted the traditional egg rolling on the White House lawn. As we waited for him to come out, I joined a group of kids waiting to greet him. He was shaking hands and talking with some of the others, and I could hardly wait for him to get to me. But when he was only two steps away, a photographer pushed in to get a good picture, bumped my basket, dumped my eggs, and then the president was gone! My big day was shattered because, not only had my basket dumped, but in the rush, my president didn't even know me.

When Isaiah entered God's throne room, he wasn't meeting the president. He stood face to face with the Creator in all of His glory. Yet God knew him! Aware of his sinfulness, the prophet felt unworthy of even being in God's presence. But the Lord graciously forgave him and called him into service.

The humanness of our leaders keeps them from knowing their people. But our great king knows us—and loves us. Thus our ministries in His name have a very personal character. He sends us forth according to our gifts and passions, guaranteeing spiritual fruit as we rely on His power.

Almighty God, thank You for knowing me and loving me. Thank You for forgiving my sins and for giving me life and a purpose. Help me to respond as Isaiah did. Amen.

What's the Source?

If what a prophet proclaims in the name of the Lord does not take place or come true, that is a message the Lord has not spoken. . . . so do not be alarmed (Deuteronomy 18:22).

Scripture: Deuteronomy 18:15-22
Song: "Standing on the Promises"

The eighteenth-century French philosopher Voltaire actively opposed Christianity, calling it a ridiculous, absurd, and bloody religion. He is said to have predicted that the faith would be extinct within 100 years of his lifetime.

Instead, within 50 years of his death, the Geneva Bible society reportedly used his house and printing presses to print copies of the Bible. Soon the Great Awakenings of the eighteenth and nineteenth centuries brought thousands of men and women to Christ in England and America. Many believe we are still seeing the effects of these revivals today.

The outcome of prophecy depends wholly on the source. We know that Christianity will never be snuffed out because of the promises God has made in His Word. In fact, the Lord himself assured us that the gates of Hell would not overcome His church (see Matthew 16:18).

Secularism continues to creep into our culture today through our schools, universities, and the media. But we need not be alarmed. Let us hold fast to the promises of God's Word, rather than the ever-changing message of worldly wisdom.

Lord, I trust the promises You have made in Your Word. They are the foundation of my life. Forgive me for being swayed by any contrary message. In Christ, amen.

July 10–16. **Lisa Earl** writes from her home in Cranberry Township, Pennsylvania. She enjoys spending time with her husband and three young sons.

By His Strength

I have made you a fortified city, an iron pillar and a bronze wall to stand against the whole land—against the kings of Judah, its officials, its priests and the people (Jeremiah 1:18).

Scripture: Jeremiah 1:11-19
Song: "Eternal Father, Strong to Save"

Bronze is a strong metal that the ancients used for tools, weapons, and buildings. Its powerful imagery abounds in Scripture.

Today's passage states that God will rescue His people by making them a bronze wall. On their own, the Israelites could accomplish nothing; when they trusted God, however, they couldn't be defeated.

The image of bronze appears elsewhere in the Old Testament. As the Israelites traveled toward the promised land, they spoke against God and Moses, complaining so much that God sent venomous snakes among them. After they pled for mercy, God told Moses to fashion a bronze snake and put it on a pole. When anyone was bitten by a snake, they could look at the bronze image and live (see Numbers 21:4-9).

In the New Testament, Jesus compares himself to that bronze snake: "Just as Moses lifted up the snake in the wilderness, so the Son of Man must be lifted up, that everyone who believes may have eternal life in him" (John 3:14, 15).

Jesus was lifted up so we could lay our burdens down. By His wisdom, strength, and abiding presence, we can then stand against any aggressive difficulty that confronts us.

Dear God, I look up to Your Son for the power to confront the enemies in my life—anything that tries to derail me along the path of discipleship this day. Help me to stand against the sin in the world and in myself. In Jesus' name I pray. Amen.

No Drought About It

You are to me like a deceptive brook, like a spring that fails (Jeremiah 15:18).

Scripture: Jeremiah 15:10-21
Song: "Come, Thou Fount of Every Blessing"

Growing up in rural central Pennsylvania, we relied on spring water for our daily needs. We weren't hooked up to the municipal supply, and our water availability depended on rainfall. Just before a drought, we'd fill up buckets, gallon jugs, and even our kid-sized wading pool with water. Once the spring dried up, we had to haul water buckets to the sinks, tub, and toilets.

I now live in the suburbs. Yet I can't boast about being any better than our unreliable spring. I may claim devotion to Christ, but when life throws me tough challenges, I may kind of dry up as far as faith and cheerfulness go.

Thankfully, Jesus fills us with something better than we could ever produce on our own. "Let anyone who is thirsty come to me and drink," says Jesus. "Whoever believes in me, as Scripture has said, rivers of living water will flow from within them" (John 7:37, 38).

As we seek to love and serve the Lord, in and of ourselves, we come up dry. Jesus is the source of living water, and any righteousness we have flows directly from Him. Just as my family had to rely on rain to relieve us from a drought, we rely on Jesus to pour out His Spirit.

Almighty and everlasting God, fill me with Your Holy Spirit. Cleanse me, renew me, and revive me so springs of living water can flow through me. When I am the driest in faith and hope, give me Your strength and peace. In the name of the Father and the Son and the Holy Spirit, amen.

No Longer Lopsided

Like clay in the hand of the potter, so are you in my hand, Israel (Jeremiah 18:6).

Scripture: Jeremiah 18:1-11
Song: "Change My Heart, Oh God"

My mom's dresser sported several lopsided clay containers when I was growing up. These less-than-perfect creations were the result of my elementary school art classes. The containers were neither attractive nor functional, as my chubby digits lacked the skill of a true craftsman.

Today's Scripture reminds us that God's people are like clay in His hands. We were formed by God, the perfect potter. Yet our sin makes us imperfect, even misshapen. Because of Adam and Eve's disobedience in the Garden of Eden, our bodies are now subject to disease, aging, and death. Our insides were also corrupted with deadly sins of our human nature: pride, envy, wrath, sloth, lust, gluttony, greed.

Thankfully, God has a plan to mold us into better shape, from the inside out. We're like jars of clay: simple, imperfect vessels, but the treasure of God's presence lives in us through the Holy Spirit (see 2 Corinthians 4:7). Because of Jesus' crucifixion scars, our imperfections can be healed.

While our exteriors may be lumpy—like my clay creations, even decaying with age—the Holy Spirit works to conform us to His image, day by day.

Dear Heavenly Father, mold me into who You want me to be in my world. Help me to trust that You are the perfect potter, and you are doing this work in my life. Forgive me for relying on myself and for doubting Your ability to change me from the inside out. In the name of my precious Savior and Lord. Amen.

Spared from Suffering

I will discipline you but only in due measure; I will not let you go entirely unpunished (Jeremiah 46:28).

Scripture: Jeremiah 46:25-28
Song: "When I Survey the Wondrous Cross"

A recent survey by the parenting website Babycenter.com found that only 49 percent of moms discipline their children by spanking, even though most of them were spanked as children. Yet that doesn't mean parents today are letting their children run wild. What are the modern techniques? Time-outs and removal of privileges said 90 percent of moms in the survey.

In today's Scripture we find that God destroyed the nations around Israel but punished Israel less severely. Because He is both loving and just, He cannot let sin simply have its way (see Exodus 34:6, 7). The Israelites were God's children. He had every right to completely destroy them for their sin; instead, He chose to discipline them out of love.

As God's children, our sins must be dealt with as well. Thankfully, God's only Son, Jesus Christ, has already borne the ultimate punishment for our sins through His death on the cross. While we may suffer the earthly consequences of our poor choices, we can avoid the ultimate disastrous effect of our sins—eternal separation from God—through faith in Jesus.

Let us take comfort in the fact that, although we face trials in this life—some of them of our own doing, we will be spared more severe suffering because of the suffering servant.

Lord, thank You for taking my punishment. Help me share Your message of grace and forgiveness with those in my world who have seeking hearts. Amen.

In the Quiet, New Life

"Come, follow me," Jesus said, "and I will send you out to fish for people" (Mark 1:17).

Scripture: Mark 1:16-20
Song: "I Love to Tell the Story"

Our local park is full of noises: The crack of baseballs on bats, the whirring of roller blades on pavement, and the cheering of proud parents at the soccer field. The only quiet spot is the fishing pond. There, people of all ages simply sit, stand, or even glide in canoes, waiting for the fish to bite.

Today's verse compares evangelism to fishing—we are to be fishers of men and women. What a contrast to our culture's typical view of evangelistic proclamation—the shouting of street preachers, the ringing of doorbells, and the banging of drums at loud concerts aimed toward youthful ears.

Maybe there's a different type of evangelism, one that is soft and subtle. The whispered prayer of a desperate parent. The silent strength of a shoulder to cry on. The faithful service of a church custodian. Men and women faithfully trusting God to bring people to Him, that they may take a first, tentative taste of His goodness.

While God uses different means to reach different people, let us not underestimate the power of subtle service wrapped in humble silence. Let us wait on God's timing with open arms, ready to catch those He sends our way, by just being a friend.

Almighty and most merciful God, help me to be willing to reach others with Your good news in any way You ask me to do it. Help me to recognize those who serve You behind the scenes and value their witness to Your love. Thank You for them today, in the name of Jesus, my Savior and Lord. Amen.

Give Me the Words

"Alas, Sovereign Lord," I said, "I do not know how to speak; I am too young" (Jeremiah 1:6).

Scripture: Jeremiah 1:4-10
Song: "O for a Thousand Tongues to Sing"

One of the greatest joys in my four years of parenting has been helping my sons learn to speak. Their pronunciation is a never-ending source of amusement in our household. Some of our favorite misspoken words have been "Wawi" for Levi, "babanas" for bananas, and "yeyyo" for yellow. Although these words are adorable, my husband and I want our children to learn to speak correctly. When they mispronounce something, we repeat the words correctly and encouragingly.

How much more encouraging is our Heavenly Father! In today's passage, He even put His words in the mouth of Jeremiah when the prophet doubted his ability to deliver God's message.

The theme of God speaking through His people abounds in Scripture. Jesus told His disciples that when they were brought before rulers for preaching the gospel, the Holy Spirit would speak through them (see Mark 13:11).

He can speak through us today, as well. When we don't know what to pray, the Holy Spirit intercedes for us through wordless groans (see Romans 8:26). Although I can only repeat words to help my children speak better, God can actually speak through you and me. Let us allow Him to spread His message through us today, whether in winsome words or helpful deeds.

Father, thank You for the gift of speech. Forgive me for failing to let Your words flow through me. Give me Your words today. In the name of the Holy Trinity, amen.

Regardless

You must speak my words to them, whether they listen or fail to listen, for they are rebellious (Ezekiel 2:7).

Scripture: Ezekiel 2:1-7
Song: "I'll Go Where You Want Me to Go"

A Caucasian man sitting next to an elderly African-American widow was the talk of the church. But after a few weeks, the white face in an otherwise all-black church was accepted without question.

What the members didn't know was that this same man had spent 15 years in prison for killing a black man! The widow had persistently visited her husband's killer in prison and led him to Christ. Now he attends services with her on Sundays.

In another setting, a former member of a notorious motorcycle gang visited a local church. He found only one friendly face, that of a 9-year-old boy in a wheelchair. "If you have any questions about our church, just ask me," Jerry said.

In time, Mike had many questions, and he always sought out Jerry first. What a strange pair they became, the 9-year-old and the ex-biker engaged each Sunday in heartfelt conversation.

A little old lady and a wheelchair-bound little boy demonstrate the call to Ezekiel: be unafraid in sharing God's message. You may encounter stubborn, unyielding hearts. You may find some receptive souls. But our commission doesn't depend on the hearer's response. Our call is to share the message, regardless.

Lord, I want to be more like Jerry or more like a daring widow who willingly witnesses to her husband's killer. What courage! Embolden me, through Christ. Amen.

July 17–23. **Dan Nicksich** and wife Donna reside in Grant, Michigan, where Dan is the senior minister of the Northland Church of Christ.

Stand Firm!

On both sides of it were written words of lament and mourning and woe (Ezekiel 2:10).

Scripture: Ezekiel 2:8-10
Song: "Stand Up, Stand Up for Jesus"

Andy has been a preacher for 25 years. But he still remembers a fifth-grade Sunday school class when he first learned about Hell. Those words of woe and warning were enough to turn him to Christ.

By Ezekiel's time, the nation of Israel had turned so far away from God that a message of lament, mourning, and woe was being sent through God's prophet. Though there is always hope and a bright future with the Lord, in this case a happier message wouldn't have sufficed to turn the people's hearts.

Ezekiel is one of a number of prophets who had to stand against the tide of public opinion. Noah, Elijah, Isaiah, and later, Jesus, all experienced cultural rejection of their messages.

We live in a time when society increasingly accepts lifestyles previously rejected as sinful, and we must be willing to speak about these things. It's not easy to travel alone when everyone else is going a different direction. Yet God's call is always to stand with Him, even if it leaves us with a minority status.

We can relate to Ezekiel in our day, with so many voices raised in opposition to moral absolutes of any kind. But let us stand firm. Human society will always experience much mourning and woe. But be of good cheer: a better kingdom is coming.

O Lord God, I thank You for those mentors and models who have stood firm and given me a powerful example to follow. May I not be swayed by changing times or difficult days. I pray in the powerful name of Jesus. Amen.

The Right Kind of Medicine

I took the little scroll from the angel's hand and ate it. It tasted as sweet as honey in my mouth, but when I had eaten it, my stomach turned sour (Revelation 10:10).

Scripture: Revelation 10:8-11
Song: "Thy Word"

A silly song from the movie *Mary Poppins* makes a relevant point: "Just a spoonful of sugar helps the medicine go down." It's much easier to partake of things that taste sweet. Sometimes, however, they still turn the stomach sour.

Several times in Scripture prophets are told to eat a scroll. The idea is to partake of—hence to accept and internalize—the message coming from the Lord. To Ezekiel the message continued certain prophecies against many peoples, nations, languages, and kings. Those prophecies were something of a bitter pill to swallow, a message that turns the stomach sour.

For Christians, the Scriptures are useful for teaching, rebuking, correcting, and training in righteousness (see 2 Timothy 3:16). The rebuking aspect isn't the most pleasant pill to swallow, but it proves necessary in the long run.

When we need to hear that word of rebuke, God's grace provides that precious spoonful of sugar and promises to bring the necessary correction. Especially when a good friend or mentor points out a flaw in your life, you will find that awful feeling in the pit of your stomach replaced with something much more pleasant: the joy of returning to the Lord and His Word.

Heavenly Father, I admit I don't like to be criticized. But I thank You for the desired effect, when I allow a loving rebuke to do its work in me. Keep me on the right path with Christ. Amen.

Power of the Word

Mordecai wrote in the name of King Xerxes, sealed the dispatches with the king's signet ring, and sent them by mounted couriers, who rode fast horses (Esther 8:10).

Scripture: Esther 8:7-10
Song: "I Sing the Mighty Power of God"

Edward Everett spoke for two hours. President Abraham Lincoln spoke for two minutes. We know Lincoln's speech as the Gettysburg Address. Few remember that Everett also spoke.

There is power in both the written and spoken word. Everett would later write to the President to say, "I should be glad, if I could flatter myself that I came as near to the central idea of the occasion, in two hours, as you did in two minutes."

Imagine the responsibility of writing a decree in the name of the king. Our Scripture today tells us that the king's decree gave God's people new life when they were headed for destruction. Imagine the joy brought by written words of deliverance!

The handwritten letter or note is no longer the norm, of course. Computers, i-phones, i-pads, twitter posts, e-mails, and the like have taken communication in a whole new direction. But there is still power in the written word. Shouldn't God's people use it for the good of His kingdom?

Send words of comfort to the grieving, words of encouragement to the depressed or hurting. Send words of insight to those still searching. They may find your words as exciting as those once sent via the fastest horses.

Lord, I want to be encouragement to those in my life. I pray You will remind me daily of opportunities to touch lives and brighten their days. Amen.

Time to Speak Up?

Son of man, I have made you a watchman for the people of Israel; so hear the word I speak and give them warning from me (Ezekiel 3:17).

Scripture: Ezekiel 3:12-21
Song: "All Hail the Power of Jesus' Name"

It was over 40 years ago, but I remember it as if it were yesterday. I was just 16-years-old, playing center field, when the batter hit a long drive off to my right. I ran hard, looking back over my left shoulder, all the while thinking, *I'm going to get that ball.* And I would have—if it hadn't been for that fence.

That pesky old fence put a damper on my plan. I hit it at full speed without breaking stride. Afterward, my normally faithful left fielder apologized for failing to shout a warning.

Ezekiel was called to be a watchman for his people. As a watchman, the prophet was accountable for the souls of those he saw going astray. Thus, he must raise his voice in warning.

Do you know folks who have unwittingly placed themselves in eternal danger? Have you tried to convince him of his error? Do you see yourself as accountable to God for her soul?

The heart of a 77-year-old woman was touched at an evangelism seminar. She took her Bible with her to visit a number of family members and friends with a word of love and invitation: consider the Lord's call to you. Only one, an aunt and retired college professor, responded. What joy! But also, what a burden relieved for the watchman: she had obeyed; she had spoken.

Lord, I want to be the watchman who gives the word of warning, but let me first look into my own life. "Search me, O God, . . . See if there be some wicked way in me." Amen.

Roots and Trees

All the trees of the forest will know that I the Lord bring down the tall tree and make the low tree grow tall. I dry up the green tree and make the dry tree flourish (Ezekiel 17:24).

Scripture: Ezekiel 17:22-24
Song: "To God Be the Glory"

Two men began meeting together in their retirement center's recreation room for a time of Bible study. They had no further plan, dream, or vision; they simply wanted to study the Scriptures. Before long, others joined them. In time, younger neighbors from outside of their retirement community also became part of the group.

The growing study group relocated, added children's classes, and eventually became a church. It all started with two men who simply met for Bible study. The power of God to take the smallest shoot, the tenderest sprig, and to produce a magnificent tree was never more evident.

Judah had been uprooted by a foreign power. King Nebuchadnezzar of Babylon had carried the people into captivity. But God promised to preserve a remnant—a shoot, a sprig—and to produce a powerful kingdom, a magnificent cedar, in which all nations could find shelter. (Some of these words relate to a coming messiah and His kingdom.)

Forty years after two men met to study their Bibles, a church of 2,300 continues to minister to their community. What a testimony to a great God who uses the smallest things for His glory!

Lord, I marvel at how You move us to simple acts of devotion, which in turn become testimonies to Your greatness and power. Here am I, a willing servant. Today, lead me into small acts of obedience with faith and joy. Through Christ, amen.

Receptive Audience

The people of Israel are not willing to listen to you because they are not willing to listen to me, for all the Israelites are hardened and obstinate (Ezekiel 3:7).

Scripture: Ezekiel 3:1-11
Song: "Just a Closer Walk with Thee"

When I traveled to Haiti, I went to lend encouragement with both physical and spiritual labor. I preached at the Sunday morning service and spoke at a weekend seminar for area preachers.

It was the first time I had to speak through an interpreter. As he translated my words, people laughed at jokes, nodded at the appropriate times, and voiced words of praise for cherished truths. They were attentive, receptive, and eager to learn.

I was told afterward that this is the norm whenever visiting preachers come to speak. There's something about the willingness to travel a distance that enhances appreciation for the guest. I'm told that American visitors are especially cherished.

Ezekiel would not have an appreciative audience. He was sent to his own countrymen who spoke the same language. They were already in exile due to their failure to repent. And now they would refuse to listen to their prophet, just as they had failed to listen to God in the past.

How can we apply all of this? For one thing, remember: Your minister has worked hard to partake of God's Word. Will he find a receptive audience, eager to hear this Sunday's message?

Lord God of all peoples, I thank You for those who have taught me and diligently spent their time in preparation to lead Your church. May I encourage their hearts in some way this day. I pray in the name of Christ my Lord. Amen.

A Thousand Generations

Know therefore that the Lord your God is God; he is the faithful God, keeping his covenant of love to a thousand generations of those who love him and keep his commandments (Deuteronomy 7:9).

Scripture: Deuteronomy 7:7-11
Song: "Faith of Our Fathers"

Family has always been important to my husband and me. We grew up in loving, churchgoing families. We chose to marry young and have three children, because we wanted to share our good experiences of being loved with a new generation. Furthermore, we chose to return to our hometown after living a thousand miles away, so our children could be close to our families. It wasn't a sacrifice but a loving decision; we simply wanted the best for them.

Today, our children are successful, happy, single adults. Thank God! But my husband and I have accepted the fact that it may be our lot in life not to be grandparents. Rather than grieve, we share God's love with the children of young friends.

Yes, as adoptive grandparents we continue to speak of God's faithfulness and the importance of following His commands, values we received from our families. We may never see a thousand generations of our family of descendants. But we can do our best with those we reach.

Father God, thank You for the wonderful upbringings with which You have blessed my husband and me. We are equipped to share Your love with others, but help us to do it wisely, lovingly, effectively. In Christ I pray. Amen.

July 24–30. **Kayleen Reusser** of Bluffton, Indiana, has written several children's books. She writes regularly for newspapers and magazines and enjoys speaking to children and adults about writing.

Which Riches?

I am about to remove you from the face of the earth. This very year you are going to die, because you have preached rebellion against the Lord (Jeremiah 28:16).

Scripture: Jeremiah 28:12-16
Song: "Riches of Earth I May Not See"

"God wants me to be rich," I repeated to myself. According to the best-selling book, if I intoned those words with confidence daily, they would affect my destiny. Apparently the words would influence my thinking and actions to the point that I would subconsciously do things that made the goal more likely. The book's popularity was mind-boggling. Several friends had purchased it and promoted its theme of "believing your way to success."

Never mind God's actual plan for my life. As long as I was sure of being one of God's chosen children—deserving a comfortable life—my destiny was sealed!

Of course, nothing even close to that kind of success happened to me. As if to prove God was truly in charge of my life, the economy soured. My writing career floundered as assignments with long-established magazines folded. Desperate to support myself, I began working at a low-paying job in a retirement community. Surprisingly, the people who lived there filled a need in my life for acceptance and purpose.

When people didn't recognize Hananiah's lies, God sent Jeremiah, an obedient prophet, to confront them. God still cared. He just wanted His followers to keep their eyes on Him.

Dear God, it's tempting to believe people who promise health, wealth, and happiness. But remind me always that only You can provide true success and true peace. I place my trust in Your riches! Thank You for Your love. Through Christ, amen.

Everyone Can Serve God

The words of Amos, one of the shepherds of Tekoa—the vision he saw concerning Israel two years before the earthquake (Amos 1:1).

Scripture: Amos 1:1, 2; 3:12-15
Song: "Called as Partners in Christ's Service"

When I began writing for publication more than a quarter century ago, I faced great uncertainty. Wasn't the craft of writing for the truly talented? the trained? the rich and famous? I was a stay-at-home mother. I didn't have the education to know how to write professionally, nor did I know anyone who could teach me. Additionally, our family had little—make that no—money to spend on my learning to write.

I prayed for God's guidance, set up an electric typewriter on a card table in a bedroom, and got to work. It was a long, painful process, but eventually my words began to sell. Years passed before I believed in my ability as a writer.

Today, I'm delighted to lead a Christian writing club. I find great joy in teaching others how to write words that please God—and I can use myself as an example (either as a way of illustrating what to do or what not to do).

Amos also was born into humble beginnings. As "one of the shepherds of Tekoa," he wasn't ashamed of his past, knowing God's hand guided him. Lack of education or experience isn't all that important. But willingness to know God and follow His plan? Crucial.

Dear Father, help me to continue to lean on You for every decision about writing. I owe You everything. Use me as You will in this ministry. In the name of Jesus, who lives and reigns with You and the Holy Spirit forever, amen.

A Future of Hope

Seek good, not evil, that you may live. Then the Lord God Almighty will be with you, just as you say he is. Hate evil, love good; maintain justice in the courts (Amos 5:14, 15).

Scripture: Amos 5:10-15
Song: "Lead Me to Calvary"

The time I'd dreaded had arrived. As editor of the local jail's chaplaincy newsletter, I interviewed inmates who had become Christians. One young female, whom I'll call Pam, had been accused of killing her infant son.

With three children of my own, I couldn't understand such an action. With neatly-combed hair and sad eyes, Pam told me her story. Six months ago, her husband had come home from work to find their infant son not breathing. He tried to resuscitate, but the baby died, allegedly from being strangled with a cord. Based on evidence at the scene, Pam was arrested. She was diagnosed as severely depressed and kept on suicide watch. A jail chaplain gave her a Bible and asked her to attend chapel.

Pam read the Bible, attended Bible studies and chapel services, and was eventually baptized. "Even though my future is uncertain," she said, "I rely on God."

Gone was the sorrowful look she had worn earlier. Her eyes glowed softly, and she looked serene. Pam understood the result of sin and repentance. Her faith reminded me of Amos's words—though God punishes sin, He makes a way for the sinner to be forgiven and start again.

Almighty and most merciful God, help us to remember that Your love and forgiveness extend to every person, for the ground is level at the cross. Teach us to love as You love. In the name of Jesus, my Savior, I pray. Amen.

Christianity Isn't for Cowards

Let justice roll on like a river, righteousness like a never-failing stream! (Amos 5:24).

Scripture: Amos 5:18-24
Song: "Nearer My God to Thee"

My college friend, Haley, had never shown an interest in God. As the years passed, I hesitated to mention my faith, as I felt it could alienate her. But eventually I contacted a minister who lived close to her, asking him to visit her.

My plan was that he would appear to drop in as he canvassed the neighborhood, asking people to come to church. "Don't mention my name," I told him, fearing Haley would be mad at me for interfering in her life.

Thankfully, the minister wisely refused to act on my terms. He pointed out that while he appreciated my interest in Haley's welfare, he wondered why I didn't share more of my belief in God. "If you do that and she wants to know more—then I'll visit," he said. "It could be your own personal story that she needs to hear."

I realized how dishonest and cowardly I had been about my unease for Haley's welfare. In a sense, I cared more for our friendship than her soul. Just as the minister saw through my weak gesture of concern, Amos saw through the hypocrisy of the religious leaders of his day. They wanted to serve God in ways that would make them look good in the community. But did they really serve Him with their hearts?

Lord, You know my heart. Keep working in me that my motives become purer and my witness more sincere. Remind me that my actions speak more loudly than my words. I pray in Jesus' name. Amen.

Harvest of Blessings

"The days are coming," declares the Lord, "when the reaper will be overtaken by the plowman and the planter by the one treading grapes. New wine will drip from the mountains and flow from all the hills (Amos 9:13).

Scripture: Amos 9:11-15
Song: "Praise the Lord"

My husband and I used to own a small farm. It was a demanding lifestyle. We worked most of our waking hours, planting and harvesting corn, wheat, and soybeans. Each year we gave our best efforts, hoping for the reward of a bountiful harvest. If the weather was in our favor, we usually enjoyed good crops.

Amos provides an interesting agricultural illustration of God's blessings to His faithful followers. In October Israelite farmers plow to prepare for planting of barley and wheat seed. In spring they harvest the crop.

Grapes are harvested from midsummer to early fall. Amos said the time would come when the treader of grapes would overtake the sower of seed. Think about it: The grape harvest would be so abundant that it would extend into the grain planting season. The hills would overflow with rivers of sweet wine.

Just as John and I were usually rewarded with an abundant harvest, God told Amos He would replenish His followers with goodness, grace, and the comfort of the Holy Spirit. That's good news to those of us who long for reassurance of God's blessings.

Lord God, thank You for caring for me through every trial of daily life. I thrill to the wonderful vision that the prophets glimpsed, and I say: "Even so, come, Lord Jesus" (Revelation 22:20, KJV). In His precious name I pray. Amen.

A Dedication of Talents

The Lord took me from tending the flock and said to me, "Go, prophesy to my people Israel" (Amos 7:15).

Scripture: Amos 7:10-17
Song: "Write These Words in Our Hearts"

For months I silently sat and listened in awe as members of my Christian writing club shared tips about publishing books and writing magazine articles. Yet when I decided to pursue my lifelong desire to write for publication, it seemed like a waste of time. Who would ever want to read my words?

I lived in a small Midwestern town on a dairy farm, and we had no money for me to invest in writing courses. I did feel blessed, though, to have an electric typewriter—and one hour a day (during the kids' nap time) to practice writing.

Still, I was resolved to try. The few times I had written creative essays in college had been pleasurable experiences, especially when a professor read my descriptive essay to the class.

The first couple of years my writing attempts were pitiful (and humiliating). However, club members taught me that a calling from God cannot be neglected. Gradually, my hard work paid off. Today, I've written 12 children's books and thousands of newspaper stories.

I knew God had designed me to work with words. Like Amos, I was willing to obey God's call and work hard to become an ambassador for Him. Hopefully, my words have blessed not only God, but other people with information and inspiration.

Dear God, You love us and bless us with spiritual gifts for the edification of Your church. Help me to use mine to the best of my ability, trusting You to produce the spiritual fruit. Through Christ I pray. Amen.

He Lives!

You will receive power when the Holy Spirit comes on you; and you will be my witnesses (Acts 1:8).

Scripture: Acts 1:1-11
Song: "Spirit of God, That Moved of Old"

I wasn't in danger when I went on two short mission trips—not unless I slipped from the deck of the medical boat into the swirling black waters of the Rio Negro. I was among them to teach Vacation Bible School to the happy-go-lucky children, distribute donations, and help those whom I believed were the real missionaries.

Though the villagers called me "missionary," I wondered if I deserved the title. To me, a missionary sacrificed years, not days, spreading God's Word throughout the world. They traveled to foreign lands with Bible in hand. They risked their lives, were exposed to disease, and sometimes were detained, beaten, or tossed in prison. Even killed.

Before Jesus was taken up to Heaven, He told His chosen apostles they would receive the gift of the Holy Spirit, after which they would spread the good news about Jesus to the ends of the earth. The apostles were witnesses to all Jesus was and is.

The apostles of Jesus' day risked everything to spread the message. Much like today, they faced imprisonment, beatings, rejection, and martyrdom. One thing kept them going: Jesus lives. Missionaries today share the same confidence. Jesus lives.

O Lord, the great I Am, I ask You to place Your cloud of protection around missionaries throughout the world. Through Christ I pray. Amen.

July 31. **Shirley J. Conley** lives in Oviedo, Florida. A member of a Christian writer's group and garden club, she's a published author of devotionals, creative nonfiction, and fiction short stories.

DEVOTIONS®

▶ **August**

The same Lord is Lord of all and richly blesses all who call on him, for, "Everyone who calls on the name of the Lord will be saved.

—*Romans 10:12, 13*

Gary Wilde, Editor | Margaret K. Williams, Project Editor

Photo © iStock | Thinkstock®

DEVOTIONS® is published quarterly by Standard Publishing, Cincinnati, Ohio, www.standardpub.com. Copyright © 2016 by Standard Publishing. All rights reserved. Topics based on the Home Daily Bible Readings, International Sunday School Lessons. Copyright © 2013 by the Committee on the Uniform Series. Printed in the U.S.A. All Scripture quotations, unless otherwise indicated, are taken from the *HOLY BIBLE, NEW INTERNATIONAL VERSION*®. *NIV*®. Copyright © 1973, 1978, 1984, 2011 by Biblica, Inc.® Used by permission of Zondervan. All rights reserved worldwide. Scripture quotations marked (*KJV*) are taken from the *King James Version. New American Standard Bible (NASB)*, Copyright © The Lockman Foundation, 1960, 1962, 1963, 1968, 1971, 1972, 1973, 1975, 1977, 1995.

Pick Me

Then they cast lots, and the lot fell to Matthias; so he was added to the eleven apostles (Acts 1:26).

Scripture: Acts 1:15-17, 20-26
Song: "Leaning on the Everlasting Arms"

Will they accept me? I've never been much of a joiner, especially in a group where my peers could either vote me in or out. Yet, when a friend suggested I join the garden club, I immediately knew it was something I would enjoy.

I met with the membership chairwoman, who attempted to put me at ease with tea and cake. Nevertheless, I wondered what impression I was making. The application asked questions about my gardening interests and experience, and at last I attended my first meeting, where the chairwoman introduced me. I stood in front of 20 or more strangers and told about myself. *God help me!*

I left the meeting with by-laws in hand. Now I was required to attend two more meetings before my fate was decided by a vote. At the biannual plant sale it was announced: I was in.

Jesus' original inner circle numbered 12, but now the apostles needed to replace Judas Iscariot. A specific criteria for making their choice was outlined, so they prayed for guidance and wisdom, narrowing the choices down to Barsabbas and Matthias from the many followers. Lots were cast. Matthias was chosen.

But what of Barsabbas? Did he feel sad, dejected, left out?

Father God, please comfort those on the outside looking in—the sad, dejected, and brokenhearted. Thy will be done in their lives. In Christ, amen.

August 1–6. **Shirley J. Conley** lives in Oviedo, Florida. A member of a Christian writer's group and garden club, she's a published author of devotionals, creative nonfiction, and fiction short stories.

The Gift of Faith

All of them were filled with the Holy Spirit and began to speak in other tongues as the Spirit enabled them (Acts 2:4).

Scripture: Acts 2:1-13
Song: "Open My Eyes"

As a teen I was invited by my girlfriend's family to go with them to their church in downtown San Diego. We attended Sunday school and worship, and then we teens hung out in Balboa Park before returning for youth group and evening service. Jackie's parents often visited friends afterward.

One Sunday some months later, I was told I could no longer ride with them—their plans didn't include me. With no other transportation, I was heartbroken and even began to question the teachings of the church. Great emphasis was placed on speaking in tongues in that congregation, so I began to wonder whether I really was a Christian, as I'd never spoken in tongues. Yet, Sunday after Sunday I witnessed others doing so.

The disciples spoke in tongues when the Holy Spirit filled them. It was a miraculous ability to utter a foreign language understood by citizens of neighboring countries.

In light of my experience—and that of the early disciples—for me the big question remains: Was tongues to be a normative experience for all the Christians who would follow? Or is Acts a transitional book—bridging the way between the old covenant and the new—ushering in the gospel age with signs and wonders that would soon cease (see 1 Corinthians 13:8)?

Holy Spirit, You gave me the gift of faith. Open my eyes and ears to Your voice today. Open my heart and fill it with love and compassion for others. I worship You. Amen.

My Neutral World

They devoted themselves to the apostles' teaching and to fellowship, to the breaking of bread and to prayer (Acts 2:42).

Scripture: Acts 2:37-44
Song: "Show a Little Bit of Love and Kindness"

When I read the Scripture telling of the fellowship of the early believers, it makes me think of the 1960s hippie movement. Two forms of fellowship, two kinds of collective experience. As to the early church, all the believers were together and enjoyed everything in common. They shared their possessions with anyone in need. They worshipped together, ate together, and took care of each other.

This kind of living was a goal of the hippies too. It was a communion. But without the Lord at the center, it became thoroughly self-centered (the "Me Generation").

Also, the Vietnam War threw this generation into a rather depressed state in which people seemed to seek happiness at all costs—tune in and drop out. For the first time, clips of the ongoing war were televised. When my younger sister began to lose her friends to the foreign battles, she ran off to join a hippie commune, stating it would be a religious experience.

But only a religious experience can be a religious experience. That is, the Lord of religion must live at its heart. The hippies missed this; the early church embraced Him and lived for Him. True spiritual fellowship followed.

Father God, help me to care not only for believers in the family of God, but for all those You call. Let my generosity lean toward the needy. Teach me to love my neighbors as I pray for peace in this turbulent world. In the name of Jesus, amen.

Not Guilty!

They seized Stephen and brought him before the Sanhedrin. They produced false witnesses (Acts 6:12, 13).

Scripture: Acts 6:8-15
Song: "God Is So Good"

Crunch! It happened so quickly. Stuck behind a line of cars turning right, I signaled and inched my way into the left lane. Then I saw the white pickup behind me pull out. With no place to go, and partway in the other lane, I froze. The driver scraped the side of my Saturn and knocked off the side mirror.

When he told the officer I pulled out in front of him, a young lady confirmed it. I, on the other hand, contended I was already partly in the lane before he pulled into it. Did he not see me?

The officer, unimpressed with my years of a clean driving record, wouldn't listen. The citation read Reckless Driving. "Pay the fine," I was told, "or request a hearing in traffic court."

I'm innocent. How would I convince the judge? When the clerk called my name, I stood on wobbly legs in the crowded courtroom and waited while the formalities of my case were read. The officer responded when his name was called, but the other driver and witness did not. "Case dismissed for failure to appear," stated the judge.

Imagine the anxiety of standing before the Sanhedrin knowing you're innocent. Stephen's face shone like an angel, mine only showed fear and then relief.

God is good. God is so good.

Heavenly Father, though I go through times of anxiety, fear, and sometimes pain, I know You are always near. Nothing is too difficult as You guide my way. You care for me and will be my final judge. Through Christ I pray. Amen.

Verbal Stones

Saul approved of their killing him (Acts 8:1).

Scripture: Acts 7:54–8:1
Song: "In the Hour of Trial"

Have you ever stood by while someone was persecuted? Saul stood and watched as Stephen was stoned. He did nothing to stop it.

Today, it's no longer necessary to physically bend down and pick up stones to cast at another. Through social media, for instance, we can persecute someone without facing him. With a tap of fingers, words of hate spew across a screen from mouths on fire with hatefulness. Cyber bullying is the result.

I once left a church when conflicts over doctrine became too much to bear. Certain changes went against the beliefs of many, and my timing coincided with others who were leaving. Suddenly, my name was linked with them in an ensuing media outbreak—complete with a verbal stoning that exacerbated the situation as both sides experienced confusion and misunderstanding.

Yes, I joined those who left, and we called ourselves "The Seekers," as we searched for a church to fill the empty space in our hearts. Among the many things I learned: We need to speak truth, of course—but winsomely, gently and in a spirit of good will. Never should our intention be to hurt or antagonize, but to call for accountability as we seek it in ourselves.

Almighty God, I desire to follow Your will as taught in Your Word. Take my hand and lead me. Help me to stand against those who choose to sway others. Give me the courage of Stephen and the heart of Jesus. In the name of the Father and of the Son and of the Holy Spirit, I pray. Amen.

Listen and Pray

Brothers and sisters, choose seven men from among you who are known to be full of the Spirit and wisdom. We will turn this responsibility over to them and will give our attention to prayer and the ministry of the word (Acts 6:3, 4).

Scripture: Acts 6:1-8
Song: "Cups of Cold Water"

One of seven who completed 50 hours of training to become a Stephen Minister, I stood in front of the congregation in a special recognition ceremony. I cringed when asked to speak first. Any form of public speaking scares me. Yet, here I was trying not to look at the people as I shared why I chose to become a lay caregiver, reading to them John 15:5-8. Both group and individual prayers were offered, and the elders laid hands on us. At last, diplomas were distributed, along with many hugs.

I was ready to receive my first care receiver. My years of widowhood qualified me for the role of caregiver for a recently widowed women. Taught to listen and pray, the one-on-one relationships suited me.

What is Stephen Ministry? Did you know it's used in congregations and organizations worldwide and named for the biblical Stephen? Scripture tells us the number of Greek disciples increased. In order to allow the apostles to continue preaching, they needed help from men of wisdom to oversee food distribution to the widows. Stephen, a man of faith, was one of seven presented to the apostles, who prayed and laid hands on them.

Lord, fill my heart with compassion for others. Teach me Your way so I can serve You. May I be an instrument of Your love to those who are hurting. Through Christ, amen.

A Mother's Prayer

"Woman, you have great faith! Your request is granted" (Matthew 15:28).

Scripture: Matthew 15:21-28
Song: "My Faith Looks Up to Thee"

Barbara left messages on her adult son's voice mail. She texted him: "I love you." She did this for five years, but he didn't respond. She asked our Sunday school class to pray for him.

Many parents can relate to this mother's request. Like the Canaanite woman in today's Scripture, they're desperate for answers to their words of love and to their prayers, which seem to fall on deaf ears. Yet Jesus gave us hope when He reached out to the Canaanite woman and healed her daughter.

One of the men in our class addressed Barbara. "Don't ever stop praying," he said. "Although my mom prayed for me for many years, she never saw the answer to her prayers that I would have a relationship with God." We were encouraged to keep praying for our adult children, hoping that some day they would experience and respond to God's amazing love.

Like the Canaanite woman, we will not give up but persist in faith, knowing God loves our families more than we ever could. He is merciful and patient with our loved ones. He will not give up on them as He did not give up on us. He wants all of us to be together with Him.

Lord Jesus, please intervene in the lives of my children, that they would experience Your love in a way that will bring them into a relationship with You. In Christ, amen.

....

August 7–13. **Sue Tornai** lives with her dog, Maggie, in California. She has two children and seven grandchildren. Sue enjoys reading, writing, knitting and making jewelry.

Free

Before the coming of this faith, we were held in custody under the law, locked up until the faith that was to come would be revealed (Galatians 3:23).

Scripture: Galatians 3:23-29
Song: "Love Came Down"

How had I strayed so far from God? I went back to church in a town far from where I grew up. Every Sunday brought tears of despair.

I talked to the minister. "When I was a girl, our family was part of the bigger family of God," I said. "I long to be a part of the church again, but I'm not worthy."

"No one is worthy," he said.

"You don't understand. I've walked away from marriage and broken relationships. Everyone here looks perfect."

The minister smiled. "We cannot live in this world of sin without it touching us, but Jesus died for sin. You can accept what He did on the cross to forgive you of sin and give you eternal life or you can keep beating up on yourself."

Could the God of the universe give His only Son for someone like me? The minister's words changed my life, and I accepted God's love. I began to read the Bible, and it seemed like every verse jumped off the page and into my heart. I talked to God in prayer too. Sometimes all I could say was, "Thank You, Jesus. Thank You, Jesus." No longer bound by the law, I was free to live for Him and tell His story.

Thank You, **Father God,** for sending Jesus into the world to save people like me from dying in their sin. Surround my friends and family with Your presence that they will know Your love. In Jesus' name, amen.

Hearing the Good News

How can anyone preach unless they are sent? As it is written: "How beautiful are the feet of those who bring good news!" (Romans 10:15).

Scripture: Romans 10:9-15
Song: "I Come to the Garden Alone"

I sat on a bench near the Garden Tomb in Jerusalem. Crowds of people waited in the midst of lush red, white, pink, and violet flowers. I imagined Mary Magdalene meeting the angels in the tomb and then Jesus suddenly facing her in the garden. I heard sounds of voices singing hymns and thought, *Surely this is what Heaven is like.*

Our cheerful guide spoke of our need of a Savior and how that need was met by Jesus. The man's words were profound and sweet to my ears. He was more than a guide. He preached the good news of Jesus Christ. Days after my visit I remembered his face, his joy and peace, his simple but true message. He was a shining example of Romans 10:15. I don't know if he had beautiful feet, but his face was lit up with the beauty of His Lord. I believe this guide was sent by God, and if anyone stood in that place and didn't know the love of Jesus, surely that person would have felt His love through the spoken words.

God's love is too wonderful and active to hold inside us for long. It is something we give away so it can do its work, just as the guide at the Garden Tomb gave. We know that God replenishes the love we share, so we can keep on giving.

Thank You, **Lord,** for people who bring good news, who share Your love that others might know You. Help me to follow the example of that man in Jerusalem, who clearly follows the God-man in whom I pray. Amen.

Thrive During Persecution?

A great persecution broke out against the church in Jerusalem, and all except the apostles were scattered (Acts 8:1).

Scripture: Acts 8:1-3
Song: "God Is My Refuge"

The early church grew in numbers by the thousands during periods of persecution. Today, under church planting organizations like The Timothy Initiative (TTI), the church continues to expand. In the past eight years, TTI has planted 27,764 churches in 40 countries and 499,752 lives have been changed for God's glory to date.

However, the church doesn't always grow while suffering persecution. According to Opendoorsusa.org, one hundred million Christians in 60 countries are currently persecuted. The greatest concern is the suffering induced by extremist Islamic terrorists. "The abuses in China and North Korea are alarming but in some Middle Eastern countries, there are few, if any, Christians left," says Dan Weber, president of the Association of Mature American Citizens.

"If the world hates you, keep in mind that it hated me first," Jesus said, and "If they persecuted me, they will persecute you also" (John 15:18, 20).

Yet, He encouraged His friends and us: "When you are brought before synagogues, rulers and authorities, do not worry about how you will defend yourselves . . . , for the Holy Spirit will teach you at that time what you should say" (Luke 12:11, 12).

Father God, I pray for an end to the abuse and atrocities committed against our Christian brothers and sisters. Please send release, rescue, or escape. May they know You are always with them. In Jesus' name, amen.

God's Word

When they believed Philip as he proclaimed the good news of the kingdom of God and the name of Jesus Christ, they were baptized, both men and women (Acts 8:12).

Scripture: Acts 8:4-13
Song: "O Word of God Incarnate"

It was Jordan's Independence Day when we visited Jerash, an ancient ruin near the capitol of Amman. Many local families visited the site along with tourists. The young people welcomed us and loved talking with us. So I felt at ease when we climbed the hill and entered the Temple of Zeus.

Then I heard a bagpipe band playing "Amazing Grace"! What a contrast between a landmark dedicated to a long-ago mythological god and adoration dedicated to a living Savior.

I thought about how easy it would be to become distracted from the truth in the days when such beautiful buildings were centers of active worship. Could someone like Simon the sorcerer have deceived me too?

But Philip demonstrated the power of a risen Lord, preaching the good news of Jesus Christ amid a pantheon of lifeless deities. People believed him, even Simon.

God gave us eternal truth, so we won't be deceived by falsehoods that die out in the end. But let us know that truth! Then we'll be prepared to give reasons for what we believe, compelling reasons that can melt the hardest hearts.

O Eternal Lord God, guard my heart from deception and keep me focused on the truth conveyed in Your Word. I love You and I'm committed to worshipping only You. So this day I renew my dedication to the truth conveyed in Your living Word, my Lord and Savior, Jesus Christ. In His name, amen.

Power or Humility?

Simon answered, "Pray to the Lord for me so that nothing you have said may happen to me" (Acts 8:24).

Scripture: Acts 8:14-25
Song: "Sheltered in the Arms of God"

Masada awesomely displays the genius of Herod the Great. He feared enemy attack, so he wanted a fortress; however, he also feared running out of food and water within castle walls. That is why—through sheer power and intellect—he built a palace fortress on a cliff overlooking the Dead Sea. It had no access except for a snakelike path up the side of the steep mountain. And there was no fresh water for any enemy who might besiege him—not within the countless miles of surrounding desert.

But food and water for Herod? He filled huge storehouses with food from the crops grown on the sky-high palace grounds. And he collected rainwater into large mountainside cisterns

Like Simon in today's Scripture, Herod thought his wealth and power could buy him whatever he needed or wanted. He could produce his own pleasure, safety from his enemies, and unceasing food and water.

Simon was humbled, though, when Peter exhorted him, "May your money perish with you, because you thought you could buy the gift of God with money!" In contrast, Herod's arrogance was his downfall. God loved him and would have been his provider, protector, defender, and refuge. He chose instead to rely on his own resources.

Thank You, **Father God,** for Your faithfulness to humble me when necessary. Please open my eyes to any pride that keeps me from knowing the truth of Your love. In Jesus' name I pray. Amen.

Read for Life

Philip ran up to the chariot and heard the man reading Isaiah the prophet. "Do you understand what you are reading?" Philip asked. "How can I," he said, "unless someone explains it to me?" So he invited Philip to come up and sit with him (Acts 8:30, 31).

Scripture: Acts 8:26-39
Song: "Read It Over Again to Me"

Gaza means "strong" or "stronghold," but the city has been conquered many times and has come to have a negative meaning: Hell. This sheds light on our Scripture reading today. The Ethiopian eunuch had been to Jerusalem to worship God, but was on his way to Gaza! He stopped his chariot to read the prophetic words of Isaiah, and God sent Philip to him at just the right time. He said to the man, "Do you understand what you are reading?"

As a Christian, I'm called to put my faith into action as Philip did. He loved Jesus and was ready to share the truth of the gospel. How can I be more like Philip—ready to explain the truth about God's love? Knowing we are all on our way to Hell, until Jesus intervenes in our lives, gives me a sense of urgency.

I am thankful for the faithfulness of those who shared God's love with me and prayed for me so that today I have the hope of eternal life. They inspire me to use my faith and pray for opportunities to talk with people about what their greatest need is, the need of a Savior in Jesus Christ, our Lord.

Father God, ignite my faith so I will speak the truth of Your gospel in a way that is joyful and attractive. And help me to be ready to give good, solid reasons for my faith wherever I am. In the name of Jesus I pray. Amen.

Turn Here

I persecuted the followers of this Way to their death, arresting both men and women and throwing them into prison (Acts 22:4).

Scripture: Acts 22:1-5
Song: "Jesus, Still Lead On"

"Turn! Turn!" Three men hollered at my husband as they traveled home from a fishing trip. With seconds to spare, Chet swerved right.

"Phew!" Chet took a deep breath. "Never saw the road sign."

"No wonder you didn't catch any fish," Jack said. "Better get your eyes checked. Like tomorrow."

Tom joined in. "This side exit is new. Just finished last month. No wonder you didn't notice."

My husband had driven this road many times. He took the route for granted. But then his eyes and the new exit betrayed him. Sometimes, just as a glue-backed stamp sticks to a letter, we stick to the old way. The way we've always done it. The way we've always believed. We don't realize a change has occurred—likely a change for the better.

Chet's friends kept him from taking a longer way home. When they hollered, he made the turn just in time.

God doesn't holler at us. Instead, He gently guides us in so many ways. How great to find His direction in prayer, in His Word, and in association with others who trust Him.

Dear Gracious God, how wonderful to be able to come to You and find guidance for my life. Left on my own, I would surely take the wrong way. I can never thank You enough for guiding my pathways through life. In Jesus' name I pray. Amen.

August 14–20. **Elizabeth Van Liere,** of Montrose, Colorado, published her first book at age 87. Now, at age 91, her second book, *Dare to Laugh,* has also been published.

Blameless? Who, Me?

Since an overseer manages God's household, he must be blameless (Titus 1:7).

Scripture: Titus 1:5-9
Song: "O Lamb of God Most Blameless"

We have two lovable but naughty dogs. First, there's Uber, my grey and black Aussie. I adopted him from a box outside a grocery store. Such a cute puppy. Now, seven years later, he weighs 75 pounds—no longer cute, but handsome. He is the alpha dog—he runs the show.

Then there's Bear, a miniature, brown Aussie. When we pet him, Uber, the herd dog, barks a "No" and nips Bear on his back. Also, sometimes when I enter my bedroom, Bear scrambles down from the bed. "Naughty Bear," I say. "You know you aren't supposed to be up there."

The same goes for Uber. He often jumps off the living room couch just as I walk in. "Off limits, Uber," I shout.

Another nasty trick: both dogs love wastebaskets, love to shred tissues and strew them along the hallway. *Who is the culprit?* They both get that hang-dog look when I scold them.

It's a good thing these dogs aren't in line to oversee God's household (even though they oversee mine)! They would never qualify.

But how about me? I am a Christian writer. I am a Bible teacher. I am part of God's household. Do I jump when I know I've sinned? Am I blameless?

Dear Heavenly Father, I'm far from being blameless, but I stand before You forgiven. This doesn't excuse my sinning today. So may Your great love light my path and keep me from wrongdoing. In Jesus' precious name, amen.

He Saw It First

His followers took him by night and lowered him in a basket through an opening in the wall (Acts 9:25).

Scripture: Acts 9:21-25
Song: "Little Is Much When God Is in It"

"Is this absolutely necessary?" I asked. Two men had come to deliver six bottles of oxygen.

"Well," Adrian said, "your oxygen level tested low a week ago at your checkup. Try it when you walk the block to your mailbox."

"But I haven't noticed anything. I was doing fine."

Adrian shook his head. "You wouldn't realize it until it was too late. Did you know a lack of oxygen can hurt your heart?"

I shrugged my shoulders.

"Try it for a month," he coaxed. "I bet you need to rest after even a short walk. And afterwards you gasp for air. Right?"

The next day I hauled the oxygen canister out of the box, turned it on, and hooked the tube over my ears and to my nose. Then I slung the carry-on over my right shoulder and, with a woe is me feeling, I began my five-minute walk.

How odd, I suddenly thought. I needed a renewal on the night-time oxygen concentrator and needed a checkup to receive it. Result: Given day-time oxygen too. Was this all coincidence?

Foolish woman, I told myself. *Can't you see? This is God's doing—He cares for you! He saw your need before you knew it.*

Almighty Father, You rescued Your apostle Paul because You cared for him so deeply. I experience that same love coming to me too. In every moment help me trust in this: You know my needs before I do. Your ways are always for my good. I thank You for all You do for me, through Christ the Lord. Amen.

Mentors, Barnabas and Me

Barnabas took him and brought him to the apostles (Acts 9:27).

Scripture: Acts 9:26-31
Song: "Am I a Soldier of the Cross?"

Love horses? Here's a job for you: horse trainer. Every year the Bureau of Land Management captures about a hundred wild horses. Experienced trainers bid on the animals, and once they arrive at their new home, a long taming and training process begins. A great video, "Wild Horse, Wild Ride," takes you to the farms of such trainers, who each use their own particular techniques. But they all spend many hours with their horses.

They know wild mustangs don't respond to harsh or aggressive treatment. The animals must be handled in a positive manner that leads to a willing obedience.

First, the horse eventually lets the trainer pat its nose. But put a blanket on its back? "Hey! Who said you could do that!" The horse bucks, and the blanket falls to the ground.

Repeat and repeat. Over and over, until at last a saddle covers the now-accepted blanket. We know the horse and man will become friends—almost. Several days later the trainer is allowed to climb aboard, and a wild ride begins.

Patience wins, though, and soon the horse is ready to be adopted. The once wild mustang is now gentle, perfect for even a child to ride.

Lord, I want to mentor others in discipleship, just as Barnabas initially mentored Paul. Help me to be gentle and patient with new Christians—even those who seem a little wild at first. Remind me of my own youth. Keep me encouraged with the words to speak and the modeling of Your matchless character. In Christ, amen.

Healing

All those who lived in Lydda and Sharon saw him and turned to the Lord (Acts 9:35).

Scripture: Acts 9:32-35
Song: "Turn Your Eyes upon Jesus"

I'll call her Sandra. Drugs and alcohol had ruled her life for several years, so her parents had been awarded custody of her 5-year-old son we'll call Robbie. Yet Sandra resolved to change. Before long, she'd found a job, decided to stay away from her old drug-using pals, and went to see Robbie at least once a week.

One day my daughter, who lives with me, brought a concern. "Sandra needs a place to stay at night. Could she stay with us?"

We took her in. We gave her rules: No drugs. No drug-user friends allowed near our house. Home each night by 10 p.m.

She agreed. But one day she blew it with those "friends." My daughter told her, "Sorry, Sandra. You have to leave."

A year later Sandra called. "May I come back? I won't disappoint you again." We prayed and said, "Yes. Get squared away. Aim for the end of the year. By then, you should be able to be on your own."

Sandra kept her word. Our prayers accompanied hers on her journey to well-being. She worked hard, saw her son often, and stayed clean. A year later she moved into a rental house.

How we rejoiced when she told us she'd gotten a promotion at work! And then, and then . . . a car accident took her life. It was as though God said, "You're OK now, Sandra. Come home."

Heavenly Father, how glad I am I took part in helping someone come to You. May the struggle she endured, and the victory she won, be the means of turning many to You. In the holy name of Jesus, my Lord, and Savior. Amen.

Choose Life

As he neared Damascus on his journey, suddenly a light from heaven flashed around him (Acts 9:3).

Scripture: Acts 9:1-9
Song: "Holiness unto the Lord"

Last Sunday I spent two hours in prison No, I hadn't been incarcerated; I joined others to show support for 30 inmates. In a program called Kairos, these 30 candidates partook in an intense Bible study. Classes began on Thursday evening and through late Saturday. Closure came on Sunday afternoon.

The men entered the chapel singing, "The Spirit of Jesus is in this place." I grabbed a tissue and blotted my tears as I watched the men separate into five groups, each named after a Gospel writer or Peter. A designated leader read four questions and received answers from the men:

In what state did I come here today? "I felt abandoned, lonely." "Broken."

What did I expect on Thursday evening? "I came with my heart open wide."

What did I find? "Friends." "Forgiveness." "Love."

What am I taking away from this experience? "New life." "Faith." "Trust."

Some men had been brought up in Christian homes but wandered away. Others were new to faith in God. Each one had found forgiveness, learned to forgive those who had hurt them, and — more difficult—learned to forgive themselves.

Lord Jesus, Like these prisoners I am so glad to know You have forgiven me. Help me respond by sharing Your precious love with others. In Your name, I pray. Amen.

God Stepped In

At once he began to preach in the synagogues that Jesus is the Son of God (Acts 9:20).

Scripture: Acts 9:10-20
Song: "I Surrender All"

"It was the loneliest year of my life," Steve said to the audience. "Being a freshman in a new high school was bad enough, and having my dad as principal didn't help. But something good was around the corner." He paused and shouted, "Football!" (This is Bronco country, and the audience cheered and clapped). "I couldn't wait to meet the athletes," Steve said. "I would become one of them."

He cleared his throat. "It wasn't long before I realized something was wrong. Every one of the guys was stoned. I was the only Christian in the bunch."

Steve's shoulders drooped. "The whole school year dragged by. The guys hardly spoke to me, and I felt totally alone. At school's end I made a resolution. Next fall I would join the crowd. Do what they did. Laugh. Have a buddy—even if it meant no more good guy."

He paused and held up his hands as if in surrender. "But then, God stepped in. Some teachers had moved away during the summer and had to be replaced. So who did my dad hire? Several Christian teachers."

And what became of Steve? He is now the senior minister of the church I attend.

Loving Lord, Steve's story tells me of Your steadfast guidance. It has given me such a wonderful insight into Your love. You are always ready to lead me on the pathway of life. Thank You, in Jesus' name. Amen.

The Big Picture

He says, "It is too small a thing that You should be My Servant to raise up the tribes of Jacob . . . I will also make You a light of the nations so that My salvation may reach to the end of the earth" (Isaiah 49:6, *NASB*).

Scripture: Isaiah 49:1-7
Song: "This Is My Father's World"

In college I took a lifeguard class. Watching the entire pool is a challenge. You can't just focus on a few, you have to keep an eye on everybody. Isaiah might have been a good lifeguard—he was called not only to Israel, but to the ends of the earth. Why? Because not only was Israel drowning in sin, but the entire earth was in trouble.

We want God to work in our church or in our town, but God's grace reaches far beyond our boundaries. Yet it is neither the size nor scope of the move of God that matters, but that it is genuine. He can do great things with a sincere faith.

In our crazy everyday lives, we can get distracted by our problems. In our frustrations we may in a sense downsize God by our lack of faith. That is when we need to clear our heads and hearts to gain a new perspective.

Walking outside and looking up at the sky on a clear night can give us an idea of how big our Creator is. For the wonders of the night sky didn't just happen, they were set in motion by God. The God who watches over us also watches over everyone.

Lord, please help me expand my view of Your grace. Today help me see beyond my station in life and catch a glimpse of how You view things. In Jesus' name, amen.

August 21–27. **Danny Woodall** writes from Port Neches, Texas. He is a physical education graduate from Lamar University; his hobbies are chess and fantasy sports.

Never out of Touch

For this reason I did not even consider myself worthy to come to You, but just say the word and my servant will be healed (Luke 7:7, *NASB*).

Scripture: Luke 7:1-10
Song: "Only Believe"

During summer camp I stood on the edge of the campground, glanced at the sky, and dialed the number, hoping there was enough clear space to receive a signal. Sometimes I got through, and sometimes the connection failed.

The centurion in our Scripture today recognized that Jesus' word was dependable. The connection never fails.

The military leader also knew the importance of rank and of obedience. Jesus had more power than he did, and the centurion took Jesus at His word.

Today we can hold God's Word in our hands as we read the Bible. We kneel down in prayer and sense God speaking. All we have to do is obey His commands.

I notice how obedience and trust made the centurion's faith a simple faith. No hoops to jump through, only a childlike acceptance was needed. And I remind myself: a simple faith is a strong faith. Yet it's the power of the object of faith that matters, not the strength of my sincerity—or my ability to keep the connection.

Our cell phones may lose a connection, but God never fails. He isn't bound by time, distance, or anything else.

I know, **Father,** that I'm never beyond Your reach. No matter what I have to deal with, You always keep track of where I am and what I am going through. Time and distance is no problem for You. In Jesus' name, amen.

Long-Term Faith

A devout man and one who feared God with all his house-hold, and gave many alms to the Jewish people and prayed to God continually (Acts 10:2, *NASB*).

Scripture: Acts 10:1-8
Song: "Faithful Remain to Thy Savior and King"

As the baseball season winds down, a few teams have given up on the pennant; others are fighting for a playoff spot. The teams that will make the postseason have their stars, but they also need players who are good at the fundamentals. They do the basic things right—all of the time. It's not the dazzling shortstop that carries the team through a long summer, but the guy who consistently fields the routine grounder and makes a good throw to first.

Cornelius was this kind of solid, dependable man, good at the fundamentals of faithfulness. He prayed, read the Bible, and gave to the church. Nothing flashy, but a solid believer, the kind God uses. Because of his faithfulness, God used him to open up the gospel to the Gentiles.

We might want to be a missionary in a foreign land, but if we have difficulty living for the Lord amid the comforts of home, we will struggle overseas too. We may imagine standing for our faith in front of a firing squad, willing to die for Christ in one heart-searing moment. However, the most effective witness is a life lived for Christ over an entire lifetime. That's a faith that stands true, through all the ups and downs.

Lord, You show favor on the ones who are faithful in small things, and You use the ordinary to accomplish the extraordinary. Help me to be faithful in the little things, that I may live a life that endures through the good times and bad. In Christ, amen.

God Approved

Again a voice came to him a second time, "What God has cleansed, no longer consider unholy" (Acts 10:15).

Scripture: Acts 10:9-18
Song: "Higher Ground"

Nothing is more frustrating: we finally get the latest computer or gadget—but it's missing wires or connectors. We pore over the instructions again, dig through the box, and then panic.

Of course, if you're like me, you'll soon find everything you need right there where the instructions said they'd be. One thing is certain: I could never make my own parts for the most current devices; only factory made and approved parts will do.

The difference between something being clean or unclean in Scripture is this: God's approval. We try to make Christianity a color-by-numbers faith. When the colors and numbers don't match, we are confused. We either stop painting or try to make it work on our own.

Then things can break down. We need to remember: God created everything, and He has no trouble putting the pieces of our lives back together again.

Peter had many faults, often charging ahead of the Lord. Yet he had one redeeming quality: persistence. Eventually he would obey, giving his whole life to the cause of Christ.

We bolt down dead-ends, run in circles, and crash into walls. After all of our missteps, God waits for us to follow Him. If He approves, it is good to go.

Dear Heavenly Father, let me always remember that You are God and I'm not. Your ways are higher than mine. Help me climb higher in my walk of faith. Amen.

What Do You See?

Opening his mouth, Peter said: "I most certainly understand now that God is not one to show partiality" (Acts 10:34, *NASB*).

Scripture: Acts 10:34-43
Song: "All Ye Gentiles, Praise the Lord"

It's late, and you missed your exit. Now you're in a part of town where you'd normally only drive in the daylight: graffiti-covered buildings, boarded windows, and a lonely figure up ahead. Her clothing makes it clear she's familiar with the streets.

You shake your head: Disgust? Compassion? *Lord, have mercy on her and on all of us.* Just as the Jews in our Scripture were amazed when the Holy Spirit was poured out on the Gentiles, we might be shocked if we knew the whole story of this woman on the street.

Gentile believers accepted by God? The local religionists prescribed certain steps that foreigners must follow before being accepted into God's family. However, they could not deny the Gentiles received the gift of the Holy Spirit. Acts 10 is the Gentiles' emancipation proclamation. Salvation is for all.

We have our own ideas as to how acceptable people must look and act. The girl on the street corner might indeed be just that—a girl, as in a minor. Human trafficking is a growing problem. A few bad choices, and girls can end up trapped in a hideous slave trade. Disgust? No, compassion.

Lord, You can transform any life. Today I ask that You protect those caught in the modern-day slave trade and bless those who work to free these victims from the clutches of evil. If I can help—show me how! In the name of Jesus Christ I pray. Amen.

Wonderful Grace

All the circumcised believers who came with Peter were amazed, because the gift of the Holy Spirit had been poured out on the Gentiles also (Acts 10:45, NASB).

Scripture: Acts 10:44-48
Song: "My Hope Is Built"

In his early years, my dad thought church was only a place for baptisms, weddings, and funerals. As a young soldier returning from World War II, he was surprised that the girl he was interested in wanted to go to church. Most of the people in the congregation that Sunday morning probably didn't give the uneasy serviceman much of a chance to meet their standards.

The Jewish people also had standards for Gentiles to follow if they wanted to be a part of God's chosen people. When the first group of believers realized that God had poured out the Holy Spirit on the Gentiles, they were amazed. The recently converted Gentiles helped spread the gospel all over the known world in a few decades.

Today God is still amazing people. Over 70 years later, the uneasy serviceman would be remembered for having served as Sunday school superintendent for over 50 years. My parents totaled over 100 years of Sunday school service. Add the years of their three children, and it is over 200 years of service.

Not bad for a nervous serviceman and a determined little lady. We never know how God might work in someone's life.

Lord, I thank You that You aren't limited by our expectations. Help me to see others as You see them and to work with all who wish to advance the cause of Your Son, Jesus. Through Christ my Lord. Amen.

Beyond the Boxes

He said to them: "You are well aware that it is against our law for a Jew to associate with or visit a Gentile. But God has shown me that I should not call anyone impure or unclean" (Acts 10:28).

Scripture: Acts 10:19-33
Song: "How Great Thou Art"

Life can get crazy. So in order to maintain control, we may put things and people in boxes. Sometimes we try to put God in a box. As a result, the box gets crumpled or remains empty. We wonder what went wrong. Often we repeat the same process and end up with the same results.

God is not limited to our boxes. He is God. We want a flowchart faith, neatly packaged in dos and don'ts: holy do this, unholy do that. If God follows our plan, all is right with our world. We forget that God's ways are not our ways.

Thanks to the Pharisees, truly religious people could no longer visit or associate with a foreigner. They had their set of man-made rules. When we open our boundaries, we open ourselves up to more of God's blessing.

The problem with our boxes is this: God thinks outside of our boxes. Well beyond our boxes, in fact! And when we decide someone isn't fit for God's work, we only hurt ourselves. In trying to limit God, we limit our blessings. I'm thankful Peter learned this lesson, because salvation's gate was swung wide open for everyone as a result.

Lord, help me never seek to limit Your grace. Help me understand that Your love is for everyone and live in a way that extends Your love daily to all. In the name of the Father and of the Son and of the Holy Spirit, I pray. Amen.

Spot the Sprout

Noah found favor in the eyes of the Lord (Genesis 6:8).

Scripture: Genesis 6:1-8
Song: "Take Time to Be Holy"

I wanted to throw the plant away because it looked lifeless and ugly. With its dry and withered leaves, it was hopeless!

I walked toward the trash can as I heard my mom say, "Wait a minute. Look here at this." She grabbed the container and pointed out a small green sprout near the base of the brown plant. "This plant still has potential," she said. "It still has some life left in it. You just needed to spot the sprout."

Mom saw the positive in a seemingly negative creation. She saw good when all I saw was bad.

God spotted the sprout in Noah. Thus, in a world that abounded with evil, Noah found favor with God. He was the positive influence in an era filled with wickedness. God's whole creation seemed to be lifeless except for the sprout of Noah. As he followed God's commands, Noah's life was spared, and he ultimately enjoyed the Creator's great blessing.

Perhaps you face a difficult situation in which you need to spot the sprout? Ask God to help you find the blessings in even the most trying circumstances. Be encouraged by Noah's example and ask yourself, "What can I do today to please You, Father?"

Lord, thank You for the many blessings You have given me. Help me be a positive influence in my world, as I seek Your wise guidance each day. In Jesus' name, amen.

August 28–31. **Alisha Ritchie**, of North Carolina, enjoys spending time with her husband (of almost 20 years) and two children. She has published numerous devotions and articles over the years.

Early Morning Nature Show

Noah did all that the Lord commanded him (Genesis 7:5).

Scripture: Genesis 7:1-10
Song: "All Things Bright and Beautiful"

Sitting on my deck in the morning sunlight, I hear the birds sing. In the distance, two squirrels playfully rustle amid the trees. My dog runs through the grass, picks up a stick, and then sits to gnaw on it for a while. I enjoy watching the bustling nature show performed by all of God's creatures.

With my love for animals, I'm thankful Noah faithfully followed God's commands: He must collect seven pairs of clean animals, one pair of unclean animals, and seven pairs of every kind of bird to bring along with him on the ark. Gratefully, Noah followed those instructions meticulously. He demonstrated true faith and obedience to God's will for his life, following the plan precisely.

Following the Lord isn't always an easy task! Sometimes it's tough to be faithful, doing what we know is right, but God promises to help us. He gives us everything needed for faithfulness through the Bible, fellowship with other believers, regular worship, and His indwelling Spirit.

But are there areas in your life in which you'd like to demonstrate a deeper surrender to His will? Let us pray for discernment: "If any of you lacks wisdom, you should ask God, who gives generously to all without finding fault, and it will be given to you" (James 1:5).

Dear Father, thank You for the blessings of the beautiful earth and all of the animals in it. You alone are worthy; I bow my will to Yours. Through Christ, amen.

Waiting on the Moth

God said to Noah, "Come out of the ark, you and your wife and your sons and their wives" (Genesis 8:15, 16).

Scripture: Genesis 8:13-19
Song: "Those Who Wait on the Lord"

I found the chunky caterpillar crawling on the garage floor and knew my daughter would want to keep him. We filled a plastic container with leaves and twigs, bringing the container in the house for the night.

Much to our surprise, the next morning, we discovered our new friend had encased himself in a cocoon. We were so excited because we knew it was just a matter of time until a beautiful moth would emerge.

Now, my daughter and I are waiting and waiting.

We check the plastic container daily for signs of change in the cocoon—but we've seen no activity yet. It's hard to be patient and continue to wait. We want to see this amazing new creature.

I'm reminded that Noah had to wait. After the rain stopped, he looked out from the ark and saw dry land. Surely he was ready to leave the ark after being cooped up for so many days. But Noah demonstrated patience, waiting on the Lord to determine when it was safe to venture out. Waiting is never easy, but Noah trusted God to give him patience.

Is there a "moth" in your own life that keeps you waiting? Ask God for patience in the midst of the stress. He is our peace.

Lord God, thank You for giving me biblical heroes to emulate—like Noah, who showed fortitude and patience. Give me patience as I learn to wait on Your perfect timing. In the precious name of Jesus, amen.

Fruitful Dreams

As for you, be fruitful and increase in number; multiply on the earth and increase upon it (Genesis 9:7).

Scripture: Genesis 9:1-7
Song: "Oh, the Lord Looked Down"

When I was young, I dreamed of being a mother of two children—a boy and a girl. Fast forward 20 years: I was indeed blessed with an adorable, brown-eyed son and then, two years later, with a beautiful, curly-haired daughter. My husband and I were satisfied that we had been fruitful, and it's my hope that one day my children will also become parents, providing lots of little grandchildren to love and cherish.

In today's Scriptures, we read the beginning verses of God's covenant with Noah. The Lord blessed Noah, commanding him and his family to be fruitful and multiply. They had the important task of populating the earth since there were only eight humans left following the flood. It was vital that Noah and his family follow God's command so that the whole earth could eventually be filled. The Lord took this command so seriously that He mentions it not once, but twice in these verses. Once again, Noah and his family proved to be faithful in carrying out God's plans.

When the Lord tells us to do something, no matter how big or small, it's important that we listen. God wants to bless our surrender to Him, just as He blessed the obedience of Noah.

O Lord, thank You for all the ways You have blessed me. Now help me to be fruitful in my witness to the gospel, that I may gain spiritual children, through the new birth, who enter Your church with joy! Through Christ I pray. Amen.

DEVOTIONS®

► **September**

In the image of God
has God made mankind.

Genesis 9:6

Gary Wilde, Editor | Margaret K. Williams, Project *Editor*

Photo © iStock | Thinkstock®

DEVOTIONS® is published quarterly by Standard Publishing, Cincinnati, Ohio, www.standardpub.com. Copyright © 2016 by Standard Publishing. All rights reserved. Topics based on the Home Daily Bible Readings, International Sunday School Lessons. Copyright © 2014 by the Committee on the Uniform Series. Printed in the U.S.A. All Scripture quotations, unless otherwise indicated, are taken from the *HOLY BIBLE, NEW INTERNATIONAL VERSION*®. *NIV*®. Copyright © 1973, 1978, 1984, 2011 by Biblica, Inc.® Used by permission of Zondervan. All rights reserved worldwide. Scripture quotations marked (*NKJV*) are taken from the *New King James Version*®. Copyright © 1982 by Thomas Nelson, Inc. Used by permission. All rights reserved. Scripture quotations marked (*NASB*) are taken from the *New American Standard Bible*®. Copyright © 1960, 1962, 1963, 1968, 1971, 1972, 1973, 1975, 1977, 1995 by The Lockman Foundation. Used by permission. (www.Lockman.org). All rights reserved. *Holy Bible, New Living Translation (NLT)* Copyright © 1996, 2004, 2007, 2013 by Tyndale House Foundation. Used by permission of Tyndale House Publishers Inc., Carol Stream, Illinois 60188. All rights reserved. *Contemporary English Version (CEV).* Copyright © 1995 by American Bible Society.

Lazy Gardener

So you also must be ready, because the Son of Man will come at an hour when you do not expect him (Matthew 24:44).

Scripture: Matthew 24:36-44
Song: "In Our Dear Lord's Garden"

I dream of having a gorgeous flower garden. I see hydrangea bushes bringing forth blossoms of blue and lavender, brilliant buttercups and pansies sprouting close to the ground. My garden is a spectacular canvas of vivid color and texture—absolutely breathtaking—inviting you to abide there all day long.

In reality, my flower garden pales in comparison to my dream. No buttercups or hydrangeas bloom, because I haven't taken the time to plant them. The flowers and bushes growing are sparse, lacking the attention of one with a green thumb. I admit I am a lazy gardener. I want the benefits and beauty of a wondrous flower garden but don't want to invest the time or energy to nurture one. I put off growing my dream garden, because there will always be tomorrow.

Am I a lazy gardener when it comes to my personal walk with God? Do I want all the benefits of a close relationship with Him without devoting myself to what's required? The Bible tells me in Matthew that I don't have time to be sluggish; Jesus may return at any time. Perhaps I will sit here in the quietness and till the garden of my faith for awhile.

Dear Father, help me realize I need to be a good steward of my time, growing my faith in You. Guide me in following Your will for my life, helping me to prepare for the day when Your Son returns. In His' name, amen.

September 1–3. **Alisha Ritchie** writes from Stanfield, North Carolina, where she enjoys spending time with her husband of almost 20 years and with her two wonderful children.

Treasure Hunt

In the days when the seventh angel is about to sound his trumpet, the mystery of God will be accomplished, just as he announced to his servants the prophets (Revelation 10:7).

Scripture: Revelation 10:1-7
Song: "God Moves in a Mysterious Way"

Don't you just love a treasure hunt? No matter how old I grow, I still get excited with the challenge of a scavenger hunt. There's just something about deciphering those clues and trekking from one destination to another—until finally . . . the prize!

Our growth in Christ is much like a treasure hunt. We're constantly journeying with the goal of uncovering deep riches. The ultimate prize, our treasure, is Christ, in whom all knowledge and wisdom are hidden.

Of course, we may experience obstacles and trying times, which will (hopefully, if we make good use of them) draw us closer to Him. Other times, we receive blessings in the form of deepened fellowship, more heartfelt worship, and answered prayers. These special gifts are tiny glimpses into God's ultimate plan—the mystery of His will—letting us know He is constantly at work on our behalf.

We may not understand why certain things happen now, but God is sovereign and in complete control. So until the day comes when all things are revealed, let us enjoy the treasure hunt, growing in a more intimate relationship with Him.

Lord God of Heaven and earth, I want to seek You in all areas of Your life, being alert to the treasures You've planted along my path. Thank You for giving me the ability to know You, and help me to become more and more aware of Your abiding presence. In Christ, I pray. Amen.

Faithful Through the Seasons

As long as the earth endures, seedtime and harvest, cold and heat, summer and winter, day and night will never cease (Genesis 8:22).

Scripture: Genesis 8:20-22; 9:8-17
Song: "O Day of Rest and Gladness"

Autumn is my favorite time of year. I love the crispness in the air that lets me snuggle up in all my favorite sweaters. Nature's glory shines forth as the tree leaves turn to brilliant shades of red, orange, and gold. Bright pumpkins and luscious mums flourish in every direction I look. To me, no season is more beautiful than autumn.

However, no matter the time of year, the seasons will inevitably change. Each rotation into a different season serves as a reminder of God's faithfulness to His promises. Just as sure as fall turns to winter, and winter to spring, and then spring to summer, God is loyal to His Word.

We are reminded of this truth in Genesis, which speaks of God's decree after the earth had been devastated by floodwaters. The Lord assures all humankind that He will never destroy the earth again in this manner. We can count those words a blessing and rely on them completely.

Such great, cosmic promises have the most personal implications for me. I wonder today: What area of my life am I still afraid to turn over to God? As king of the universe, can He not meet my every need?

Lord God of Creation, I thank You for the promises that You make—and for always keeping Your Word. Help me to mature in my faith as I learn to trust You more completely. I pray in the name of Christ, my Savior and Lord. Amen.

Changing Names and Other Things

As for Sarai your wife, you are no longer to call her Sarai; her name will be Sarah (Genesis 17:15).

Scripture: Genesis 17:15-17
Song: "I Will Change Your Name"

Over 30 years ago, my wife changed her last name to my last name. That's not unusual, because changing names means wanting to identify with a new situation. For example, adopted children often change their names when they've been received into a new family. It's not done lightly. After all, such a change means loads of paperwork and court appearances. It's a big deal.

Earlier in Genesis 17, God changed Abram's name to Abraham. Now, He's changing Sarai's name to Sarah. In Sarai's case, her name is changed by only one letter. Still, the change is significant. God goes on to explain that He was going to bless her richly, and she would become the mother of many nations. She goes from Sarai to Sarah—and from being childless to becoming a mother of many nations. Big change! But our God changes things dramatically: from a seemingly insignificant name change to changed lives and changed circumstances.

Perhaps your life was changed by the Savior, whose name means "Wonderful Counselor, Mighty God, Everlasting Father, Prince of Peace" (Isaiah 9:6). If so, your name is written in the lamb's book of life. What a wonderful change!

O God, You are the author of change. Thank You for saving me. Help me to influence others who are searching for the truth. In Christ's name, amen.

September 4–10. **Pete Anderson** lives in Florida with his wife of 33 years. He has two adult boys who live nearby. When not teaching fifth grade, he enjoys mission trips, traveling, and writing.

Just Fruitful?

As for Ishmael, I will bless him also, just as you have asked. I will make him extremely fruitful and multiply his descendants (Genesis 17:20, *NLT*).

Scripture: Genesis 17:20-22
Song: "Here I Am to Worship"

Ah, adjectives! Don't you just love them? I am having a day. I am having a nice day. I am having a wonderfully nice day. I am having an exciting, wonderfully nice day. I am having a wonderful, exciting, thrilling, eventful, nice day. OK, enough with the adverbs and adjectives.

But I do so enjoy it when God uses these tools of speech as He shares what He's planning for the future. Thousands of years later, the reader can still receive a pleasant literary jolt, along with a little more insight into God's being.

When the Lord told Abraham He would bless Ishmael, He didn't merely say that Ishmael would be fruitful. No, He told Abraham that Ishmael would be *extremely* fruitful. Fruitful is good. But "extremely fruitful" must be even better, right?

But why the additional modifier? Well, if I were to hazard a guess, I might say that we can discover the answer in a later chapter of Genesis: chapter 25. There, we learn that Ishmael had 12 sons who became 12 tribes (imagine all the children). More than just fruitful, Ishmael was truly extremely fruitful. God always keeps His promises—adjectives, adverbs, and all.

Dear Lord God, I worship You because every good thing comes from above. You have my best at heart, and You keep Your promises. How grateful I am! So help me to be faithful in the promises I make with others, as a reflection of Your matchless character. I pray in the name of Jesus my Savior. Amen.

On That Very Day

On that very day . . . (Genesis 17:23).

Scripture: Genesis 17:23-27
Song: "One Day"

"On that very day . . ." It doesn't take a rocket scientist to figure out that those words mean something happened immediately.
Somebody predicted it, and "on that very day" it occurred. Futurist
writers have made many predictions of what lies ahead, and sometimes their predictions have come to pass.

The biblical prophets, though, far surpass the futurists in seeing
into the last days. Zechariah, for instance, in the fifth century BC,
declared the Messiah would be betrayed for 30 pieces of silver
and that the money would be thrown to the potter (see Zechariah
11:12, 13). Just as predicted, Judas Iscariot was paid 30 pieces of
silver for betraying Jesus. And the money, which Judas threw on
the ground, was used to buy a: "Potter's field," or burial site. It
happened on that very day.

December 25 was glorious for me as a kid. My family joyfully observed Christmas time with gifts, visiting relatives, hearty meals,
sing-alongs, and just plain fun. We even went caroling together
on Christmas eve. But on Christmas day—that very day—we ate,
opened presents, and spent the entire day together in a spirit of
thankfulness. As I grew older, I realized the real importance of the
day and the gratitude it invites. Yes, we still get together and eat
and open presents. But we also celebrate the Savior's birth, for the
whole world changed *on that very day.*

Lord Jesus, I am grateful that You know what tomorrow will bring. You know the
future. Take my life and let it honor You in everything I do this very day. Amen.

Not Even One Square Foot

God didn't give him any part of it, not even a square foot. But God did promise to give it to him and his family forever, even though Abraham didn't have any children (Acts 7:5, *CEV*).

Scripture: Acts 7:1-8
Song: "Days of Elijah"

I am a public school elementary teacher. I've collected money from my class for yearbooks, field trips, and fund-raisers. I've had to count, record, and give receipts for the collected funds and turn in the money to our school secretary. Do you know how much of the money collected was mine? None of it; not one dime!

Yes, I do receive a paycheck and (besides taxes, insurance, and various payroll deductions), the money is mine. I can't physically count it anymore since my pay is automatically deposited in my bank account (and they count it for me, I hope). So, some money belongs to me, and other money belongs to the school. Maybe you've had to count someone else's money or possessions?

In our Scripture today, God promises Abraham land, but he didn't get to own it, not even one square foot. He was promised, however, that the land would be given to his family, forever. And forever is a long time, extending the promised blessing even to you and me today. After all, "If you belong to Christ, you are now part of Abraham's family, and you will be given what God has promised" (Galatians 3:29, *CEV*).

Dear God, You are the giver of such great blessings. Fill my heart with gratitude—and my life with good deeds—in response to Your matchless grace. In the name of the Father and of the Son and of the Holy Spirit, amen.

Just Tell My Wife, Please

He did not waver at the promise of God through unbelief, but was strengthened in faith, giving glory to God (Romans 4:20, *NKJV*).

Scripture: Romans 4:13-25
Song: "Lord, I Lift Your Name on High"

My wife and I raised two children, both boys. Our first child was born when Barb was 27, and our second was born when she was 36. The boys are now 31 and 22, so their births were a quite a number of years ago. I can't imagine what my wife would say—or what I would do—if God decided to bless us with yet another child. We're old enough to be grandparents. Besides, I'm looking to retire in the foreseeable future, not raise another child.

That wasn't Abraham's outlook, though. Abraham was almost 100-years-old, and Sarah was 90—not exactly childbearing ages. Yet Abraham knew that God would keep His promise to give him a child through his wife.

True, Abraham laughed at the thought of having a child at such an age, but he never wavered in his belief that God could actually make them parents. Luke 1:37 states that "with God nothing will be impossible" (*NKJV*). It could well be impossible in human terms, but with God?

What God promises, He does. We need not waver with unbelief, but accept that God knows what He is doing. (And should He decide we will have another child? I'll let Him tell my wife.)

Help me, Lord, to trust You in all things. You not only have tomorrow in Your hands, but You also have today. Help me remember that nothing that happens today will surprise or shock You. I can rest in Your love. Through Christ, amen.

No Serving? Not an Option!

We do have such a high priest, who sat down at the right hand of the throne of the Majesty in heaven, and who serves in the sanctuary, the true tabernacle set up by the Lord, not by a mere human being (Hebrews 8:1, 2).

Scripture: Hebrews 8:1-8
Song: "All Creatures of Our God and King"

As a teacher, I have the principal as my supervisor. She's in charge, but subject to the area superintendent. We have an American president and, although he's "in charge," he's still subject to the voters and Congress. Every company has a boss, but even that person is subject to stockholders or the ruling board and ultimately even the customers. I can't think of any job or person that doesn't have some sort of higher authority. When you get right down to it, we all serve somebody.

Except for Christ. He's the high priest, subject to no one. He is the absolute authority, and all honor goes to Him. What He wills, happens. His word is law, acknowledged or not.

In the Old Testament, the high priest was the supreme leader of the Israelites. Aaron, brother of Moses, was the first high priest, and the office was hereditary in the Levite tribe. Today, our high priest is not an office to attain, but Christ Jesus who asks to be the sovereign ruler of our lives. It is He to whom we make petitions and offer thanks and praise. But will we serve Him alone? We may serve the devil, we may serve the Lord, but we will serve somebody.

Thank You, Jesus, for saving my life and interceding for me forever at the right hand of the Father. Help me to glorify You in everything that happens today. Alleluia! I praise You, my great high priest, Jesus Christ! Amen.

Walk Faithfully and Be Blameless

When Abram was ninety-nine years old, the LORD appeared to him and said, "I am God Almighty; walk before me faithfully and be blameless" (Genesis 17:1).

Scripture: Genesis 17:1-14
Song: "Walk Beside Me, O My Savior"

Not long ago I returned from a trip to Europe. My wife and I traveled with another couple and spent 17 days exploring the continent. And we walked and walked and walked. When we weren't taking a train to another country, we walked and explored. Did I mention my tired feet? and knees? and ankles? Did I share that we walked nearly everywhere?

I'm thrilled that God doesn't call us to walk *perfectly*. That's not the form of the word used in today's verse. God asked Abram to walk before Him faithfully and blamelessly.

Our walk with God is to be the same. With faith. Blameless. *Blameless* means innocent of doing wrong. Although we have sinned (done wrong things), we can walk blameless before Him when we admit our sin and He "forgets" our wrongdoing. We still suffer the consequences of any sin, but before God, we can be blameless. And we walk with faith, believing—depending on it! "As far as the east is from the west, so far has he removed our transgressions from us" (Psalm 103:12).

As we walk with Christ, our feet, ankles, and knees won't get tired. For He walks with us and, when necessary, carries us. We're not alone. We walk with Him everywhere we go.

Father, help me to walk in Your ways. Keep me close for I am prone to wander. Forgive my sins. Open my eyes to the needs of others. Amen.

A Cure for the Overwhelmed

He rested on the seventh day. Therefore the LORD blessed the Sabbath day and made it holy (Exodus 20:11).

Scripture: Exodus 20:8-11
Song: "Holy Sabbath Day of Rest"

I felt wrung out. Drained. Running my own business and balancing family time, church work, and home care left me depleted, snappish, and downright grumpy. Life seemed to be moving in fast forward.

Something has to change, I thought while scrubbing a dirty pan in a sink full of bubbles. *But what?* I couldn't delegate my work or say no to new projects. We needed my income, plus I love my work. I couldn't afford to hire a housekeeper or chef. Was there a way to make time to rest each week?

I suggested our family try a "screen-free" day each Sunday. Two-plus years later, we are still enjoying this form of Sabbath rest. We aren't perfect at it. What a difference, though, even an imperfect rest gives our souls.

What do we do with all the free time? We hike, go on birding adventures, or just rest and play and read. And when the work and school week begins, we feel ready to reenter the fray, knowing that another day of rest will come again in just six short days. Celebrating Sabbath in this way adds a beautiful rhythm to the week, giving us a chance to pause and reset.

Father God, thank You for the gift of rest and the promise that I don't have to "do it all," all the time. Help me to follow in Your footsteps, allowing myself to enjoy Your gift of holy rest. I pray in the precious name of Jesus. Amen.

September 11–17. **J. P. Choquette** writes, encourages other creatives, makes junk art, and takes walks from her home in Swanton, Vermont. She enjoys Sabbath rest weekly (and chocolate daily).

Do I Work Harder Than God?

Observe the Sabbath day by keeping it holy, as the LORD your God has commanded you. Six days you shall labor and do all your work, but the seventh day is a sabbath to the LORD your God. On it you shall not do any work (Deuteronomy 5:12-14).

Scripture: Deuteronomy 5:12-15
Song: "'Tis So Sweet to Trust in Jesus"

I grew up in a congregation that celebrated the Sabbath from sundown Friday to sundown Saturday. I now attend a different church where worship is held on Sunday mornings. Still, I try to keep the entire day free from work. A devotional I read once said something to this effect: Even God rested on the seventh day. Is your work more important than God's?

That question pierced my heart. The truth of the matter is that often I get so tangled in my to-do's and should-do's and better-get-a-head-start's that I miss out on the rest that God promises me. Not just once a year on vacation, but once a week. A chance to slow down, reflect, notice things that, in the rush of the week, I pass right by.

Sipping a glass of water at the kitchen sink one Sunday, I noticed the fountain that sits on our kitchen counter. Water burbled over the stones. At that particular moment, sunlight caught the water and made iridescent shimmers. I stopped for several minutes, just drinking in the beauty. And I felt God nudging my heart—"See the beauty all around you? Stop and enjoy."

Father God, please help me go beyond just living so that I may truly experience the moments of life. Help me to slow down long enough to notice the beauty around me and to enjoy the opportunity to truly rest in You. In the name of Christ, amen.

Rules Versus Relationship

If any of you has a sheep and it falls into a pit on the Sabbath, will you not take hold of it and lift it out? How much more valuable is a person than a sheep! (Matthew 12:11, 12).

Scripture: Matthew 12:9-14
Song: "Blessed Assurance"

How I wish that becoming a Christian made me perfect! Instead, I feel as if I must be on guard constantly, being careful that I don't make a bad impression or do or say things that will cause others to see me as in a less-than-favorable light.

It's easy—incredibly easy—for my thoughts to go from being joyfully careful in my Christian walk to focusing merely on rules: who's breaking them and who isn't. Like the Pharisees in Jesus' time, I find it easy to fall into legalism. "She shouldn't be wearing that," or "I can't believe he said that!" too often bubble up in my mind. Instead, suppose my thoughts turned to God's grace: for me and my fellow brothers and sisters in Christ.

Instead of judging others or myself so harshly, I want to spend precious minutes relaxing in God's love. Instead of whipping out the old mental holy/sin meter, let me instead be thankful that my Father loves me, no matter what, and forgives me when I mess up.

I'm so grateful that God's grace transcends all the rules and regulations that I worry about. I'm glad that He wants to maintain a meaningful relationship with me, not a score sheet to see how well I keep the rules.

Father, thank You that instead of rules You want a relationship. I'm grateful that You want to experience life together, rather than keep a checklist of my shortcomings. Praise You for the gift of grace and the cross of atonement. In Jesus' name, amen.

Afraid to Offend?

Many who heard him were amazed. "Where did this man get these things?" they asked. . . . "Isn't this the carpenter? Isn't this Mary's son and the brother of James, Joseph, Judas and Simon?" . . . And they took offense at him (Mark 6:2, 3).

Scripture: Mark 6:1-5
Song: "New Song Arisin'"

I loathe causing offense. Maybe it's ingrained in my nature—I've been shy since birth—or due to experience. If politics or religion or other hot-button issues are being discussed loudly at an event, I quickly find my way out of the room.

Our verse today reminds me that talking is actually a *choice* that someone makes. In Jesus' time, people in His hometown chose to reject Him. Why? Because He was "the carpenter," and "Mary's son," and the brother of regular old men and women whom they knew.

Does that mean Jesus' message was wrong? That He shouldn't have done what God called Him to, because He might offend a person or group? Of course not. So what really lies behind my deep desire to avoid being offensive? Is it fear? Worry that I will be rejected or might be called out on my beliefs or actions?

As it says in 2 Timothy 1:7, God didn't give me a spirit of fear. Allowing myself to be caught up in the anxiety of possibly offending thrusts me into a type of prison. And God definitely doesn't want a child of His living behind bars.

Father, thank You for equipping me with a courageous spirit. I know that You are there beside me, willing me to speak the truth, even if I feel uncomfortable. Thank You for being the Spirit of truth, and help me to walk in Your Son's bold footsteps. In His name, I pray. Amen.

The Gift of Rest

On the Sabbath we went outside the city gate to the river.
. . . We sat down and began to speak to the women who had
gathered there. One of those listening was a woman from
the city of Thyatira named Lydia, a dealer in purple cloth.
She was a worshiper of God. The Lord opened her heart to
respond to Paul's message (Acts 16:13, 14).

Scripture: Acts 16:11-15
Song: "To Thee, O Lord, Our Hearts We Raise"

One of the important lessons I've learned as a *solopreneur*—a
fancy word meaning that I wear every hat in my business—is to
take time to work *on* my business not just *in* it. The difference is
this: when I'm working *in* my business, I'm carrying out the day-
to-day activities. When I'm working *on* my business, I'm pulling up
out of these tasks to look at the bigger picture.

Lydia was a busy businesswoman. Yet she took time out of her
hectic week to observe the Sabbath, to go to "a place of prayer."
She opened herself up to God, and He met her there. The text says
that "The Lord opened her heart."

It's nearly impossible to open my own heart, if I keep myself so
busy that I can't hear His voice. If I don't make time for Him—regular,
ongoing time—then I will soon find myself treading water spiritually.

Every week I'm given the gift of a Sabbath rest. On this day I
choose not to work; instead, I pull up out of my hectic life for a few
precious hours and look at God's bigger picture.

Heavenly Father, thank You so much for your promise of rest every seven days. I'm
grateful that in this noisy, chaotic world, I always have time set apart to just *be*. Thank
You for the gift of renewal through Your abiding presence. In Christ, amen.

Blindfolded by Busyness

You make me glad by your deeds, LORD; I sing for joy at what your hands have done (Psalm 92:4).

Scripture: Psalm 92
Song: "The Lord's Prayer"

I stumbled from bed, rubbing gritty eyes. How could it be time to face another day when the troubles from the previous one still swirled in my mind? I hadn't slept well. Maybe I'd skip my morning walk and jump into my work; get a head start.

Or . . . an abbreviated walk: once around the cul-de-sac. I pulled on sneakers and headed out. Fresh air, still sweet with dew and the scent of green growing things, filled my nose and lungs. I started walking.

Still, thoughts of all that I needed to do that day pressed in. A mental tug-of-war: To-do list versus spending time with God in quiet peacefulness. Again and again I tried to turn my mind to holy things and to stop fretting about the day ahead. Finally, I felt God nudging me: "Look around you. Listen."

Birds chattered overhead, each with a different voice. Water gurgled through culverts creating little streams that splashed and trickled. The air smelled fresh and clean as a light breeze caressed my face. Everywhere I looked there was green: from dark to light and every shade in between. I breathed deeply, grateful for the Creator who cares so much about beauty—and me. He won't let me walk through the world blindfolded by busyness.

Father, help me to remember that the gift of being, Your gift of presence and peace, is mine for the taking. Thank You for the beauty of early morning walks and the world outside my window that speaks of Your love. In Christ's holy name, amen.

Giving My Soul a Rest

The Sabbath . . . will be a sign between me and the Israelites forever, for in six days the Lord made the heavens and the earth, and on the seventh day he rested and was refreshed (Exodus 31:16, 17).

Scripture: Exodus 31:12-18
Song: "Come unto Me"

On the seventh day He rested and was refreshed. I love that portion of this text. It's amazing how much better it feels to do something refreshing—say, have a tall drink of cold water—after I've done something especially tiring. Sure, water is nice any time. But after a long hike or run? After painting a fence in the hot sun? Then it's *wonderful.*

My soul needs that kind of reprieve. As a writer and introvert, I require a certain amount of quiet in my day to function at my best. Sometimes with family, work obligations, and just the noise of everyday living, the quiet I need so much is hard to find.

I'm grateful that God knew this and has built in a special time each week for humans to rest. How often I fight Him, though! I feel the pull to "just check my e-mail," or "create my weekly To Do List," or "just get a head start on my work." When I give in and do these things, the day loses a bit of its sparkle.

When instead, I take those hours to rest, renew my spirit, and gather myself for the week ahead, I start the new week off on a wonderful note. As if receiving a drink of water, my soul appreciates the chance for refreshment each Sabbath.

Father, thank You so much for the refreshing gift You offer every week. Help me to use it to reconnect with You. I'm so grateful that You know and meet all my needs. Amen.

The Masterpiece Within

I will put my instructions deep within them, and I will write them on their hearts. I will be their God, and they will be my people (Jeremiah 31:33, *NLT*).

Scripture: Jeremiah 31:31-34
Song: "The Master's Touch"

Two artists attempted to create a sculpture using a large block of marble. They both failed. The block was abandoned. It sat outside for 25 years, exposed to the weather—until Michelangelo began working on it.

He was 26 years old. For two years, he worked on that marble. What emerged was his magnificent statue of David. He took something that many deemed worthless and created a masterpiece.

Michelangelo could see the statue in the stone. To us, it would look like any other stone. To him beauty hid inside, and he just needed to set it free. In fact, he is said to have remarked: "Every block of stone has a statue inside it, and it is the task of the sculptor to discover it." He also said, "I saw the angel in the marble, and I carved until I set him free."

We are God's masterpiece, and He has written His love on our hearts. When people look at us, they see our failures and flaws. But when God looks at us, He sees a clean heart that comes from Christ's sacrifice. We can live in the security that God is working in our lives to make us who He wants us to be.

Father, I know that You chisel away to make me more like You. You know all my potential. Help me to see and trust Your work in me. In Christ, amen.

September 18–24. **Deborah Christensen**, of Streamwood, Illinois, is a freelance writer and editor. She loves spending time with her family, which includes five great-nieces and great-nephews.

What Are Your Demands?

I, the LORD, have rebuilt the ruins and replanted the waste-land. For I, the LORD, have spoken, and I will do what I say (Ezekiel 36:36, *NLT*).

Scripture: Ezekiel 36:33-38
Song: "God's Way Is the Best Way"

I thought I had the perfect job. But five years in, I felt restless. My perfect job wasn't so perfect anymore. I demanded that God provide the perfect job. I brought a shopping list of my demands to His throne and for over two years, I prayed that list. Nothing happened.

Finally, I became desperate: "Lord, I'll do anything to get out of here. I don't care. I'll wash toilets if You want me to." Submitting everything to Him, I released my grip on my demands.

Two weeks later, I interviewed for a position with a Christian ministry. As I left, the interviewer gave me a list of the job responsibilities and promised to call with his decision. When I got home, I reviewed the list. I almost dropped that piece of paper. Everything on that list had been on my list. The difference was: this time I wasn't *demanding* any of it. I got the job and worked there for the next 18 years.

It seems that God rebuilt the wasteland of my life when I stopped demanding perfection. Are you making demands to God? Could you try releasing your grip a bit? He'll start a beautiful rebuilding process. And everyone who looks at your life will know that it's God at work in you.

O Lord, forgive me for thinking I know—better than You do— what's best for me. Help me to release my grip on outcomes and enjoy the journey in Your presence. When I have You, I have everything! Praise You, through Christ my Lord. Amen.

Welcome Home!

I will put my Spirit in you and you will live, and I will settle you in your own land. Then you will know that I the LORD have spoken, and I have done it (Ezekiel 37:14).

Scripture: Ezekiel 37:11-14
Song: "Crown After Cross"

We received the call we'd been dreading. There was nothing else they could do for my grandmother. The end was near, and family gathered around her hospital bed, sharing memories and saying good-bye. When the heart monitor showed a flat line, my sister said, "Just think. She's in Heaven."

I said, "There was probably an announcement, 'Carl Christensen, please come to the front gate.'"

Carl was my grandfather, who had passed away several years before. The thought of them reuniting brought joy to us. We grieved, but we also rejoiced in lives well-lived for the Lord. We knew Heaven was celebrating as my grandmother came home.

When someone who loves the Lord steps into Heaven, those of us left behind do grieve amidst the loss. But at the same time we know our loved one is receiving everything that God promised to them. If we belong to Him, those promises await us as well. Allow God to breathe into you a passion to serve Him here below—while looking forward to the life He's prepared for you above.

Heavenly Father, I want my short time on this earth to please You, and when I reach the end of my days, I want to go home with the knowledge that I lived my life well for You. Even now, please fill me with the joys of Heaven. Through Christ I pray. Amen.

Promises Fulfilled

I, the LORD God, will gather the people of Israel and bring them home from the foreign nations where they now live (Ezekiel 37:21, *CEV*).

Scripture: Ezekiel 37:15-23
Song: "How Firm a Foundation"

For centuries, people read the prophecies that Israel would once again become a nation. Some pointed to them and laughed: The proclamations of men like Ezekiel just proved that the Bible wasn't true.

Then, around the turn of the twentieth century, Jews began to trickle into what was then called Palestine. Using irrigation techniques, they turned the desert into a garden, rebuilding a barren land. After the horrors of Hitler, something pulled God's chosen people back to the promised land. In 1948, Israel once again became a nation. Even people who had no faith felt drawn to the nation, for God was using them to fulfill His plans.

Since then, other countries have tried to destroy Israel. In fact, several nations have attacked it from all sides at once. Against all odds, Israel has survived.

God has kept His promises to Israel so far—with many more to come. We can now look at those prophecies and know that the impossible is always possible with an omnipotent Lord.

Do you ever wonder whether you can trust God's promises? Is it sometimes difficult to believe in the impossible? Look to the history of Israel; it's the story of promises fulfilled.

Father, sometimes I lose sight of the legacy of fulfilled promises You've created. I let my circumstances—rather than Your faithfulness—influence my joy. Help me remember that You are sovereign over all things, including history. In Christ, amen.

An Empty Table—or Not?

My dwelling place will be with them; I will be their God, and they will be my people (Ezekiel 37:27).

Scripture: Ezekiel 37:24-28
Song: "Leave God to Order All Thy Ways"

My father was born the day the stock market crashed in 1929. My grandparents lost everything—and gained a son—in one day. He joined his two older sisters in the family and two years later another sister was born.

The family struggled, with my grandfather taking odd jobs just to put food on the table. Yet through it all, they held onto their faith, and all four children were baptized into Christ.

One night the food ran out, ice box and pantry standing empty. Nevertheless Grandma set the table, and Grandfather called everyone to the table. They sat in front of empty plates.

Grandfather prayed, thanking God for taking care of them down through the years. As he finished, they heard someone knock on the door. And opening that door, they found a basket of food sitting there. Now, another prayer of thanks lifted to the throne of God!

Our situation may seem hopeless, but it's not. God is right there with us. He takes care of us in ways we can't even imagine. He loves us so much. I want to submit to Him this day and always: O, Lord, You are my God. How I trust You. How I love You. All glory, praise, and honor to Your name!

Almighty God my Father, I want to turn to You in any time of trouble or need. You are my God, You are always there for me. But sometimes I forget. Remind me to rely on Your abiding presence always. I pray this prayer in the name of Jesus, my merciful Savior and Lord. Amen.

Do the Right Thing

I want you to stress these things, so that those who have trusted in God may be careful to devote themselves to doing what is good (Titus 3:8).

Scripture: Titus 3:8-11
Song: "Spirit of the Living God"

When I first started working for a Christian ministry, I thought it would be heaven on earth. I forgot that we are all just flawed human beings.

Joan (not her real name) came on as office manager. She had an abrasive personality, but I didn't work directly with her. However, my office opened to the receptionist's desk, and I could hear how Joan treated the lady who worked there. I heard this woman crying after Joan slashed her verbally and then walked away.

Joan caused so much disunity that our office divided into two armed camps. People talked about others in anger, and the once-loving atmosphere of the office disintegrated. At one point, the two women ended up screaming at each other in the middle of the office! Sadly, management did nothing, as we lost sight of our mission and allowed our flawed personalities to control us. We dishonored our Lord with our pettiness.

A divisive person can rip the unity of our churches, workplaces, and families. May it never be for us, though! Choose to do the right thing: confront the divisive person in love, make sure we're not causing division, and live a life that honors God.

Dear Heavenly Father, please show me where I may be causing divisions, gossiping, or hurting other people. Help me to follow Your example and treat others with love and dignity. In the name of Your Son, my Savior, I pray. Amen.

A Softened Heart

I will put a new spirit in you. I will take out your stony, stubborn heart and give you a tender, responsive heart (Ezekiel 36:26, *NLT*).

Scripture: Ezekiel 36:22-32
Song: "Blessed Is the Man Whose Softening Heart"

Chuck Colson worked at the highest level of power. As one of Richard Nixon's closest confidants, he wielded great influence—but also committed criminal acts that put him in prison.

He fell to the lowest depths, but God reached out to him. He committed his life to Christ, and when he got out of prison, he could have stopped there, content to go to church on Sundays and leave it at that. But while he was in that lonely cell, God worked on his heart. It became tender and responsive for the prisoners he lived with.

In fact, Colson committed to ministering to prisoners for the rest of his life. He met with them, listened to their stories, even traveled around the world to serve them. He helped change their lives through his ministry. Yes, God thoroughly tenderized Colson's heart, removing his cravings for the perks of power.

How has God softened you since you gave your life to Him? He longs for us to become more like Him and to love people the way He does. All it takes is an open heart. Then He will bring people into our lives to love. Instead of turning away, we can point them to Christ.

Father, please mold and soften my heart as I grow deeper in Your love. Help me to love people the way You love them, to see them through Your eyes. I look at the outside, but You see who they really are, precious creatures and potential children through the new birth. Make me tenderhearted toward all! In Your name I pray, amen.

See It, Believe It!

By the word of the Lord the heavens were made, their starry host by the breath of his mouth (Psalm 33:6).

Scripture: Psalm 33:1-9
Song: "We Three Kings"

One Christmas Rick Larson's daughter asked him what the star of Bethlehem was. Rick didn't know but went searching. What he found astounded him. He bought astronomy software that could portray the night sky as it was at Jesus' birth. Rick discovered that astronomers of ancient Babylon (where the Magi likely lived) would have witnessed the conjunction of Jupiter with a star named Regulus.

According to Rick's website at *BethlehemStar.net*, Jupiter is known as the King Planet. The name Regulus comes from the root word for *regal*. Its Babylonian name, *Sharu*, and its Roman name, *Rex*, both mean *king*. So . . . at the beginning of the Jewish New Year, the King Planet met the King Star.

Because the earth speeds through space, whizzing first toward Jupiter and Regulus then passing and looking back at them, the conjunction moved through the constellation Leo the Lion and circled back, perhaps forming an oval like a crown on Leo's head. It then would have stopped in our sky (see Matthew 2:9).

The word of the Lord, whatever He speaks, contains or releases the infinite power that He is. What He says, He does in every detail, and the evidence is there for us to see and believe.

O Father, I thank You that Your infinite power has everything on this earth—and above it—under Your complete control. Praise to You, through Christ our Lord. Amen.

September 25–30. **Dianne E. Butts**, of Pueblo, Colorado, has written six books and is an aspiring screenwriter. She enjoys flower gardening and riding motorcycles with her husband, Hal.

Moving into God's Blessing

I will bless those who bless you, and whoever curses you I will curse; and all peoples on earth will be blessed through you (Genesis 12:3).

Scripture: Genesis 12:1-3
Song: "Blessed Is the Nation"

My friend is moving away. She and her husband have been looking for a place to live that would be easier on his health. Recently they found their dream home, so they bought it. After their purchase, their new neighbors—folks who'd been Christian mentors in their lives decades ago—told them that they had been praying they'd move to be near them.

What a wonderful surprise! No doubt the Lord has blessings in store for my friends in their new community.

When we follow God and obey what He tells us, we are blessed. Abraham set out and left his home because he believed God. His obedience led to the family and nation of Israel. The family and nation of Israel produced Jesus the Messiah, who blesses with salvation all who receive Him.

What God says, He does. Even though it's been thousands of years since God proclaimed this promise, it still applies today. Even today, nations or leaders of nations who turn against Israel, God will also turn against. For those who bless and do good to Israel, God's promise of blessing will still come to pass.

Father God, I know that no matter what nations do, individual Christians can continue to bless Israel and pray for Your people. When we do, You keep Your Word and bless us. Help me to move when and where You say. And when I think of Israel, help me to have nothing but blessing, nothing but good things in my heart and mind. Amen.

Forever Means Forever

All the land that you see I will give to you and your off-spring forever (Genesis 13:15).

Scripture: Genesis 13:14-17
Song: "Day by Day"

Some of my best childhood memories are of my family camping on a little piece of land we owned on the side of a mountain overlooking a lake. After we'd slept in a tent all night, my dad rose and cooked us breakfast over a camp stove. Then we'd all go down to the lake to search for polished rocks and shells.

When I was a child, I figured that piece of land had been in my family forever. As a child, forever was simply everything I knew. Years later, my sister and I inherited that little piece of land. We couldn't camp there any more since houses had been built on every lot, and so we sold it. Once sold, we no longer had any claim to it whatsoever.

Humans cannot promise "forever." We try. We fail.

But when God says forever, He means what He says.

The Lord promised this little piece of land known as Israel to the family of Abraham, Isaac, Jacob, and their descendents . . . *forever.*

Today nations, governments, and world leaders may argue over who has the right to that land. But surely those who do not believe the land belongs to Israel also do not believe what God has decreed. Are they not actually fighting against Him?

For with Almighty God, forever means forever.

Dear God, You have written yourself into news headlines, even in my day. Help me to be strong in seeing, knowing, and believing You and to use these headlines to witness to those who still need to trust You and Your Word. Through Christ, amen.

Vote for Good or for Evil

Do not bow down before their gods or worship them or follow their practices. You must demolish them and break their sacred stones to pieces (Exodus 23:24).

Scripture: Exodus 23:23-27
Song: "God of Gods, We Sound His Praises"

I'm a member of a small town church that belonged to a large Christian denomination which, unfortunately, had been drifting away from what many of us believe is right in God's sight. As the members of the church discussed among ourselves what the national leaders were doing, we knew there'd come a time we would have to decide whether to stay within the denomination.

Meanwhile, a group went to work to create a new denomination that would stay within God's Word. That meant when churches had to make a decision to stay or go, they had a new group to join should they vote to leave.

Many in our congregation prayed there would be a unanimous decision to leave, but that is not what happened. While the vote to leave passed, it was not unanimous. Those who disagreed with leaving the national church left our congregation.

We were saddened, but we did not allow our church to follow the practices of foreign gods. I hope that we demolished what was trying to creep in—a loss of focus on the true Lord God. Beware of any work or practice that takes your eyes away from serving and worshipping the one true God.

God in Heaven, help me recognize what is foreign and not of You. Help me see clearly so I never bow down before other gods or worship them or follow their practices. Give me courage to demolish what is not of You! In Jesus' name, amen.

My Heritage Lilies

Solomon ruled over all the kingdoms from the Euphrates River to the land of the Philistines, as far as the border of Egypt. These countries brought tribute and were Solomon's subjects all his life (1 Kings 4:21).

Scripture: 1 Kings 4:20-25
Song: "Find Us Faithful"

My sister brought me some old-fashioned orange day lilies. "They're from Aunt Sarah's garden," she told me. Though we called her Aunt Sarah, she was actually a great-aunt, our grandmother's sister. I loved the thought of having Aunt Sarah's lilies handed down to me. I call them my heritage lilies.

We hand down many things: clothes, habits, knowledge, faith. The genealogies in the Bible are for tracing the lineage of the promised Messiah from Abraham to Jesus—a great heritage handed down through centuries. Without the sacred ancestry lists, how could we know God kept His messianic promises?

The land described in today's verses is the same land described in Genesis 13:15 and Exodus 23:23—which we've looked at this week—and in Genesis 15:18, 19, which we'll consider later this week. This land is described over and over to make sure it is recorded clearly: this is the land that God promised to Abraham.

Promises kept. This is the heritage for the person who believes God. The flower of a day lily lasts only one day, thus its name. But the roots go on forever and spread, just like our faith.

Dear Heavenly Father, I thank You for the heritage of faith that has been handed down to me by other believers. Help me to be rooted in it and faithful to hand the faith on to others. In Jesus' name I pray. Amen.

Heavenly Accounting for All

What does Scripture say? "Abraham believed God, and it was credited to him as righteousness" (Romans 4:3).

Scripture: Romans 4:1-4
Song: "The God of Abraham Praise"

I try to earn enough with my writing to pay for its own expenses, but it rarely does. It used to; not so much any more. I've never made a profit I could put toward the family budget.

So when I look over my income for the year, every year I see my income is not much. It's a good thing my husband supports me in every way. He not only encourages me in my writing, he earns enough to pay for everything we need to live on.

I may not make much in earthly wealth, but I believe I'm laying up treasures in Heaven. But what about my husband? He works hard to earn money to provide for our daily needs here on earth. What about his treasures in Heaven?

I ask God to credit to his account an equal amount to whatever I'm earning in heavenly treasure. I can't do what I'm doing without him. (And, after all, work—of any kind that benefits the world—is a gift from God to all human beings.)

Abraham believed God. This is the definition of faith. This believing guided Abraham throughout his life, and his belief was credited to his heavenly account as righteousness. It is that kind of heavenly accounting that makes salvation a possibility for you, for me, and for every one of our neighbors.

Father, when You look at my heavenly account, what do You see? Help me live in such a way that my account is full of what pleases You. And thank You for the bottom line—that, by Your grace, the righteousness of Christ is credited to my account. Amen.

My Prayer Notes

DEVOTIONS®

▶ **October**

Praise be to God,
   who has not rejected my prayer
   or withheld his love from me!

Psalm 66:20

Gary Wilde, Editor | Margaret K. Williams, Project *Editor*   Photo © iStock | Thinkstock®

DEVOTIONS® is published quarterly by Standard Publishing, Cincinnati, Ohio, www.standardpub.com. Copyright © 2016 by Standard Publishing. All rights reserved. Topics based on the Home Daily Bible Readings, International Sunday School Lessons. Copyright © 2014 by the Committee on the Uniform Series. Printed in the U.S.A. All Scripture quotations, unless otherwise indicated, are taken from the *HOLY BIBLE, NEW INTERNATIONAL VERSION®. NIV®.* Copyright © 1973, 1978, 1984, 2011 by Biblica, Inc.® Used by permission of Zondervan. All rights reserved worldwide. Scripture quotations marked (*NKJV*) are taken from the *New King James Version.* Copyright © 1982 by Thomas Nelson, Inc. Used by permission. *Holy Bible, New Living Translation* (*NLT*) Copyright © 1996, 2004, 2007, 2013 by Tyndale House Foundation. Used by permission of Tyndale House Publishers Inc., Carol Stream, Illinois 60188. All rights reserved.

What God Has Set in Motion

To your descendants I give this land, from the Wadi of Egypt to the great river, the Euphrates (Genesis 15:18).

Scripture: Genesis 15:1-6, 17-21
Song: "Sweet Beulah Land"

My friend was riding with her husband, daughter, and son-in-law, driving back from meeting her great-grandchild. Nearby, as a farmer plowed his land, a strong wind blew loose dirt, creating a thick dust storm that blanketed the highway.

Drivers couldn't see. So when a car stopped in the middle of the highway just ahead of them, there was a horrendous crash. The others in the car survived, but my friend died.

At her funeral we remembered her: She had plowed up hard ground in many hearts, helping unwed pregnant girls, teaching children and moms about Jesus, loving them into God's kingdom. She was a woman of prayer. She prayed for me and my writing projects.

When someone dies, we say she has "entered her eternal reward." This is true, but only because of the Lord's promises to us. He keeps His promises even when we can't keep ours.

God promised Abraham and his offspring a land and a blessing. Through that blessing, Messiah Jesus, believers today also inherit the kingdom land. My friend received that faith and passed it on. As a result, she's now enjoying the promised land.

God of Abraham, how am I living? Will I leave a lasting heritage of faith in lives affected for You? Help me to do just that. In Jesus' name, amen.

October 1. **Dianne E. Butts**, of Pueblo, Colorado, has written six books and is an aspiring screenwriter. She enjoys flower gardening and riding motorcycles with her husband, Hal.

Oh Really, Johnnie?

What does the LORD your God require of you? He requires only that you fear the LORD your God, and live in a way that pleases Him, and love Him and serve Him with all your heart and soul (Deuteronomy 10:12, *NLT*).

Scripture: Deuteronomy 10:12-22
Song: "O Lord, How Shall I Meet You?"

Johnnie sent his sweetheart a note that read, "I'd swim the deepest river, I'd climb the highest mountain, I'd go through fire for you. Love, Johnnie. P. S. I'll be over tonight if it doesn't rain."

We may laugh at Johnnie, but how many times have I failed to love the Lord and put Him first in the normal course of my life? Have I ever known any brother or sister in Christ who really did this? And yet this is the place of blessing into which only I can place myself. No one else can love Him for me, not even God himself. He cannot bless me with this kind of a life, much as He wants to.

But He has given me Scripture, a revelation of His person and way that will help. He has given me His Spirit as an indwelling advocate to guide me into all the truth and the practice of it. So I will start again today to enter into this life of total worship of the Lord, my God. He will meet me there and draw me to himself with cords of love. Thankfully, He will surpass my highest dreams of blessing.

Lord, this is the life I desire. Change me, enable me, do anything You want, but make me this kind of person for Your glory and honor. In Jesus' name, amen.

October 2–8. **Brian Doud** is a retired minister working as the resident violin maker in a well-known Cleveland, Ohio, shop.

Get Ready

So Moses went down to the people. He consecrated them for worship, and they washed their clothes (Exodus 19:14, *NLT*).

Scripture: Exodus 19:9-15
Song: "Lord, I'm Ready"

Have you ever noticed how personalized the getting ready process is? Some people have their bags packed, unpacked, and re-packed several times before the day of departure arrives! Others wait until everyone else is in the car before they put down their book, go to comb their hair, and make minimal (or no) preparatory moves . . . while everyone else waits. And waits. And waits!

But quite a few things do require and warrant certain preparations, the getting ready to do something special. God was going to come down to the mountaintop and give Moses the Ten Commandments—a most momentous occasion in human history. The hot and dusty wandering slaves needed to prepare for an audience with the King of kings and Lord of lords. They needed to be prepared in heart and mind, so the consecration and washing were both necessary.

God has something in store for my future, part of His great eternal plan. Today's element of that may be small, but it will be there. I want to be ready, cleansed, and eager to meet Him, even in the seemingly mundane routines of my day. I want to honor Him and His presence in my life wherever I am.

Great God of the universe, and yet of the tiny details of my life today, I open my heart to Your Holy Spirit. Please cleanse me and make me ready for whatever we are to be doing together. For the sake of Your dear Son, I pray. Amen.

A Dark and Stormy Night

Darkness as black as night covers all the nations of the earth, but the glory of the LORD rises and appears over you (Isaiah 60:2, *NLT*).

Scripture: Isaiah 60:1-7
Song: "The Light of the World Is Jesus"

Have you noticed how a spiritual darkness seems to be taking over the world? It seems that all restraints of righteousness are being thrown off. The "nations of the earth," including our own, seem bent on legalizing everything—and every moral and spiritual deviation now seems possible, as though making it legal also makes it good. And so the darkness of sin begins to overshadow the light of revealed truth.

But let us rejoice in the Word of God! It is glorious to have the light of the good news of God's salvation through Jesus Christ. And what a blessing to know the fellowship and communion of the saints. Where would we be without prayer and the privilege of drawing near to the Lord?

We have Jesus, who is the light of the world. You and I may not be *with it* and *cool* according to the darkened vision of this world's citizens. But I'd far rather be walking in the light with the Lord. In fact, we live in joy and hope right now, for "we are citizens of heaven, where the Lord Jesus Christ lives. And we are eagerly waiting for him to return as our Savior" (Philippians 3:20, *NLT*).

All this darkness will soon pass away, but in doing the will of the Lord, we have the light of the Lord's glory today.

Lord of light, thank You for the inheritance of the saints to live in light. Bless me with your light as I walk in a darkening world. Amen.

My God Beats Any God!

I know the greatness of the LORD—that our Lord is greater than any other god (Psalm 135:5, *NLT*).

Scripture: Psalm 135:1-9, 19-21
Song: "Who Is on the Lord's Side?"

Have you ever seen the United Nations building and the flags of many nations arrayed in front of the building? They are carefully arranged so that no flag is higher than another, so that no country is portrayed as greater than another. And yet, each flag is distinctive and reflects the pride of its people.

In biblical days, it wasn't uncommon for warring nations' armies to taunt each other before battle in an attempt to intimidate the foe. Part of these taunts involved declaring that "our god can beat your god," so with his help, we will beat you and your god. There was some truth here for Israel—in reverse. When Israel did not honor the Lord, He did not fight for them, and they were defeated. They were thus disciplined for their unfaithfulness. Their God was still all-powerful, but He would not defend them while they were immersed in sin.

How wonderful to know that my God is, indeed, the greatest! And not by a slim margin, but by an overwhelming superiority. He is that much greater over Satan, demons, and all powers and gods put together. I am unbeatable today as I rest in Him. Romans 8:37, (*NLT*) "Overwhelming victory is ours through Christ, who loved us."

Blessed Savior, I rest in You as my complete defense against the world, flesh, and Satan. Show yourself strong in the defeat of all that is negative and in the honoring of all that is good. Please do this in the world, in Your way and time—and also within me. I pray in Your precious name. Amen.

What's That Voice?

Then a voice from the cloud said, "This is my Son, my Chosen One. Listen to him" (Luke 9:35, *NLT*).

Scripture: Luke 9:28-36
Song: "Speak, My Lord"

My mother rushed to the back door and called out, "Bru . . . Bri . . . Br . . . Kids!" My brother Bruce and I (Brian) laughed at my mother's confusion and inability to focus on one specific name to call. But any mother who has five or more children can understand that. And at her call to us "It's time for bed," if there was no immediate scurrying, my father would put down his newspaper and say, "Did you hear your mother?" The only good answer at that point was immediate action.

So many voices clamor for our attention today. We are easily distracted by commercials, teachers, employers, and family. We need wisdom: to whom should we listen?

Our verse today could serve well as our directive for all of life. Let us listen to our Lord and Savior, Jesus Christ. He alone has the authority of the heavenly Father himself backing His words, and His wisdom is otherworldly.

A wise person will choose what God chooses. God chose to speak to us through Jesus. He has chosen us out of the world to hear and trust Him. Jesus alone has our best interest at heart. There is no reason in Heaven or earth not to listen to the one who constantly calls to our hearts. Do you hear His gentle invitation to listen?

Lord of love, please forgive me for not listening to You more intently during my daily hours. I know Your words give comfort and direction in a confusing world. Speak, Your servant hears! Through the name of Jesus, amen.

Walking in Dark or Light?

You are a chosen people, a royal priesthood, a holy nation, God's special possession, that you may declare the praises of him who called you out of darkness into his wonderful light (1 Peter 2:9).

Scripture: 1 Peter 2:1-10
Song: "Send the Light"

My older brother, cousin, and I shut the door on our cabin. We headed through the dark and up a path through the woods to the road and the car. It was the darkest night I had ever experienced. We groped uncertainly along the ordinarily familiar trail. How good it felt to reach that car and some light and then to finally see the lights of home!

Most of the people I will see today are in the dark spiritually, even the most well-adjusted and emotionally secure of them. They cannot find their way home to the Lord Jesus and the truth of the Bible. They will be uneasy because they do not find their rest in Him. They can't see the value of trusting Him in the darkness of this world. They perceive that the conventional wisdom in this life is enough light for them and for facing the question of an afterlife.

How thankful I am for the light, the Lord Jesus, and for His Word, which is a lamp for my pathway. How thankful I am to be spared an eventual outer darkness because of the saving grace of Jesus! I'll do my best to show others His wonderful light and the effect it is having on my life.

Lord, shine Your light through me to those around me today. May they join me in answering Your call to enter Your wonderful light. I know the invitation will be best heard through my sincere acts of love and kindness. Help me. Amen.

Climbing the Mountain

The LORD came down on the top of Mount Sinai and called Moses to the top of the mountain. So Moses climbed the mountain (Exodus 19:20, *NLT*).

Scripture: Exodus 19:16-25
Song: "Lord, Speak to Me, That I May Speak"

Before the age of satellites, helicopters and drones surveillance of the forests in hill country was done from the top of fire towers built on the heights of the most strategic mountains. One could be seen from very near my ancestral home in the river valley. The boys in our family often climbed the mountain and the tower to see the beautiful, spectacular panoramic view. The view of the valley was our reward, but we had to climb the mountain to see it.

God could have spoken to Moses down on a plain. In fact He did, just enough to get Moses to climb the mountain to meet with Him.

I wonder whether today there might be a call from God for me to meet with Him somewhere. He could speak to me from His Word or out of the circumstances of life or by means of a fellow believer.

Wherever it is, I must be there to hear the message. I don't want to miss the view of His perspective. It may not be as big a message as the Ten Commandments which He gave to Moses. But when God called, Moses climbed. I will too.

Father God, Lord of all that I will hear today, make my ears sensitive to Your voice. I want to listen closely to whatever You say, blocking out all the rest of the noise. In the name of Jesus who lives and reigns with You and the Holy Spirit now and forever. Amen.

Hear and Do

Go near and listen to all that the LORD our God says. Then tell us whatever the LORD our God tells you. We will listen and obey (Deuteronomy 5:27).

Scripture: Deuteronomy 5:22-27
Song: "Where He Leads I'll Follow"

After 15 years of marriage, Daniel's wife was hardly speaking to him. Sitting in his minister's office, wringing his hands, Daniel didn't know what to do next. "Daniel, would your wife say that most of what you say to her builds her up?" "Would she say that you care about what's important to her?" "Would your wife say that you seek her input on things that you're facing?"

Daniel answered no to all of the questions.

"Daniel, nine times out of ten, you're going to know the right things to say and do. Just say and do those things. That's what you need to do next. And may the Lord strengthen you."

When the people of God heard Moses give them the Law, their response was simple and to the point: "We will listen and obey." As with Daniel, it's usually easy to know how to obey God in just about every situation—the challenge is actually *doing* it.

As we know from Israel's history, the peoples' actions didn't always live up to the vows they spoke. But it does not need to be so with us. When it comes to obeying God, especially in the context of our relationships, let our motto be, "We will hear and do it."

O Father, I often know the right thing to do, but sometimes I find it hard to put it into action. Please give me the ability to obey without hesitation. In Jesus' name, amen.

October 9–15. **Doug Schmidt** is a freelance editor and writer living in Colorado Springs, who loves the great indoors.

Mom and Dad

Honor your father and your mother, so that you may live long in the land the LORD your God is giving you (Exodus 20:12).

Scripture: Exodus 20:1-12
Song: "God, Our Father, We Adore Thee"

David's mom was bipolar. When she was depressed, she'd camp out on the couch and sleep. During these times, the TV would stay on 24 hours a day. When David's mom was manic, she could be exceptionally cruel. Whenever he was around her, he felt as if he were walking on eggshells.

When his mom had a massive stroke, he wrestled with all the loose ends that would never be addressed. But when she passed away, the Lord seemed to comfort him, "I have held your mom responsible to the degree to which she could be held responsible. Be at peace."

The only one of the Ten Commandments with a promise is the one to honor our parents. This was especially important for the Israelites, whose cohesiveness as a nation depended on strong family bonds. When those bonds were weak, the people of God became vulnerable.

Sometimes it's hard to honor parents, especially if they were harsh, abusive, or negligent. Even so, we can assure ourselves that God is the one who chose our parents for us. We can honor them in the roles they served. And if forgiveness is warranted, then let us extend mercy to them. To do so is to honor not only them, but God as well.

God, thank You for the parents You gave to me. In Your sovereign plan, Mom and Dad are the ones You chose for me. I honor You in honoring them. In Christ, amen.

Rest in What's True

You shall not give false testimony against your neighbor (Exodus 20:16).

Scripture: Exodus 20:13-17
Song: "Great Is Thy Faithfulness"

For 10 years, Thomas refused to talk with his dad. Why? Because after his parents divorced, family members convinced Thomas that his dad didn't care about him.

But when Thomas was about to get married, his fiancée talked him into inviting his dad to the wedding. That one act started an avalanche of revelations that convinced Thomas he'd been duped about his dad. These family members had given "false testimony" against his father—and because of that, he lost more than a decade of interacting with his father, who cared deeply about Thomas.

Throughout Scriptures, we see a myriad of examples of "false testimony" discrediting someone who had done nothing wrong. Consider Naboth, the vineyard owner—or even Jesus, during His trial. The damage caused by someone "lying under oath" cannot be overestimated. For this reason, the prohibition against lying is emphasized repeatedly in the law of Moses.

Having to face false accusations can be heartbreaking. Even so, if we focus on what is factually true and respond in appropriate ways, we can trust God to take care of the rest. Retaliation is never a God-honoring option. Simply rest in what is true.

Lord, give me the courage to confront gossip whenever I encounter it. If someone is not being represented well in his or her absence, help me to draw awareness to what's happening. In Jesus' name, amen.

The Bible's Authority

Do not think that I have come to abolish the Law or the Prophets; I have not come to abolish them but to fulfill them (Matthew 5:17).

Scripture: Matthew 5:17-20
Song: "The B–I–B–L–E"

A pastoral candidate was asked by the nominating committee why he believed that the Bible was the authoritative Word of God. He replied, "In addition to affirming the claims of the biblical writers in regard to the authority of God's Word, my primary reason for believing in this is Jesus' high view of the Scriptures. Jesus often quoted from the Old Testament as if they were indisputably authoritative. Jesus also made it clear that the Holy Spirit would speak through the apostles. For me, there is no more compelling reason to believe in the reliability and authority of the Scriptures: I take the Bible seriously because Jesus did." That was enough for the committee; they extended a call to the young man, and he accepted.

Yes, Jesus held a high view of the Bible, and in rising from the dead He gave His words eternal weight. While His enemies may have accused Him of trying to get rid of the Law, He countered by saying that He was there to fulfill it all, perfectly. To treat the Bible lightly was to invite God's discipline upon them.

In our culture the Bible is often attacked as archaic and irrelevant. Even so, because of the testimony of Jesus, we know that all biblical principles are timeless and applicable to us, regardless of their cultural manifestation.

Heavenly Father, thank You for the authority and timelessness of Your Word—and its witness to the Living Word, my Lord Jesus Christ. Amen.

The First Step

If you are offering your gift at the altar and there remember that your brother or sister has something against you, leave your gift there . . . . First go and be reconciled to them; then come and offer your gift (Matthew 5:23, 24).

Scripture: Matthew 5:21-26
Song: "What a Friend We Have in Jesus"

John's brother was murdered by a guy named Harry during a drug deal gone bad. When John heard about it, he set out to get a gun to take care of Harry, but never found him. Years later, John and Harry ended up in the same prison. John had found Christ through a prison ministry, but struggled with forgiving his brother's killer.

One day at lunch, Harry offered John something off his tray, and the supernatural ability to forgive hit John like a tsunami. Today, John and Harry attend the same church and talk freely about what happened between the two of them.

According to Jesus, once we become aware that someone has a legitimate issue with us, we need to go to that person and make things right. Quite often, simply owning up to what happened will make our relationship with that person even stronger.

Sometimes conflicts, especially in families, can go on for years because no one will take the first step toward reconciliation. If we are followers of Christ, then taking the initiative in conflict resolution is our responsibility. Even if we are the ones who were hurt, it's important to get that discussion going.

Father, I know that we can't control how other people respond, but we can be the first ones to try. As You bring memories of past conflicts to my mind, please give me the courage to take the initiative in seeking peace. Through Christ, I pray. Amen.

Vow Keeping

I tell you that anyone who divorces his wife, except for sexual immorality, makes her the victim of adultery, and anyone who marries a divorced woman commits adultery (Matthew 5:32).

Scripture: Matthew 5:27-32
Song: "Take My Life and Let It Be"

Jim was sitting in his minister's office, hoping to get a green light to divorce his wife. "Has she had an affair?" "Has she ever been violent, or threatened violence?" "Has she told you that she doesn't want to be married anymore and plans to leave?"

Jim answered all the questions with no.

"Then your marriage covenant has not been broken by your wife, and if you marry someone else while that covenant is still intact, you'll be committing adultery." Jim was disappointed; there wasn't even a shade of gray in what his minister was saying.

Back in the first century, a Jewish man could say to his wife "I divorce you" three times, hand her a certificate of divorce, and marry a "younger model" the next day. According to the Pharisees, this would close any loophole in the Law. But according to Jesus, if a man were to do this, then the original marriage covenant would still be in place.

The marriage covenant can't be nullified by boredom, disappointment, or the absence of romantic feelings. If the marriage vows have not been broken through adultery, abuse, or abandonment, then divorce is simply not a God-honoring option.

Father, You are the one who instituted marriage. Yet within the most intimate of all human relationships, a lot can go wrong. Give me the humility to seek Your wisdom in this relationship, honoring the covenant that defines its boundaries. In Christ, amen.

Not My Idol

Do not make any gods to be alongside me; do not make for yourselves gods of silver or gods of gold (Exodus 20:23).

Scripture: Exodus 20:18-26
Song: "The Doxology"

Jack loved his car. It wasn't brand new, but he kept the thing spotless, inside and out. If there was a family outing, Jack would have his wife take her car—the thought of kids eating in the back seat of his spotless sedan made him nauseous.

One day while his kids were playing kickball, the ball got away and bounced on the hood of the car. He started screaming at his youngsters and ran over to inspect the damage. When Jack found no trace of harm and saw his kids sobbing, he came to an awful realization: His car had become an idol.

The Old Testament prohibition against idolatry was repeated over and over to the Israelites. Even so, they frequently succumbed to the seduction of pagan gods who supposedly controlled the rains, the ability to conceive, and even success in the marketplace. It wasn't until after the Jews returned from the exile that all traces of pagan idolatry vanished from their day-to-day lives.

Have you noticed that anything good can become an idol to us? If we end up placing more security in a thing, or bank account, or a relationship—more than we do with God—we're dealing with an idol in our lives. Then it is time to consider replacing the good with the best.

Lord, if there's anything in my life that's taking Your place, if I'm putting my security in anything or anyone but You; please, help me to put that thing in its proper place. Let my ultimate trust reside in You—no matter the cost. In Jesus' name, amen.

The Day Everything Changes

"There is still the youngest," Jesse answered. "He is tending the sheep" (1 Samuel 16:11).

Scripture: 1 Samuel 16:1, 11-13
Song: "Step by Step"

I spent my youth preparing for a ministry in music and missions. I accompanied my choir, played clarinet in the all-state band, and earned a Bachelor of Sacred Music degree in college. From there, I went for a Master of Music degree.

At the end of my second semester, the professors decided I wasn't talented enough to continue. My world changed that day. Instead, I became a teacher and a writer.

David had a day like that. He was out tending the sheep, as he had every day. He excelled at it, killing any threats to the animals. But as the youngest son, he had few prospects for any other kind of life.

Then one day the prophet Samuel arrived at his father's front door and anointed him as Israel's next king—even though Israel already had a king. Before long, David left home to enter Saul's service as the first step on his road to the throne.

David accepted his change of roles with courage and faith. I can't say I took my change day with joy, but I did seek God's direction. Our lives may contain several days that change everything—for me, most recently, moving into a nursing home. With each change, God has gone before, preparing me for ministry.

Lord, I am so thankful that You control my days. Cleanse me of any sins and burdens that keep me from serving You wherever You lead me. Through Christ, amen.

October 16–22. **Darlene Franklin**, of Purcell, Oklahoma, spends much of her time writing at the crossroads of love and grace.

Father God

I will be his father, and he will be my son. I will never take my love away from him (1 Chronicles 17:13).

Scripture: 1 Chronicles 17:9-15
Song: "Children of the Heavenly Father"

Raising kids is never easy. My son was baptized into Christ when he was 7-years-old. At 12, he confirmed that decision. At 15, choosing an atheist as his best friend, he was arrested for possession of LSD.

Sadly, our family's story isn't unusual. But during that difficult time, God reassured me, over and over again, speaking to my heart words like these: "My heart is broken too; I love him more than you can. After all, he's my adopted son, and I *will* accomplish my plan for his life."

Now 35, Jaran is doing well, and his two older children are believers. The work God began in my grandmother's heart has produced spiritual fruit for five generations.

When David's sons committed grave crimes, God offered a promise. His son would succeed him, and God would establish His kingdom forever, a promise ultimately fulfilled in our Savior, Jesus Christ. They would enjoy a father/son relationship. God would never remove His love from David's son.

I suspect that last promise meant the most to David. It did to me; I measure my son's success by his love for the Lord. He could work any job at all, as long as he enjoys a life-long love affair with his Savior.

Father God, how thankful I am that You are also a father to everyone I care about, family and friends. Your love for them exceeds mine. Day by day, may they follow the path You have laid out for them with all their heart, soul, and mind. In Christ, amen.

Looking Ahead

"My son Solomon is young and inexperienced, and the house to be built for the Lord should be of great magnificence and fame and splendor in the sight of all the nations. Therefore I will make preparations for it" (1 Chronicles 22:5).

Scripture: 1 Chronicles 22:2-5
Song: "Who Knows When Death May Overtake Me"

The doctor's verdict: 10 years left to live, a measly 3,650 days. As those days count down, I'm striving to align my priorities with God's. And it seems to me the Lord has given me three things to strive for: Get to know Him better, so Heaven will be but a step away from life on earth. Keep writing (whenever I ask God if it's time to stop, He gives me new assignments). And create a legacy that's more than my books.

I hope to shower my family with love and share my faith all during the time I have with them. David must have reached a similar point in his life. God had established him as king over Israel, given him victory over all his enemies, and blessed him with many sons. But the king's one remaining wish—an act of gratitude—was to build a house for the "Name of the Lord my God" (v. 7).

God said no, promising that Solomon would build it instead, but David still wanted the temple to be his legacy. He couldn't build it, but he could get everything ready: workers, supplies, silver, and gold.

Lord, You are eternal, and whatever our stage in life, we can ask You to light the path to the future. Teach me to number my days, and forgive me for the times I place my will above Yours. Shine light on my days and put courage in my heart, that I may follow the path You open before me. In Jesus' name I pray. Amen.

Get to It

Now begin the work, and the LORD be with you (1 Chronicles 22:16).

Scripture: 1 Chronicles 22:6-16
Song: "Work, for the Night Is Coming"

As a writer, I often accept a contract from a publisher. The devotionals I've written for this week are one such assignment. When I looked at David's commission to Solomon to build the temple, I noticed parallels to my writing contracts:

• The publishing company gave me an assignment. I received a commission from them and the Lord to do the work of writing; God gave Solomon the job of building the temple.

• I study the assigned passages and pray for discretion and understanding before I write the devotionals, so that my words will accurately reflect God's Word. David prayed for wisdom for his son, and more importantly for a heart committed to God.

• When the writing becomes hard—and I doubt myself—I try not to give in to fear and discouragement. David told Solomon to be strong and courageous, not fearful and discouraged.

• My editor provided me with everything necessary to write the devotions: Scripture passages, format, and samples. David provided all the material and workers Solomon would need to build the temple.

Not all of God's assignments are as clear-cut as David's commission to Solomon. But whatever work God calls me to do, I will have success only as I follow His lead.

Lord, You promise to lead me in the way I should go. Once You make Your will known, help me obey with courage. I thank You that You will provide for all my needs—financial, intellectual, and spiritual—to do the work. In Jesus' name, amen.

God's Word, His Bond

Who is like you, LORD God Almighty? You, LORD, are mighty, and your faithfulness surrounds you (Psalm 89:8).

Scripture: Psalm 89:1-15
Song: "The Lord, the Sovereign King"

At a time when so many marriages end in divorce and public officials are constantly caught in scandals, we naturally feel that faithfulness is a quality in short supply. I considered some people I might consider faithful: Billy Graham, Corrie ten Boom, Teresa of Calcutta.

Then I thought of Preacher Bill. I shared my nursing home room with Brenda, and every Wednesday and Sunday Preacher Bill came to visit her. Since my home church was 30 miles away, I asked him if he'd be my minister as well. He instantly agreed.

After Brenda died, he continued his visits, buying fruit and soft drinks and toiletry items for my use. His visits continued until earlier this year: he retired, and I moved to another home. On his last visit, I bid him a heartfelt farewell.

Only it wasn't his last visit. He followed me to my new nursing home. He acted as my advocate with the administrator. He traveled to a sister church on Sunday, specifically to talk with the minister and leadership about me. They have taken over the visits, but Preacher Bill still keeps in touch by e-mail.

Imagine that kind of faithfulness, multiplied beyond our comprehension, and we'll have a tiny glimpse into the faithfulness that characterizes our great and good God.

Lord, I praise You for Your might, but I don't always recognize Your faithfulness. You are faithful to do what You promise. And because of Your great love, displayed upon the cross, I will spend eternity in Your fellowship. Thank You, in Jesus' name. Amen.

Learning Curve

David came to Saul and entered his service. Saul liked him very much, and David became one of his armor-bearers (1 Samuel 16:21).

Scripture: 1 Samuel 16:19-23
Song: "How I Love Thy Law, O Lord"

Benjamin Franklin was an inventor, scientist, and writer. He came from humble beginnings, his formal education ending at the age of 10 when he became a printer's apprentice. At 17 he ran away to Philadelphia.

He worked as a printer until the governor of Pennsylvania sent him to England to buy a printing press—without purchase money! By the time he returned to America, he had acquired experience and wealth that allowed him to buy a newspaper company. He became the official printer for the colony and began *Poor Richard's Almanac.* He also played a role in the creation of a fire department and the University of Pennsylvania and served as clerk at the state assembly.

By the time he became a leader in the Revolutionary War, Franklin was prepared to speak, write, and intercede on behalf of the fledgling nation. No wonder he was involved in the Continental Congress, sent as the American ambassador to Paris, and wrote the preamble of the Constitution of the United States.

David didn't go straight from sheepherder to king. From the time he entered Saul's service until God placed him on the throne, God prepared him. He will do the same for us.

Sovereign Lord, You've called me for a purpose, and You will bring it to pass. Wherever You lead me today, may I work with all my heart, knowing You are preparing me for the future. Forgive me when I skip ahead of Your plan! Through Christ, amen.

The Loving Disciplinarian

I will be his father, and he will be my son. When he does wrong, I will punish him with a rod wielded by men, with floggings inflicted by human hands (2 Samuel 7:14).

Scripture: 2 Samuel 7:1-6, 8-10, 12-16
Song: "Just as I Am"

Many states define parental abuse in language similar to this: "Parents . . . can use reasonable and appropriate physical force, if it is reasonably necessary and appropriate to maintain or promote the welfare of the child." There are many countries in Europe that prohibit the spanking of children altogether, whether at home or at school.

Beatings with rods and flogging wouldn't meet the definition of "reasonable physical force," of course; that crosses the line! Yet there were times when I, as a parent, had problems finding that line—and I know I'm not alone.

If any court were to judge God as to whether He is a loving father based on the verses above, He would be found guilty of unconditional love toward His children. Yes, what God told David holds true today: He loves us as our Father; we are His children. The next verse adds that He will never, ever take His love away from us.

But when we stray, He will discipline us; that, also, is an outflowing of His love. He knows exactly what kind of discipline, the timing and the amount, that is "reasonable and appropriate." With such a Father, how can we not want to love Him back?

O God my Father, I thank You that You love me enough to set boundaries for me. Forgive my sin, and lead me in the way of righteousness. When Your discipline seems greater than I can bear, I cling to Your loving purposes. In Jesus' name, amen.

The Rewards of Worship

"Stand up and praise the LORD** your God, who is from ever-lasting to everlasting"** (Nehemiah 9:5).

Scripture: Nehemiah 9:1-5
Song: "Time Now to Gather"

A man once said that his parents drugged him when he was a boy. They drug him to Sunday school and to church on Sunday morning. They drug him back to church on Sunday night and to church at midweek. They drug him to church whenever the church doors were opened.

We may smile, but today church attendance has been replaced by sports events, trips, and work. It's not that these are bad things, but when they become replacements for worshipping with other believers, how will families learn to "stand up and praise the Lord"?

The Israelites gathered in the same place on the same day of each October and repeated the same rituals. They fasted, wore sackcloth, and put dust on their heads as a sign of grief. They read from the Law, confessed their sins, and worshipped for hours.

God doesn't reward us just because we have an unbroken record of worship, nor is God interested in our developing a legalistic religion where we feel compelled to attend every event sponsored by the church. However, there are great rewards awaiting those who humble themselves before God and worship Him with other gathered believers who have a habit of doing so.

God, thanks for the opportunity to gather with others each week in praise of Your greatness. I freely express my love, my needs, and my thanksgiving. In Christ, amen.

October 23–29. **Michael Helms**, author of four books, is senior minister in Jefferson, Georgia. He and his wife, Tina, have two sons, John and Ryan, and a daughter-in-law, Alyssa.

God Knows You by Name

You made the heavens, . . . and all their starry host, the earth and all that is on it, the seas and all that is in them. . . . the multitudes of heaven worship you (Nehemiah 9:6).

Scripture: Nehemiah 9:5-8
Song: "He's Everything to Me"

Our solar system has eight planets: Mercury, Venus, Earth, Mars, Jupiter, Saturn, Uranus, and Neptune. Pluto was demoted from the list to dwarf planet status in 2006. Poor Pluto. The Kepler Space Telescope recently helped discover another planet, bringing the number of identified small worlds potentially suitable for life to 12.

Nearly 2,000 exoplanets that orbit stars other than the sun have been discovered since 1988. With 200 billion stars in the Milky Way, astronomers estimate there could be as many as 11 billion habitable earth-size planets in our solar system. It is estimated that there are one hundred billion galaxies in the universe. *Wow!*

The God who made all of these planets knew Abraham by name. He chose him to leave Ur of the Chaldeans and promised to give him a land, a people, and a blessing.

The God who made the heavens and the earth knows you by name too. That God seeks to establish a relationship with you. He wants to lead you and use you to accomplish His work.

So the next time you look up and see the stars, ponder the wonder of the God who made the heavens, the God who knows you by name and calls you to join His mission plan.

Lord, the heavens remind me of You, not just because I see Your handiwork in the midst of the darkness, but because of its infinitude. I cannot comprehend its vastness, nor can I cannot comprehend the vastness of Your love and mercy. In Christ, amen.

Loving Without Understanding

In your great mercy you did not put an end to them or abandon them, for you are a gracious and merciful God (Nehemiah 9:31).

Scripture: Nehemiah 9:26-31
Song: "Down by the Riverside"

In the movie, *A River Runs Through It*, Norman Maclean says, in reference to his wayward son, "It is those we live with and love, and should know, who elude us. You can love completely without complete understanding."

Parents whose children have gone astray understand this statement. They may be left scratching their heads, unable to understand their child's destructive decisions. Yet despite such poor choices, the love of parents usually remains unshaken.

Might that describe God's ways with us? Might our decisions leave God shaking His head in disbelief? Take those stubborn Hebrews in today's text as examples. How many times did they find themselves in a mess? Yes, there were consequences for their poor choices, for love doesn't mean the absence of consequences. However, God, the loving parent, was unable to stay away, unable to abandon them because of His deep compassion. Time and time again He came to their rescue.

Let us praise God that He loves us so much, so completely. The river that runs through our lives is a river of grace and mercy, understood most completely in Jesus Christ our Lord.

Lord God, as Jesus stood in the River Jordan to be baptized, He prayed. As He did, Your Spirit descended upon Him. Demonstrate Your love to me in such a way. Empower me, lead me, and help me so I will find my way. Through Christ, amen.

Wiping the Slate Clean

If you, LORD, kept a record of sins, Lord, who could stand?
(Psalm 130:3).

Scripture: Psalm 130
Song: "Create in Me a Clean Heart, O God"

As a small child I remember the joy of being chosen to wash the schoolroom chalkboards after a week of class work. The task consisted of taking an empty gallon can (once filled with beans or peas) from the lunchroom, filling it up with water, and dipping a rag in it to wash the old, black slate.

It was a satisfying feeling to see a nice, clean board. There was no longer any record of what had been written there, no record of class work, or even words of punishment some of us may have written 50 times or more, such as "I will not pass notes in class."

The psalmist pondered this question: "If you, Lord, kept a record of sins, Lord, who could stand?" He realized the importance of having his sins forgiven, his slate wiped clean, and the feeling that comes from knowing that the mistakes he had committed against God could remain in the past. Just as we could enter a new day with a clean chalkboard, the psalmist could enter a new day with a clean heart.

Because of God's unfailing love, and because God did not abandon him when he made mistakes, the psalmist was filled with hope . . . and so can we.

Almighty and most merciful God, thank You for the feeling that comes with sins forgiven. Thank You for wiping my slate clean and giving me a chance to start this day anew. I pray I may serve You in gratitude, always. In the name of the Father, and of the Son, and of the Holy Spirit. Amen.

I'm Not Exaggerating Here

It would be better for them to be thrown into the sea with a millstone tied around their neck than to cause one of these little ones to stumble (Luke 17:2).

Scripture: Luke 17:1-4
Song: "Footsteps of Jesus"

"I'm starving; I could eat a horse; wow, this thing weighs a ton; she's older than the hills; I could sleep for a year, I'm so tired; he's got tons of money; I've told you a million times I don't like seafood." What do all these expressions of speech have in common? They're all instances of *hyperbole,* otherwise known as exaggerations. People don't use these expressions of speech *literally.* Rather, they are used for emphasis or effect.

Everyone knows you are not literally starving or that you could actually consume a real horse. No, your friend simply understands that you are really, truly hungry.

Jesus used hyperbole in the same way, to bring emphasis to things He wanted to stress as important. Our Lord didn't want anyone to literally end up in the bottom of the sea with a millstone around his neck because he or she caused a "little one" (a phrase used for a follower of Jesus) to stumble or sin!

Jesus spoke this way in order to emphasize the seriousness of leading another believer away from doing what is right. It's a stern warning. "Watch yourselves," He says. And He's not exaggerating.

Father in Heaven, help me to live a consistent life so that people who see me at church, the tennis courts, the ball game, the movies, or out with friends will see the same person—someone seeking to do what is right in Your eyes. I pray this prayer in the name of Jesus, my Savior and Lord. Amen.

A Reward for the Persistent

God "will repay each person according to what they have done" (Romans 2:6).

Scripture: Romans 2:1-8
Song: "We'll Work Till Jesus Comes"

As a teenager I only got a small taste of what it was like to be a day laborer. Though I worked a hot job for several summers in a lumber yard in South Alabama, I once did a couple of the hottest and nastiest days of work ever: picking cucumbers for a man who'd planted about 20 acres of them.

We each got paid according to the amount of cucumbers we picked. So, the harder we worked, the more money we made. And even now, every time I pass a field where people are picking vegetables, I can only imagine what it's like to do that work every day, year after year.

Paul reminded the Romans that the Lord will give a reward to those who are persistent in doing good. This isn't a passage that sells cheap grace, but neither does it tell us we earn our salvation.

Salvation still comes by the grace of God. However, the Lord seems eager to bless those who remain persistent in doing good, and the blessing for them is eternal life. In contrast, the warning is clear: for those who live a life that is purely self-seeking—and who reject the truth and follow evil—well, instead of the blessing of eternal life, only wrath and anger can remain. Thankfully, we get to choose.

Lord, I know that my goodness cannot earn me a heavenly home. However, I see that You expect goodness from me and want to bless me because of my care for others. So, may my life be a living sacrifice for You. Help me by your grace, I pray. Amen.

Life-Giving Binding

These now join their fellow Israelites the nobles, and bind themselves with a curse and an oath to follow the Law of God given through Moses . . . to obey carefully all the commands, regulations and decrees of the LORD (Nehemiah 10:29).

Scripture: Nehemiah 9:32-38; 10:28, 29
Song: "Blest Be the Tie That Binds"

For centuries in countries all over the world, children have played a game called "mercy." It is also known by other names, such as "Uncle" and "Peanuts." To play, two players face each other and hold each other's hands, left hand to left hand, right hand to right hand. On the word "go" each tries to bend the other's fingers and wrists and inflict pain until the other cries out the word of the game.

For millennia, people have reached out to take the hand of God, but then they've sought to go their own way. Rather than submit to God's will, they've arrogantly believed God should submit to theirs. Guess who ends up crying for mercy.

The result in Nehemiah's day was that the people lost their freedom. That's the result today as well, because we become enslaved to sin when we go our own way.

Eventually, the people relented, crying out for mercy, realizing that doing things their way only brought more pain. Then they bound themselves to God, so He would lead them.

They realized that being bound to God wasn't constricting, but life giving. That's the blessed lesson for us, as well.

Forgive me, **Lord,** when I am arrogant and believe that I know what is best in my life. Forgive me for pushing off into my days without consulting You or listening to You. May I submit to Your will so I won't have to cry for mercy later. In Jesus' name, amen.

Not by Sword

I will not trust in my bow, nor shall my sword save me. But You have saved us from our enemies, and have put to shame those who hated us. In God we boast all day long, and praise Your name forever (Psalm 44:6-8, *NKJV*).

Scripture: Psalm 44:1-8
Song: "He Is Able to Deliver Thee"

During a difficult time I faced a battle that pressed me against a wall of gigantic proportions. My giant wasn't a 9-foot-tall soldier named Goliath. But it was a giant-sized problem I couldn't handle on my own.

I thought of David and Goliath—as we all do when faced with such looming difficulties. In the blink of an eye, I could see David reaching for the five smooth stones and placing one in the slingshot, the others in a pouch. He'd been offered a traditional soldier's armor and sword, but this wasn't a traditional fight. David knew this victory would only come from God, so he chose a familiar weapon and walked forward by faith.

Shouldn't I make the same choice David did when Goliath called him out? My hope comes from the Lord.

God gave David the victory when He sent that one smooth stone sailing like a missile into Goliath's head. I know my victory will also come from God, and I praise Him for the mighty works He does on my behalf.

Lord, thank You for being my hope and source of strength when I face the large battles in my life. Strengthen my heart to always trust You. In Christ's holy name, amen.

October 30–31. **Kathy Cheek** writes devotions, inspirational stories, and poetry appearing in various publications. She and her husband live in Dallas, Texas, where two daughters also reside.

Give My Heart

A woman came to Him having an alabaster flask of very costly fragrant oil, and she poured it on His head as He sat at the table (Matthew 26:6, 7, *NKJV*).

Scripture: Matthew 26:6-13
Song: "Have We Any Gift Worth Giving?"

I don't have an alabaster flask of costly fragrant oil. So although this biblical account is a beautiful story, I ask myself, "What do I have of value that I can give to God?"

The poor widow gave everything she had with an offering of two mites. She didn't have a costly possession to her name, but God was very pleased with her offering (see Luke 21:1-4).

In O. Henry's beloved short story, "The Gift of the Magi," a husband and wife sell the only worthy thing they have in order to buy each other a gift. But in the end, their sacrifice turns out to be their gift of love to each other.

In the "Little Drummer Boy," we see the best gift a poor drummer boy could give a newborn king: to play his best on his drum.

In a Christmas poem, "In the Bleak Midwinter," Christina Rossetti declares her gift in these words.

What can I give Him, poor as I am?
If I were a shepherd, I would bring a lamb;
If I were a Wise Man, I would do my part;
Yet what I can I give Him: give my heart.

Isn't that what the Lord wants from us, after all?

O God, as a sacrifice of love for You today, I give You all of me, I give You my heart. Let me be Your hands and feet of compassion today. Through Christ, amen.

DEVOTIONS®

▶ **November**

> The LORD your God is God; he is the faithful God, keeping his covenant of love to a thousand generations of those who love him and keep his commandments.
>
> *Deuteronomy 7:9*

Gary Wilde, Editor | Margaret K. Williams, Project *Editor*

Photo © iStock | Thinkstock®

DEVOTIONS® is published quarterly by Standard Publishing, Cincinnati, Ohio, www.standardpub.com. Copyright © 2016 by Standard Publishing. All rights reserved. Topics based on the Home Daily Bible Readings, International Sunday School Lessons. Copyright © 2014 by the Committee on the Uniform Series. Printed in the U.S.A. All Scripture quotations, unless otherwise indicated, are taken from the HOLY BIBLE, NEW INTERNATIONAL VERSION®. NIV®. Copyright © 1973, 1978, 1984, 2011 by Biblica, Inc.® Used by permission of Zondervan. All rights reserved worldwide. Scripture quotations marked (NKJV) are taken from the *New King James Version®*. Copyright © 1982 by Thomas Nelson, Inc. Used by permission. *Holy Bible, New Living Translation (NLT)* Copyright © 1996, 2004, 2007, 2013 by Tyndale House Foundation. Used by permission of Tyndale House Publishers Inc., Carol Stream, Illinois 60188. All rights reserved. Scripture quotations marked (KJV) are taken from the *King James Version*. Scripture quotations marked (NASB) are taken from the *New American Standard Bible®*. Copyright © 1960, 1962, 1963, 1968, 1971, 1972, 1973, 1975, 1977, 1995 by The Lockman Foundation. Used by permission. (www.Lockman.org). Scripture quotations marked (CEV) are taken from the *Contemporary English Version*. Copyright © 1991, 1992, 1995 by American Bible Society. Used by permission. All rights reserved. Scripture quotations marked (TLB) are taken from *The Living Bible* copyright © 1971. Used by permission of Tyndale House Publishers, Inc., Carol Stream, Illinois 60188. All rights reserved. Scripture quotations marked (ESV) are from ESV® Bible (The Holy Bible, *English Standard Version®*), copyright © 2001 by Crossway, a publishing ministry of Good News Publishers. Used by permission. All rights reserved.

Pray for One Another

Be kindly affectionate to one another with brotherly love, in honor giving preference to one another: . . . rejoicing in hope, patient in tribulation, continuing steadfastly in prayer (Romans 12:10, 12, *NKJV*).

Scripture: Romans 12:9-18
Song: "Sweet Hour of Prayer"

I am blessed to be part of a November gathering of women from my church. We are just a small group, and we meet once a November in one of our homes, but we come together to pray—and we're serious about it. We take praying for our church, our ministers, and our teachers and missionaries very seriously. We take praying for our country seriously. We take praying for one another seriously.

One of our ladies recently lost her husband to an 18-year battle with cancer. Another lady is getting ready to go to Haiti on a short-term mission trip, and she knows we will be back here praying for her. One lady's husband has been out of a job for several Novembers, and he is very discouraged. We trust God with every prayer request, knowing He hears each one.

Together we bear one another's burdens, and together we lift each other up in prayer. We may come with a heavy heart but we leave with a lighter heart. I count it a privilege to pray for others, and I am thankful to know that others pray for me.

Lord, thank You for Your attentiveness to our prayers. We know You hear our prayers and You are at work on our behalf. I pray this prayer in the name of Jesus. Amen.

November 1–5. **Kathy Cheek** writes devotions, inspirational stories, and poetry appearing in various publications. She and her husband live in Dallas, Texas, where two daughters also reside.

For Love's Sake

Yet for love's sake I rather appeal to you—being such a one as Paul, the aged, and now also a prisoner of Jesus Christ (Philemon 9, *NKJV*).

Scripture: Philemon 8-16
Song: "And Can It Be That I Should Gain"

When I read in Philemon how Paul pleads on behalf of Onesimus—and I read these words, "yet for love's sake I rather appeal to you"—I hear an echo of other words Paul has written in his letters.

I am reminded of his impassioned words on love in 1 Corinthians 13, for instance. In the Philemon story we witness Paul living out the message he wrote in Corinthians. I feel the impact of this in my own life when I struggle to reach someone with the message of love.

Sometimes we fail to show love or give it effectively. But I also think of the people in our lives who seem unable to receive the love we offer them. Is there a relative in the family who ridicules you when you try to talk to them about the Lord? Is there someone at work who makes fun of the Bible that pokes up from the top of your tote bag?

Many people carry deep wounds from the church or from life in general. And wounded, hurting people tend to wound others. What is needed? Continued compassion. For the sake of love, we keep trying and we keep loving the world around us, no matter the response. It is what Paul teaches us in the famous love chapter of the Bible, and it is what Christ exemplified in His life.

Lord, I ask You today to fill my heart with love for everyone who crosses my path. May I speak Your love in word and deed to those around me. In Jesus' name, amen.

Modern Day Idols

They invited the people to the sacrifices of their gods, and the people ate and bowed down to their gods. So Israel was joined to Baal of Peor, and the anger of the LORD was aroused against Israel (Numbers 25:2, 3, *NKJV*).

Scripture: Numbers 25:1-9
Song: "Be Thou Exalted"

Idol worship has always landed God's people in trouble. From the days of ancient Israel to our present culture, mankind is prone to wander from God. In place of the infinite Lord, we substitute something finite and make a god of it.

There are parts of the world where physical idols still exist. In our American culture our idols aren't usually carved from wood or other materials, but they nevertheless show what is of highest value for us. Anything that we make of ultimate concern—our unconditional value—is our god. It will drive a wedge between us and our almighty Creator.

It isn't wrong to love our families, but let us praise God as the source of all family joys. It isn't wrong to have money and wealth, but let us give as much as we can to kingdom causes. Garnering fame and status may be the natural result of excellence in any area. But let us acknowledge our gifts as coming from the Lord.

The simple fact is: God wants first place in our lives, and it starts in our hearts. When we have this priority right, it makes all the difference in our relationship with God.

Lord God Almighty, help me today to reorder any priorities that make You less supreme in my life than You deserve to be. Give me wisdom in all things! In the holy name of Jesus, my Lord and Savior, I pray. Amen.

Believe It? Respect It!

Now the sons of Eli were corrupt; they did not know the LORD. . . . Therefore the sin of the young men was very great before the LORD, for men abhorred the offering of the LORD (1 Samuel 2:12, 17, *NKJV*).

Scripture: 1 Samuel 2:12-17
Song: "Believe in the Lord Jesus Christ"

Eli's sons didn't know the Lord. They were evil and had no respect for God's laws regarding sacrifices and offerings. So they abused those laws. If you don't believe in something, then you probably won't treat it with respect.

The reverse is true, as well. For example, I love the American flag because I respect the courage and sacrifice of so many who have given their lives to keep our country free. That's why, when I see a torn and tattered flag, I wonder why the owner hasn't replaced it with a new one. Don't they care enough to honor our flag and all it represents?

When I see a news story where someone has burned a flag, I will admit that my heart churns with indignation. I can't understand their action. But I do understand that they do not respect our flag.

I find the same holds true for any symbol of God's sovereignty in our world. For instance, do we treat the Bible with respect? Do we enter places of worship with hearts bowed in adoration? Do we approach the elements of the Lord's Supper with reverence? The list could go on: if we believe in it, let us respect it.

O Father, thank You for the freedom we have in the liberation, the redemption that comes through the cross of Jesus. May America always be a people of prayer who love Your life-giving values. In Christ's name I pray. Amen.

A Life That Honors God

The Lord God of Israel says: . . . "Those who honor Me I will honor, and those who despise Me shall be lightly esteemed" (1 Samuel 2:30, *NKJV*).

Scripture: Numbers 25:10-13; 1 Samuel 2:30-36
Song: "Holy, Holy, Holy"

Ever heard someone refer to God as "the Big Guy" or "the Man Upstairs"? Not exactly terms of honor!

For our hearts to truly honor God, we must acknowledge who He is—the omnipotent Lord of the universe. With that kind of resumé, our God is clearly worthy of our deepest respect, worship, and adoration. He is holy and majestic, powerful and sovereign.

How can we honor God? We can follow His commands. We can strive to live according to the teachings of the Bible. He gave us His written Word to guide our ways so that we can live a life that honors Him, enhancing His reputation in the world.

And a God-honoring life has its rewards. Our Scripture today tells us that God will honor those who honor Him, and I want to take those words to heart each day.

The blessing can go beyond the personal and affect national life as well. John Haggai put it like this: "God is concerned with nations, but nations also need to be concerned with God. No nation can have a monopoly on God, but God will bless any nation whose people seek and honor His will as revealed by Christ and declared through the Holy Spirit."

O God, the King of glory, may I never lose sight of Your awesome holiness, Your power and glory. You dwell quietly in my heart. How great You are, and how I wish to love You with all my being! Through Christ I pray. Amen.

Why, Lord, Why?

**I have loved you with an everlasting love; I have drawn you
with unfailing kindness** (Jeremiah 31:3).

Scripture: Jeremiah 31:1-6
Song: "If Thou But Suffer God to Guide Thee"

Some days truly feel surreal. Such was the case when my daughter was diagnosed with an incurable disease. I remember trying to listen intently to the doctor's prognosis, while inside I kept asking, "Why, Lord, why?" I couldn't imagine how God could allow such frightening circumstances to invade my family. I couldn't believe we were chosen to live out this kind of future.

I didn't receive the answer to my question that particular day. Two years later, I still don't have the answer. Yet, after a short time, my questioning shifted from begging to prayer, and finally, I settled in to listening for His still, quiet voice inside this wilderness. Then He gave something more valuable than I originally asked for. I discovered our history with God.

He showed me how His love has been everlasting. I could see Him clearly at work in the hard places of the past. From that point forward, as we moved through days of difficulty or of ease, the Lord continually reminded me of where we'd been as well as where we were going together.

We often seek the source of our troubles. But could the solution lie in seeking our God and His lifelong commitment to us?

O Lord and Father, I ask that You help me know and feel this very day Your personal presence and immense love. All praise to You. Amen.

November 6–12. **Melanie Stiles,** of Spring, Texas, is a Christian life coach and author. She loves mentoring others in discipleship, writing, and playing with her granddaughter.

Many Happy Returns

I will bring them from the north and from the distant corners of the earth. I will not forget the blind and lame, the expectant mothers and women in labor. A great company will return! (Jeremiah 31:8, *NLT*).

Scripture: Jeremiah 31:7-9
Song: "Even Me"

The Bible teacher in our class asked a simple question, yet I was timid about raising my hand in response. "How many of you have family members who have turned away from God?"

I had family members in exactly that state, but I didn't want to be the only one in the room who raised a hand.

I had a quick minute to decide how honest I wanted to be with the group. Were my prodigals a statement against my own faithfulness? Before I could process my thoughts completely, hands started rising into the air.

To my surprise, most of us were in the same situation. Instead of feeling vulnerable, the admission made a way for all of us to join together in prayer for the return of God's people to His kingdom. Now, we periodically stand in a circle, holding hands, as each person vocalizes the first names of their loved ones. As a group, we lift to Heaven our intentions for them.

Our God knows His people. He hears our prayers concerning them and causes the right people to cross their paths who will draw them in. Upon their return, He will welcome them with His endless love.

Dear Father, I know that, along with us, You look forward to the homecoming celebration of any of Your children who stray from Your care. Thank You for your continual love when I fail You. Amen.

What's the Next Thing for You?

I will feast the soul of the priests with abundance, and my people shall be satisfied with my goodness, says the LORD (Jeremiah 31:14, *ESV*).

Scripture: Jeremiah 31:10-14
Song: "I Am Satisfied with Jesus"

We live in a world where the next best thing is always just around the corner. If you were born to the group now referred to as the "Baby Boomers," you've seen everything from televisions to credit cards to wet suits to buffalo wings come along. The creative invention possibilities, in our culture today, seem to be endless.

Conversely—even though our homes are constantly being filled and refilled with gadgets of one sort or another—we still struggle with living in personal peace. Somehow, we haven't managed to find it in our new cell phone or hi-def television setup. Our quest to find what really matters never seems to end in a soul-deep satisfaction.

While we continue to change our focus and adjust our goal-seeking, our God hasn't changed at all. He "is the same yesterday and today and forever" (Hebrews 13:8, *ESV*). We can only find peace within a sincere relationship with Him. We can't drive through and pick up time to spend with Him; instead, we're invited to carve out a quiet space for Him in our busy lives. We can't buy an app and expect Him to respond; we'll need to pray. His abundance will always supersede any next best thing we can create or buy.

Dear Father, You've reminded me today that all I need to live a life of contentment and joy is to walk with You. Thank You for the invitation to know You in close personal fellowship. Through Christ my Lord, amen.

With Grace, Unity

"There is hope for your future," declares the LORD, **"and your children will return to their own territory"** (Jeremiah 31:17, *NASB*).

Scripture: Jeremiah 31:15-20
Song: "My Hope Is in the Lord"

For the first time in their adult lives, my two daughters agreed to an all-girl trip. I felt as though their consent was an answer to prayer, as the communication between us had dwindled to a bare minimum over the years.

Each of us led very different and distinct lives, so I asked God to open avenues of commonality among us. It didn't take long before our differences started surfacing: While one or two liked a certain activity, the other didn't . . . and on it went. Everyone voiced an opinion, from politics to parenting. For a day or two, I feared we were going to experience a very negative family vacation.

Slowly, but surely, God's grace bubbled to the surface. As we waited on one person to shop in the homemade soap store, the other two talked and waited patiently. If two agreed to dine, the other would come on board in unison. By the end of the trip, we were functioning in cohesion, giving and taking as each situation arose, with no one leading the pack.

I witnessed the uniqueness of God's kingdom through my girls. Their strengths varied, yet they could lay those down for the sake of another they loved. I came to respect them greatly as children of the heavenly Father with purposes of their own.

Thank You, **Dear Father,** for the challenges of family living—which can give rise to very special workings of Your grace. Through Christ I pray. Amen.

Stow the Phone

I will betroth you to me in faithfulness and love, and you will really know me then as you never have before (Hosea 2:20, *TLB*).

Scripture: Hosea 2:16-20
Song: "Blessed Quietness"

As I walked into my ministry leader's office one Sunday afternoon, she surprised me by saying, "I so envy you and your stay-cations!"

I had to smile. A few years ago, I realized that the hustle and bustle of my world pulled more from me than it gave back on most days. At the end of perpetually encroaching deadlines and responsibilities, I found myself out of energy and, even more important, out of compassion for others. That's when I decided to regularly schedule spiritual stay-cations. My goal was to seek God and replenish myself back to the human being He intended me to be.

Since then, I've learned how to stow the phone and turn off the television. I've walked labyrinths while reading the Psalms. I've danced all over the house to worship music. I've plopped myself on the patio, coffee in hand, and watched the birds, lizards, the sunrises and sunsets.

These quiet times, with no expectations either from or for me, have served to still my spirit. They have opened up my heart to receive what God has planned for my life. Mostly, they have enabled me to continue to be a kind servant to others around me.

Dear Heavenly Father, when my days become too hectic, call me to a peaceful place. I am so thankful that You speak in the stillness. Open my heart to hear! I pray in Jesus' name. Amen.

Take It Personally

Likewise also the cup after supper, saying, This cup is the new testament in my blood, which is shed for you (Luke 22:20, *KJV*).

Scripture: Luke 22:14-20
Song: "Nothing but the Blood"

The main message of the media today seems to be: *Your life should be easy!* And people in our American culture seem to have a great deal of trouble distinguishing between actual needs and particular wants.

Yet, for some of God's children, that is not the case. Christians are persecuted severely for their faith all over the world these days. The battles rage on for Jesus—even if in distant lands.

We prefer to avoid the word *sacrifice*. Yet it is the essence of our new life as Christians. Had Jesus not shed His blood for us and sacrificed His very life, we would still linger in death's power.

Just because it may be easy for us wherever we are, that does not mean we aren't meant to participate in the ongoing faith challenges of other peoples. For the sake of Jesus, the sacrifices continue, and those who suffer are part of our body of Christ.

As believers in a land where faith has its freedom, we can still contribute by sacrificing our time in volunteer efforts. Or we may send our money as we feel led. In any event, let us pray for those who struggle to be able to drink the cup as openly as we do.

Father, Your Son sealed the testament—Your covenant with us of promised forgiveness—by offering His blood on the cross. In the Lord's Supper I am honored to acknowledge Your sacrifice . . . and take it personally. Praise to You, in His name. Amen.

Ready to Forgive?

No longer will they have to teach one another to obey me. I, the LORD, promise that all of them will obey me, ordinary people and rulers alike. I will forgive their sins and forget the evil things they have done (Jeremiah 31:34, *CEV*).

Scripture: Jeremiah 31:27-34
Song: "Laden with Guilt, and Full of Fears"

We all seem to carry some kind of past emotional baggage. In my case, it was a childhood of abuse, which led to all kinds of teenage rebellion. Although I am quite adult today, there have been times when guilt about my past behavior has cropped up to cripple me.

The idea of *doing* better when you *know* better gets totally ignored on a guilt trip. The voice inside my head wants to reassure me I am an overall lousy individual—all for some act long ago committed.

The Lord never intended that I relive my transgressions. After all, He receives my confessions of sin and then forgets they ever happened. Will I accept that it can be that simple?

Through prayer, I was able to recognize the core of the problem: It seems I was willing to allow God to forgive me, but unwilling to do the work of forgiving myself.

I thank God for helping me see the difference between real guilt and feelings of false guilt. The one has forgiveness; the other needs it.

Father of all compassion, You have reminded me that my forgiveness is free but came at great cost to You at the cross. Thanks for Your mercy and grace. Now help me let go of lingering false guilt. I pray in Jesus' name, amen.

Awesome—or Not?

How awesome are your deeds! So great is your power that your enemies cringe before you (Psalm 66:3).

Scripture: Psalm 66:1-4
Song: "Awesome God"

Awesome is an overused word in our culture today. Just the other day I saw a YouTube video of two women fighting at a Walmart, and the guy recording the video took a moment to declare the whole episode as awesome. We've got awesome food, awesome performances, awesome cars, and awesome people. You name it—we've got an awesome version.

Trouble is, much that we call awesome simply isn't. Is the spectacle of two women swearing at each other and launching haymakers in the store aisles really awesome? How about last night's pizza or the fact that your favorite team won the game? I'd submit to you that none of these qualifies as awesome. *Awesome* is beyond all of that.

God is awesome. Parting the Red Sea is awesome. Raising a man from the dead is awesome. Restoring someone's sight is awesome. An ax head that floats is awesome. When used in that context, the word makes a lot more sense. It fits. After all, who can look on God's body of work and not be filled with awe?

It's an adjective of a higher order. God's deeds are a cut above. Other things might be cool or good or entertaining.

But God? *Awesome!*

Lord God of All, I stand in awe of You today. Thank You for all Your wonderful deeds that flow from Your matchless character. In Jesus' name, amen.

November 13–19. **Von Mitchell** teaches business and coaches basketball at his alma mater in Delta, Colorado.

Help Needed!

Blessed are the pure in heart, for they will see God (Matthew 5:8).

Scripture: Matthew 5:1-12
Song: "O to Be Like Thee"

I've been spending a lot of time in nursing homes lately. With all due respect to the patrons, some of them are seriously grumpy. In all fairness, I don't know all of their stories. Maybe some of the folks have a reason for tormenting the night help. Possibly they are justified in complaining nonstop.

Whatever the case, they are motivating me like crazy. I've determined that if God wills it for me to live to a ripe old age, I want to be one of the sweetest of senior citizens.

I see plenty of challenges ahead, though. I'm already less than patient. I'm often critical. I'm getting terribly set in my ways. But I'm declaring right now that I'm willing to put it all down. I want to be like Jesus.

I'm so glad He gave us the red-lettered instructions, aren't you? The Beatitudes provide the blueprint for us to have a beautiful attitude. We can cultivate a humble demeanor. We can hunger and thirst for righteousness. We can extend mercy and strive for peace.

We can do it all by the grace of God through Christ who gives us strength (see Philippians 4:13). And I don't know about you, but I'm going to need the help.

Dear Lord God, I seek to be pure in heart today. Yet I realize that only through Your inner influence can I do so. Help me to walk close to You. Then Your character qualities have a chance to become my own. Thank You for this blessed potential for growth. In the name of Jesus, amen.

At the Altar of Opinion

Be careful not to forget the covenant of the LORD your God that he made with you; do not make for yourselves an idol in the form of anything (Deuteronomy 4:23).

Scripture: Deuteronomy 4:21-24
Song: "Come, Let Us Worship and Bow Down"

When people think of idolatry, they may recall the golden calf of Moses' day or think of a statue to which other peoples have bowed down and paid homage. In our society we may think of money or a new car, or a weekend hobby or work, and of how it takes the place of God Almighty on the altar of our lives.

But what if your opinion were to become an idol?

Let me explain. The Bible abounds with good news about how we are made—"fearfully and wonderfully"(Psalm 139:14) as you may recall. Yet many of us don't really believe that. We speak poorly of ourselves and harbor low thoughts about our makeup. In other words, we let our opinion trump God's Word.

Here's another one: we look at some situation and deem it impossible. In our opinion: case closed. We've rendered a judgment. But God's Word says, "I can do all this through him who gives me strength" (Philippians 4:13). "For with God nothing shall be impossible" (Luke 1:37, *KJV*).

The Bible says not to make an idol for ourselves, but we do when we place more weight on what we think than on what God thinks. Our opinions are never facts until they line up with God's truth.

Lord, I pray that Your truth would reign supreme in me. Please help me to line up my thinking with Your Word. When I am in doubt, give me pause to consult Your indwelling Spirit. In Jesus' name I pray. Amen.

The Power of a Testimony

Come and hear, all you who fear God; let me tell you what he has done for me (Psalm 66:16).

Scripture: Psalm 66:16-20
Song: "Miracle of Grace"

My wife was "Facebooking" the other day when she came upon an incredible post. It all happened in a Sam's Club. An elderly gentleman cried out for help in the store as his wife slumped over—the victim of a diabetic seizure. She was dying. But another woman and her sister saw the commotion and went to pray for the lady. They prayed that she would live and not die, in Jesus' name, and the woman literally came back from the brink of death.

One of the sisters immediately went to her car and recorded a transcript of the event and posted it to social media. Still bubbling with energy, she made it readily clear that God did something amazing in her life as well. She humbly and sincerely witnessed the power of God. The power of her testimony now serves as a witness to others who view the video.

I'm convinced that hearing about what God has done for others bolsters our faith. Do you agree? How many times has it been the case for you?

If you're the kind of person who struggles to speak about your faith, you can start where you are by describing what God has done for you. May your story then serve as a witness to the great goodness of your Lord.

Dear Heavenly Father, thank You for all You've done in my life. May the story of what You've done for me encourage others. Simply give me the courage to share it. I pray in the name of Jesus. Amen.

The Right Thing

This is the covenant I will make with them after that time, says the Lord. I will put my laws in their hearts, and I will write them on their minds (Hebrews 10:16).

Scripture: Hebrews 10:11-18
Song: "O Love That Will Not Let Me Go"

It's been said that character is doing the right thing, even when no one is watching. But isn't it just living up to the code of right and wrong that the Creator has put into every one of us?

Rick Reilly, the great sportswriter, tells the story of four college football players who went into a store after-hours thinking it was open. They picked up a video cord and some batteries in the store—which had been left open by mistake—and waited at the counter to pay someone. When no one appeared, the players took out some money and waved it at a surveillance camera before placing it on the counter. One of the young men even took $.80 out of his pocket to pay the sales tax.

We live in a day when athletes are reported in the news for everything . . . except for doing the right thing. Domestic abuse. Blood-doping. You name it, it's been on the front page. How refreshing to read about young people making headlines for a different reason!

We all know right from wrong, due to natural law. It's the moral "ought" written within the human spirit, so that we are without excuse (see Romans 1:20). Let's all show character today by doing the right thing.

Dear Lord, please help me always live up to Your code of right and wrong. I know what's right, but please give me the power to do it. In the name of the Father and of the Son and of the Holy Spirit, I pray. Amen.

Once for All

He did not enter by means of the blood of goats and calves; but he entered the Most Holy Place once for all by his own blood, thus obtaining eternal redemption (Hebrews 9:12).

Scripture: Hebrews 9:11-15
Song: "Jesus Paid It All"

My wife and I recently enjoyed some vacation time up around the Grand Tetons and Yellowstone National Park in Wyoming. On our first day of exploring, we turned left off the main tourist artery to avoid a stretch of road construction. That took us straight to one of those ranger gate/toll booth–type bottlenecks where you quickly realize once again: the best things in life might be free, but this particular experience isn't going to be.

As I reached for my wallet to pay for entrance into the Grand Tetons, the thought occurred to me that I'd probably have to pay a similar fee the next day for the privilege of touring Yellowstone Park.

Long story short, I got a special discount for entrance into both parks for seven days. That made me happy. I paid one time, and from then on, all I had to do was show the receipt.

I hope you see the analogy I'm trying to draw here. Jesus, by His own sacrifice, paid for our entrance into grace . . . one time. He did it for us all. That's "*once* for all." All we have to do is trust Him. He paid the price.

That, my friends, is the greatest receipt of all time.

O Gracious God, thank You for coming to earth in the person of Your Son, Jesus. Thank You for the sacrifice of the eternal, spotless lamb on my behalf. Praise You that His work of atonement, offered once for all, lasts for all eternity. Help me, as I seek to give my life to Him in return. Through His precious name I pray. Amen.

Peace . . . Possible?

Make every effort to live in peace with everyone and to be holy; without holiness no one will see the Lord (Hebrews 12:14).

Scripture: Hebrews 12:14, 15, 18-29
Song: "Holiness"

We have so much hatred in the world today. Just days ago (as I write this) a gunman went into a South Carolina church and killed nine people. Apparently the crime was racially motivated, white on black. It's absolutely tragic. But the people of that congregation are moving forward. I've read accounts of them encouraging each other to love and forgive. It gives me hope.

And isn't that what we all need? We need hope that things can be different—that race relations, for instance, can be based on love and respect, kindness and understanding, and hopefully, trust. Trouble is, once that trust is broken—and it just keeps getting broken—our Christian walk is challenged. Will we love instead of hate?

I mean, could you blame members of that church for hating the gunman? They lost loved ones. But if they retaliate, the cycle continues. White on black. Black on white. No one will have peace.

Add any other race that you want to the mix. Only love wins.

I admire and applaud anyone who encounters hatred yet chooses to love in return. They are the ones who demonstrate what it means to "make every effort to live in peace with everyone."

Lord, how my heart longs for peace among all peoples! I pray for victims of hatred-inspired crimes and pray that we'd all demonstrate more of Your loving ways. In Jesus' wonderful name I pray. Amen.

Favored by Association

He has rescued us from the dominion of darkness and brought us into the kingdom of the Son (Colossians 1:13).

Scripture: Colossians 1:9-20
Song: "Lord, Thou Art with Me"

When I was 9-years-old, my family moved from Florida to California. I was the only new kid in my fourth-grade classroom, so getting to know Catherine significantly changed my lonely world. Our teacher seemed old and tired to me, but Catherine claimed that Mrs. B. would let us put on a play for extra credit. Without Catherine, I never would have asked for special favors. But because she was so obviously liked by all, I agreed.

With Catherine leading the way, we boldly approached Mrs. B's desk to present our proposal. Yes! The office staff let us copy programs on the mimeograph machine; we were welcomed into the classroom during recesses to practice; and we received keys to the supply closet for prop-making materials. Catherine and I organized and performed two puppet shows, a play, and a musical review that year.

With Catherine's friendship opening doors, the intimidating school became a secure haven for me. As a Christian, I now have someone even more beloved and influential in my life. Jesus Christ is His Father's beloved Son, and when I tag along with Him, I am free to walk as a favored child allowed to explore the kingdom. I am Jesus' friend. I am favored by association.

Thank You, Jesus, for reconciling me to God the Father and making me a welcome, favored child of Your kingdom. In Your name I pray. Amen.

November 20–26. **Tanya T. Warrington** is a freelance writer residing in Fort Collins, Colorado. She enjoys writing about God—the healing and freedom of walking in His love daily.

Our Blemished Record

In the following directives I have no praise for you, for your meetings do more harm than good (1 Corinthians 11:17).

Scripture: 1 Corinthians 11:17-22
Song: "I Am a Vessel"

My neighbor and I were walking when she asked, "How can you go to church with those hypocrites?" How to help her accept that both lambs and wolves attend churches, and even the sheep go astray?

I prayed for wisdom and gently waded into the river of anger and fear that I heard in her voice. "When I was younger, I was disillusioned about all the hypocrites in church," I told her. "I learned through painful experience that I was no different. I want to be like Christ in all things, but I don't succeed—I let fear gag me, I rationalize my poor behavior, I have good intentions that never materialize into action."

I felt sadness as I confessed how imperfect I am and how I fail to live up to my own standards. And then, I remembered Christ's redeeming work. I heard the gratitude in my voice as I described how unfailing God's love is, even when we fail; how He forgives us and still utilizes our willingness to serve Him. Yet I was unsure of how my friend received my words.

Later she shared with me that she had begun trusting Christ as her Savior. She said our talks had helped open her heart. How amazing that our perfect God uses such imperfect believers in the process of bringing lost sheep into the fold!

Heavenly Father, thank You for correcting me and forgiving me when I go astray. I am amazed You are able to use sinful people such as me to tell others about You. Through Christ my Lord, amen.

Be Merciful

Be merciful to those who doubt; save others by snatching them from the fire; to others show mercy (Jude 22, 23).

Scripture: Jude 1-4, 17-25
Song: "God, We Praise Thee for Thy Mercy"

One of our children was having a tough time accepting a big change, and her behavior showed it. At the end of one particularly difficult week, I suggested that we "get the situation under control." I was ready for action—ready to improve life for the rest of the family. My husband listened to me and then announced, "I'm going to take her out for ice cream."

I was shocked. I was ready for a battle plan; he was ready to extend mercy. I felt suspicious that his way wouldn't help. Nevertheless, he followed through on his idea and her behavior improved. She felt understood and loved. Mercy triumphed.

In the years since, I've seen other teenage hearts soften when I've listened to their angst—without trying to fix them or their problems. I've seen my own attitude improve also when another has refused to judge me for a mistake. In fact, I've often found that listening with patience is more helpful than defensively protecting God's reputation.

Even when someone is on a destructive path and I attempt intervention, I've still found that words of mercy and acts of service are the best course (along with remembering my own shortcomings). Grace extended helps the drowning person receive God's forgiveness and saving help.

O God of Grace and Mercy, please prompt my heart to be merciful as You have been to me. Help me to see people with Your eyes and respond to them with Your compassion. Amen.

Just As Advertised

The disciples left, went into the city and found things just as Jesus had told them (Mark 14:16).

Scripture: Mark 14:12-16
Song: "I Believe the Promises of God"

Libraries were among my most favorite places as a child. I loved reading, adored the smell of books, and luxuriated in the quietness. I delighted in reading titles and selecting a book. I liked opening file drawers and flipping through alphabetized cards, searching for new treasures.

When I'd read everything written by a specific author, I found the librarian to be an invaluable resource for guiding my next selections. Often she knew other authors I would likely enjoy, based upon whom I already liked. Invariably I'd find her whispered book recommendations to be just as wonderful as promised.

In so many other situations in my young life, however, asking questions and getting answers wasn't as rewarding for me. For example, when I asked about dinner I was fooled more than once by a name—I thought shepherd's pie would be sweet and fruit-filled, and I expected I'd like something called brussels sprout. But at libraries, books were just as good as librarians said they were.

When God's Word tells us how things are—or will be—we can trust Him. God's knowledge far exceeds even the best librarian's. He knows what was, what is, and what will be.

Dear Heavenly Father, You know me, inside and out—what I need, what I'll ask, and what is best. And with You, things are always just as You promise. I rejoice in Your unchanging goodness, and I thank You for guiding my steps today. I pray in the name of Jesus my Lord. Amen.

Forever Covenant

"This is my blood of the covenant, which is poured out for many," he said to them (Mark 14:24).

Scripture: Mark 14:22-25
Song: "There Is Power in the Blood"

Mary and I were 7-years-old when we decided to become blood sisters. She suggested it. I was the oldest kid in my family and had never heard of such a thing, but she was the youngest of five siblings and had lived in a foreign country. I'd only lived in the United States.

I had only a vague understanding of why the blood was necessary, but I liked Mary and was amazed by her superior knowledge of the world. So we met in her father's shed to become extra special friends forever. Sitting there in the dirt next to the lawn mower, we pricked our fingers with a needle and made our vow, rubbing our spots of blood together. We then made up a secret handshake to make things extra official.

Her family moved a few years later, and I never heard from her again. I don't know if she remembers me or the solemn pledge we took. Our *forever* as blood sisters was rather short-lived!

The blood Jesus shed for the forgiveness of all people, however, is truly forever. He knew exactly what He was doing and for whom. That sacrifice was sufficient for all and effective for those who simply receive its benefit. We can count on it now and for all eternity.

Lord Jesus, I am so grateful for Your willingness to spill Your very blood in order to fulfill the Father's plan for a new covenant of mercy with humankind. I am awestruck by Your love and faithfulness. In Your name, amen.

Under Construction

Do not conform to the pattern of this world, but be transformed by the renewing of your mind. Then you will be able to test and approve what God's will is (Romans 12:2).

Scripture: Romans 12:1-8
Song: "Glory Be to God the Father"

Recently, my husband and I purchased an old, neglected house. Everywhere we looked there was an urgent project begging to be done, so we hired some workers to help with the initial push. I learned quickly that there are many construction decisions to make each day as new situations arise.

One of the early, intimidating decisions we faced: What to do with a distressed ceiling? In a burst of uncharacteristic confidence, I instructed the workmen to pull it down; I was hoping to find some good beams underneath that we could stain to complement exposed wood beams in other rooms.

The workmen took a small section down and looked at me dubiously. "Are you sure?" they asked. "Yes," I answered. "Do it. If we don't find what I'm looking for, we can always put up new dry wall and finish it."

When they removed the ceiling, it exposed the good beams and two lovely triangle windows that had been hidden by former owners' remodeling. They were cheap panes but the structure was there.

Work? Yes. Messy? Yes. Beautiful, once the beams and windows were renewed and transformed? Yes!

Dear God, You are renewing my mind with Your Word and Your Spirit, transforming me over time. May I cooperate humbly with Your efforts. Help me remember that even when I feel like I'm a big mess, You see my potential. In Jesus' name, amen.

For Our Own Best Good

Nevertheless, when we are judged in this way by the Lord, we are being disciplined so that we will not be finally condemned with the world (1 Corinthians 11:32).

Scripture: 1 Corinthians 11:23-34
Song: "Teach Me Thy Way, O Lord"

Sitting on our porch, my husband and I laughed over memories of our children's reactions to chores. Those kids are now hardworking adults, but we wondered if they would ever accept correction and learn to work well. Over a decade ago, one of the girls said we "liked bossing kids." She wanted to play and saw no value in work.

She was convinced we made her labor for our personal enjoyment, but in reality, we would've rather done it ourselves. It's a hassle motivating a resistant child and waiting for a job to be finished at a snail's pace.

Another daughter decided she was Cinderella because she had to dust a stairway railing. One of our sons decided that moving some rocks constituted slavery. At the time it was discouraging. We knew that if our children didn't learn, though, they'd suffer in the future. If they remained immature, they were the ones who would be fired, would suffer for lack of funds, or would feel dissatisfied, no matter how fair their employer.

I wonder how many times I've resented the Lord's correction due to my immaturity? How many times has He saved me from serious consequences through careful parenting of my soul?

Lord, I am shortsighted sometimes when You prune away pieces of my sinful nature. Like a child, I can be sure my goals are right and fail to see the big picture. Please continue to teach me and discipline me, through Christ. Amen.

He Won't Let You Down

It is better to take refuge in the Lord than to trust in humans (Psalm 118:8).

Scripture: Psalm 118:1-9
Song: "'Tis So Sweet to Trust in Jesus"

My eyes welled up with tears as my best friend's harsh words echoed in my ears. *How could she talk behind my back like that?* I wondered.

I was hurt, confused, and feeling betrayed by one of the closest people in my life. So I prayed for guidance about how to move forward and heal the deep wounds of deceit and betrayal.

I am reminded of a crucial biblical principle: no matter how much we trust in people, they will fail us. After all, none of us is perfect; we are human. And no matter how good our intentions, it's inevitable we will fail at some point to carry through on our good intent. And when we fail, others can get hurt.

We have faith that the Lord will never fail us. We put all our trust in Him, having complete confidence He will never let us down. We turn to Him with all of our problems, knowing He will provide us with safety and protection. His love is enduring, persistent, and forever.

Even though it's difficult to suffer life's hardships and betrayals along our journey, peace can be found when we put our faith and hope in God. He remains constant and true, even when our world is not. Put your trust in the only one who endures forever.

Lord, thanks for being the one who remains good and true always. Lead me to trust in You completely, healing my hurts from those who have failed me. In Christ, amen.

November 27–30. **Alisha Ritchie** writes from Stanfield, North Carolina, where she enjoys spending time with her husband of almost 20 years and with her two wonderful children.

Failing to Fall

I was pushed back and about to fall, but the LORD helped me (Psalm 118:13).

Scripture: Psalm 118:10-14
Song: "Children of the Lord"

As a physical therapy assistant, I work with patients who sustain falls because of difficulties with balance. One patient recently told of her latest fall which caused a trip to the hospital and a very sore knee.

"I was walking into the bathroom when my knees felt weak. I lost my balance and just kept falling backwards, like I was being pushed. I tried to grab hold of the counter to catch myself, but at that point, there was nothing I could do to stop myself from falling," she said.

Ever felt like that—as if you were being pushed back? There are days when nothing seems to go right, as if we just can't make any progress toward our goals. Or one door after another closes, barring access to the cherished places we long for.

Our key verse reminds us, however, that God is always there to help us. The key is to admit our need. I like how Christian psychiatrist David F. Allen says it: "We don't want to feel helpless, so we use fear, anger, addiction, or unbridled sexuality to block out our helpless feelings. The fact is that if we cannot openly face our feeling of helplessness, we cannot receive help. It is important that we accept our helplessness, taking it to God and allowing Him to be strong where we are weak."

Lord, thank You for loving me and being my stability when it seems the world is against me. Guide me in trusting You as You provide support, never letting me fall from Your grasp. In Jesus' name, amen.

Prophets Still at Work

When God raised up his servant, he sent him first to you to bless you by turning each of you from your wicked ways (Acts 3:26).

Scripture: Acts 3:22-26
Song: "Be Love in Me"

The ancient biblical prophets were God's messengers to His people. Often their proclamations focused on turning people away from their sin so they could turn back to God.

In some ways, Christian friends can be like those prophets. For instance, I have a friend who leads by example. She doesn't use words to lecture me, but she is certainly prophetic in demonstrating by her actions what the Lord wants to see in my own life. In fact, she proclaims the goodness of God's will to all who observe her.

In light of her example, my heart is convicted when I lose patience with my children after a long day. Other times, I realize I've harbored a poor attitude in certain situations after talking with her about those times. My friend has a positive influence on me, often causing me to have a change of heart, just as the prophets affected the Israelites.

Who has God placed in your life, that special someone who helps guide you in the right direction? Thank God for that person and their ministry of servanthood toward you. Then resolve to be a positive influence on others for God's kingdom.

Heavenly Father, thank You for loving me enough to send people into my life who help me in my walk with You. Guide me in making good choices for friends and mentors. Help me to be a positive Christian influence on others for Your glory. Through Christ I pray. Amen.

Faithful GPS

Those who sat at the table with Him began to say to themselves, "Who is this who even forgives sins?" Then He said to the woman, "Your faith has saved you. Go in peace" (Luke 7:49, 50, *NKJV*).

Scripture: Luke 7:44-50
Song: "Day by Day"

Recently, my mom and I went on a day-trip to a place we had never been before. I relied on my trusted GPS to help us navigate to our destination. Mom, not having any experience with GPS, was totally amazed at how the little device guided us. When we finally arrived, she exclaimed, "You had faith that this machine would get us here, and it did. That is so amazing!"

Faith is wonderful, especially when it resides in Jesus. Trusting in God, even though we do not see or realize His full plan, helps our faith grow and mature.

The sinful woman in today's Scripture trusted Jesus enough to know she just wanted to be in His presence. She longed to show her love by serving Him, even though she was a sinner and, no doubt, felt unworthy. Yet she must have believed that Jesus loved her despite her shortcomings.

Jesus yearns for us to place all of our trust in Him so He can guide us on our journey of life. So it's crucial for us to ask ourselves, continuously: What or who am I placing my faith in today? My own goal is to make a commitment to trust God with all of my heart, releasing total control to Him.

Lord, thank You for loving me, even though I am a sinner and have failed You. Help me to have complete confidence in Your plan for my life. In Jesus' name. Amen.

My Prayer Notes

DEVOTIONS®

▶ **December**

For the LORD is good and his love endures forever; his
faithfulness continues through all generations.

Psalm 100:5

Gary Wilde, Editor | Margaret K. Williams, Project Editor | Photo © iStock | Thinkstock®

DEVOTIONS® is published quarterly by Standard Publishing, Colorado Springs, Colorado,
www.standardpub.com. Copyright © 2016 by Standard Publishing, part of the David C Cook fam-
ily, Colorado Springs, Colorado. All rights reserved. Topics based on the Home Daily Bible Readings,
International Sunday School Lessons. Copyright © 2014 by the Committee on the Uniform Series.
Printed in the U.S.A. All Scripture quotations, unless otherwise indicated, are taken from the *HOLY
BIBLE, NEW INTERNATIONAL VERSION®. NIV®.* Copyright © 1973, 1978, 1984, 2011 by Biblica,
Inc.® Used by permission of Zondervan. All rights reserved worldwide. Scripture quotations marked
(*NASB*) are taken from the *New American Standard Bible®.* Copyright © 1960, 1962, 1963, 1968, 1971,
1972, 1973, 1975, 1977, 1995 by The Lockman Foundation. Used by permission. (www.Lockman.org).
All rights reserved. *Holy Bible, New Living Translation (NLT)* Copyright © 1996, 2004, 2007, 2013 by Tyndale
House Foundation. Used by permission of Tyndale House Publishers Inc., Carol Stream, Illinois 60188. All
rights reserved. *Holman Christian Standard Bible (HCSB).* Copyright 1999, 2000, 2002, 2003, 2009 by Holman Bible Publishers, Nashville, Tennessee. All rights reserved.

You're Invited

I have made you a light for the Gentiles, that you may bring salvation to the ends of the earth (Acts 13:47).

Scripture: Acts 13:44-49
Song: "Come and Dine"

"Why are we eating off the fancy plates?" my 12-year-old daughter asked. She glanced at our table as the beautiful porcelain plates sparked her interest. A glass vase filled with daffodils made the perfect centerpiece—stark contrast to our normal routine of eating on paper plates! "We're having special guests for dinner, and I wanted to use our fine china," I replied.

"Well these must be some pretty special guests. Do I have to dress up? I don't want to wear anything fancy," my daughter continued. She assumed she too must do something special to prepare for dinner with our friends. But really, all she needed to do was come as she was.

Similarly, God invites everyone, not just His chosen people, to dine at the table of grace. He extends His gift of salvation to each of us who will receive it. We're assured there's always an available place at His table—no matter what we're wearing, where we're from, or how many scars have marked our hearts. Come dine at the table of grace with your heavenly Father. There is a place set especially for you.

Lord God of all, thank You for offering Your gift of life-saving grace. I come to Your table just as I am, only needing to accept Your invitation. Guide me to make decisions today that bring me closer to You. I pray this prayer in the name of Jesus. Amen.

December 1–3. **Alisha Ritchie** writes from Stanfield, North Carolina, where she enjoys spending time with her husband of 20 years and with her two wonderful children.

Flash

Taking him by the right hand, he helped him up, and instantly the man's feet and ankles became strong (Acts 3:7).

Scripture: Acts 3:1-10
Song: "Christ, the Great Physician"

I looked at my husband's right temple in horror. The incision was much bigger than either of us had expected. I was thankful the surgeon was able to remove all the skin cancer, but I knew he hated that huge gash near his eyebrow.

What's more, the repair work done to his skin left him with a zigzagged wound that closely resembled a lightning bolt. Thus, my kids and I affectionately nicknamed him "Flash"—which, surprisingly, he took a liking to.

The healing process took longer than anticipated. Secretly, I wished I could magically heal the wound on my husband's face, saving him all the pain. I wanted to take the mark from him, making it better quickly.

Even though I couldn't heal his wound, there is a great physician who heals all wounds. Today's Scripture assures us that God cares deeply about His children, so much so that He tends to our hurts with love, patience, and compassion.

Our wounds come in many different forms. Sometimes we break a bone; at other times we're nursing a broken heart. What is it for you? Your place of brokenness is prime territory for the Lord's healing powers.

Lord, You bring healing to my hurts and sustain me in my difficulties. Thank You. Today I place all of my wounds in Your care. Saturate my injuries with Your Words, and increase my faith as You give the care I need. Help me extend Your care to others. Amen.

Etch-A-Sketch Heart

Repent, then, and turn to God, so that your sins may be wiped out, that times of refreshing may come from the Lord (Acts 3:19).

Scripture: Acts 3:11-21
Song: "Is Thy Heart Right with God?"

The cutest brown-eyed girl in the world beckons me to play with her. She picks up her Etch-A-Sketch toy as we sit together on the fluffy rug on her floor. She makes swirls and patterns, deftly turning the knobs, and then forms a heart over the patterns. As quickly as she draws it—shake, shake, shake, and it's gone.

"Why did you erase it?" I asked.

"It looked messy, so I want to make a new one," she replied.

I realize I feel that way about my own heart at times. I try doing the "right" things by going to church and reading the Bible. I pursue bringing my children up with good values and treating people nicely. But somehow, my heart continues to get messy; I make mistakes, give in to moodiness, and harbor resentment.

Sin invades my heart because I'm human—there's absolutely no way to be perfect. But there's one, my Savior, who makes me new. Yes, my heart's purified through the sacrifice of Jesus on the cross. No matter how dirty and ugly my life may become, Jesus' blood is the cleansing stream that makes it pure. I love how the apostle John put it: "If we confess our sins, he is faithful and just and will forgive us our sins and purify us from all unrighteousness" (1 John 1:9).

Lord, thank You for the atoning work of Your Son on the cross. Thank You for the gift of salvation and forgiveness. Cleanse my heart and make it pure in Your sight. Help me to live in a way that brings honor and glory to You. In Jesus' name, amen.

Giving Ministry Away

The LORD said to Moses, "Now the day of your death is near. Call Joshua and present yourselves at the tent of meeting, where I will commission him." So Moses and Joshua came and presented themselves (Deuteronomy 31:14).

Scripture: Deuteronomy 31:14, 15, 23; 34:9
Song: "Giving It All Away"

I serve as a team leader at our congregation's information center. Because our church is portable, meeting in a school building, much preparation is required on Sunday mornings. Arriving early and setting up is the responsibility of the team leader and frankly on some Sundays, I find it difficult to get out of bed.

It was such a pleasant surprise to get a message one Friday from a team member, Liz. A friend of hers had requested that, in lieu of birthday gifts, random acts of kindness be offered to others. Liz let me know that she was able to show up early on Sunday and would handle setting up for me. I was thrilled and welcomed the extra sleep.

Liz did a great job, and I had enjoyed the break. It started me thinking. Liz has been a faithful team member, and perhaps it was time to give away the ministry of team leadership. Liz was eager to take on more responsibility while I moved on to other ministry areas. Had I been too caught up in wanting to preserve a title—or afraid that things wouldn't be done just right? Liz and I both would have missed out on great opportunities.

Lord, help me to be willing to give ministry away, releasing any feeling of control or selfishness. Your work is not about me, but You. In Jesus' name, amen.

December 4–10. **Carla Edmisten** is a social worker and freelance writer living in Spotsylania, Virginia. She enjoys collecting antiques and traveling with her family.

Have I Missed a Blessing?

Eli told Samuel, "Go and lie down, and if he calls you, say, 'Speak, LORD, for your servant is listening.'" So Samuel went and lay down in his place (1 Samuel 3:9).

Scripture: 1 Samuel 3:1-9
Song: "God Calling Yet"

When my children were young, my husband, Jeff, and I had a few disagreements on the topic of children and obedience. I credited his zero tolerance for disobedience to his former military days. He would patiently remind me that if one of our children were in a dangerous situation, disobedience could be a matter of life and death.

One afternoon Jeff was doing yard work, as our then 3-year-old daughter happily played on the front porch. Taking a break, Jeff looked up to the porch and calmly said, "Shelby, stand up and slowly come to me, right now."

She didn't question the command; down the steps she went. Her father sat her safely away and killed the copperhead snake that had wound its way to the rocker where Shelby had been sitting. What could have happened had she argued—had she merely lifted her hands in exasperation—was unthinkable.

Although Samuel didn't know at the time that God was calling him, he still answered without argument. Time after time, he practiced obedience. It makes me wonder. What blessings have I missed because I questioned, procrastinated, or threw up my hands in exasperation?

Lord, I know that Your call for obedience is for my good. Help me to obey Your call. I want to respond to You without question, always. Help me to put away my doubt and my fear at each step. In Christ I pray. Amen.

The Unseen Battle

You, dear children, are from God and have overcome [un-godly spirits], because the one who is in you is greater than the one who is in the world (1 John 4:4).

Scripture: 1 John 4:1-6
Song: "In Christ Alone"

Recently, my family vacationed in an area known to have a large pagan population. There has been much written about one small tourist town in particular, some even calling it the satanic capital of the country.

We'd visited years prior without this knowledge, and without noticing anything out of the ordinary for a typical small tourist town. However, our then 9-year-old daughter, while we visited a shop along the main street, became pale and asked that we leave. Questioning her, we found she couldn't identify any specific thing, but she had "a bad feeling; something feels bad here." Fast forward to a recent trip with my son.

In order to get to a particular attraction, we had to pass through this same town. Getting ready in the hotel that morning, my son said, "Maybe we shouldn't go; I don't feel like battling demons today." I almost let fear win—until today's Scripture verse came to mind. It was a comfort to remind my son that we don't have to battle. Jesus already fought that battle against every anti-Christ spirit and false prophet. Now the Lord invites us to live with joy in His world-conquering victory.

Lord, I thank You for defeating every spiritual enemy of Your kingdom. I am grateful that I can walk in victory over the evil one through countless battles that I cannot even see. I pray for those who do not know You as their conqueror and ask that You make Your grace and mercy known to them. Through Christ the king, I pray. Amen.

Lofty Glances

Some of the Pharisees said, "This man is not from God, for he does not keep the Sabbath." But others asked, "How can a sinner perform such signs?" So they were divided (John 9:16).

Scripture: John 9:13-17
Song: "Does Anybody Hear Her?"

As we were growing up, my dearest friend, Lisa, and I had many things in common. One thing we didn't share, though, was her very strict Christian home. Anyone who knew Lisa knew that her family was "very religious." Along with myriad other restrictions, she wasn't allowed to attend parties or school dances or to use Sundays for anything but rest.

Lisa often struggled with the fear of disappointing her parents if she didn't live up to their ideals. One of those disappointments came in the form of her college boyfriend, Steve, who did not share her family's faith.

On a Sunday afternoon visit to her house, I arrived to find Lisa and Steve in the front yard washing his car. We were having a great time, chatting and catching up, and then Lisa's parents arrived. Her mother's first words as she bolted out of the car were, "Never again embarrass me by doing such a thing as washing your car at my home on the Sabbath! But, I don't suppose you would know anything about the Sabbath."

I wonder: Did this Christian woman's proclamation entice Steve to want to know more about her faith?

Lord, help me when I'm tempted to judge others. Let me display Your compassion, mercy, and grace instead of lofty glances. I pray. Amen.

The Power of Words

I long to see you so that I may impart to you some spiritual gift to make you strong—that is, that you and I may be mutually encouraged by each other's faith (Romans 1:11, 12).

Scripture: Romans 1:8-12, 16, 17
Song: "Overcomer"

For weeks I'd been looking forward to a night out with several girlfriends. I had envisioned a relaxing dinner with much laughter, because we always so enjoyed getting together. No matter how long it had been since being together, we could pick up right where we left off and catch up with each others' lives.

On this particular night, a few new acquaintances joined us. It was wonderful to see everyone, meet new friends, and enjoy a delicious dinner. But on the drive home I realized I didn't feel energized as I usually do; instead, I felt drained.

There had been a different dynamic, I reasoned, because "new" ladies had joined us. I thought back on the conversations we had shared; they were not uplifting. Much of what we'd talked about was negative and critical. Our words did not build each other up. We were certainly not "mutually encouraged by each other's faith."

Paul longed for that encouraging communion with fellow believers and the pleasure and strength that comes from sharing our lives. He knew the power of our words when we meet. They can lighten the burden that comes with kingdom work and strengthen us to keep moving forward in God's grace.

Lord of the church, I want to be more intentional with my words within my fellowship. Help me offer encouragement to others—while controlling my tongue when tempted to let a critical spirit have its way. Through Christ I pray. Amen.

Everyday Blessings

On arriving there, they gathered the church together and reported all that God had done through them and how he had opened a door of faith to the Gentiles (Acts 14:27).

Scripture: Acts 14:21-28
Song: "Count Your Blessings"

I'd been waiting in the emergency room most of the day. Then, the medical tests to determine the cause of my miserable symptoms finally came. The results? Food poisoning.

I was given intravenous fluids and allowed nothing by mouth for hours. My desert-like mouth only added to my misery. Despite my pleas, I was denied even an ice chip. Hours later, though, I was finally given a small, single-serving container of apple juice. It was the sweetest, coldest, most delicious apple juice I had ever tasted.

Despite my weakened state, I had to know the source of this miracle nectar. I rolled back the foil lid and told myself, "I must buy this brand from now on." Days later, back at home, I moved some pitchers around in the refrigerator and saw a bottle of apple juice hiding in the back. Immediately I recognized it as the same brand of juice from the hospital.

When God "shows up" at the times when I need Him so desperately, it is truly a sweet time, and I am eager to share that experience. But my blessed apple juice reminded me: He is there, every day, working for my good. I want to be able to draw from those defining moments so I can share them with others.

Lord, help me to pay attention to Your hand in my life and recognize the day-to-day mercies You lavish upon me. I ask that You help me share the countless stories of Your faithfulness with others. In the name of Jesus, amen.

Set Apart

While they were worshiping the Lord and fasting, the Holy Spirit said, "Set apart for me Barnabas and Saul for the work to which I have called them" (Acts 13:2).

Scripture: Acts 13:1-12
Song: "Voice of Truth"

I knew, without question, that the Lord had called me to minister to women who needed healing from abortions. He had set me free from the guilt and shame that had haunted me for years, and I knew He wanted me to lead other women to that same freedom.

It wasn't an easy journey, though. In order to accomplish that mission, I had to "go public." I had to bear the judgment of what had been my secret for so many years. While my true friends were lovingly supportive, some women began to avoid me. Others weren't at all shy about their feelings, asking how I could kill a baby.

I had moments of questioning God. "Is this really what you want me to be doing? If this is your will, shouldn't it be easier?" I did not yet have the courage of Paul to call my doubt what it was: an enemy.

When a woman approached me after worship with tears in her eyes, I braced myself for condemnation. But all she said through her tears was, "I thought I was the only one." Any hurt I had to endure was well worth the hope I soon saw in her eyes.

Lord, I know You have set me apart for a purpose. Help me listen to Your voice and boldly do the work to which You have called me. When opposition forms against me, help me to be strong in stepping forward in Your strength, remembering: I am called for a purpose by the one true king. In His name I pray. Amen.

How Does Prayer Work?

My goal is that they may be encouraged in heart and united in love . . . that they may know the mystery of God (Colossians 2:2).

Scripture: Colossians 1:24–2:5
Song: "The Mystery of Faith"

A friend told me that alcoholism was a major factor in his family of origin. "My brother and I grew up with a sense of foreboding," he said, "knowing the smallest thing could turn our family into a war zone. The situation was bearable because we had each other as we went through it all." But years later, he and his brother parted . . . on bad terms.

Then he saw "The Tempest," a play about a man who was wronged by his brother. The man was able to forgive when he realized the suffering his brother had endured in life. From that night on, my friend began praying for his brother. "I didn't want to see him; I just wanted him to be all right."

Two months later, he received an unexpected call from his brother. There was a different attitude; something had changed in him. Slowly, over time, the relational tensions evaporated.

Was my friend's heart opened because he began to pray for a brother he didn't even want to see? Was the brother's heart opened by those prayers, though he didn't know about them? "And did God put me in the audience of that play," my friend asked, "in order for this whole process to unfold?"

Lord of Heaven and earth, as I continue to pray, I find encouragement growing in my heart. May You reunite us all through our prayers! In the holy name of Jesus, amen.

December 11–17. Gary Wilde, editor of *Devotions*, lives with his wife, Carol, in Venice, Florida. They have twin adult sons, recently married, who work as industrial engineers in Denver and San Diego.

Example of Faith

"In him we live and move and have our being." As some of your own poets have said, "We are his offspring" (Acts 17:28).

Scripture: Acts 17:22-33.
Song: "A Stronger Faith, Dear Savior"

One day my friend told me about his grandmother: "She lived a very painful life, yet you wouldn't know it by her peaceful and loving manner. Orphaned as a young girl, she worked as a live-in maid. She married a wonderful man, but he suffered from bouts of severe anxiety and died young. My grandmother struggled with alcoholism for much of her early life. Her last 20 years were spent as an unwanted guest, shipped off between the homes of her two daughters. Yet somehow she emerged from these experiences with the feeling that God was by her side.

"One of my earliest childhood memories of her was when we'd feed the birds, and she'd tell me stories about St. Francis. She exuded a gentle sense of loving-kindness that extended to animals as well as to difficult people."

After that conversation, I almost felt as if I knew this wonderful lady. We all "live and move and have our being" in the Creator, but it seems that some folks grow so close to Him that His beauty becomes clearly visible in their personalities. I want examples like that to emulate. And I hope, by the workings of God's grace, to be an example to others as well. As my friend said: "The memory of my grandmother always gave me hope that—someday—I could have a faith like hers."

Heavenly Father, may I continue to encounter people in my life whose example points me to You. I pray in the name of Christ Jesus. Amen.

Christ Answers Our Dilemmas

Whatever happens, conduct yourselves in a manner worthy of the gospel of Christ (Philippians 1:27).

Scripture: Philippians 1:27-30
Song: "O Scattered Seeds of Loving Deeds"

I know a lady who was a visiting nurse for over 20 years, and she always put much effort into caring for her patients. But in order to maximize their profits, the home health care company she worked for told all the nurses that they would have to greatly increase the number of their daily visits. She was never afraid of hard work, but she realized that no one could possibly perform the required number of visits—and still provide quality care to the patients.

It would be very difficult for her to leave her job. Because she had specialized in home care for so many years, she questioned whether she had the technical experience to be hired for other facets of nursing.

Yet she faced a fact she couldn't ignore, as a disciple of Jesus: she just couldn't work for an agency that disregarded the welfare of patients. So she quit her job and eventually worked at an adult day-care center where patient care was the top priority.

When making difficult life decisions, we can review how the options before us are in line—or out of kilter—with Jesus' teaching. WWJD? "What Would Jesus Do?" can be a reliable guideline when we seek wisdom from above. As we keep an open heart to His leading, the best decision will soon emerge.

My Father in Heaven, please help me to recognize Your guiding hand as I make decisions during times of change and uncertainty. I am reminded today that You have my best at heart, and I am thankful. Through Christ my Lord, amen.

Learning from Physical Pain

Join with me in suffering, like a good soldier of Christ Jesus (2 Timothy 2:3).

Scripture: 2 Timothy 2:1-10
Song: "Who Will Suffer with the Savior?"

Most people believe that if you're suffering, it means that you must be doing something wrong. And sometimes we're told that all our problems can easily be solved if we'd just "live right." Indeed, certain "life coaches" seem to think that pain and suffering are unnatural states, a sign of failure.

Is this how life actually works? For most of my adult life I've been living with chronic headaches. I work hard at trying to maintain my health in all areas, yet receive mixed results at best. In this area of life, I feel like the mythological character who struggles to roll the big rock up the hill, only to have the rock roll back over him as he gets near the top.

Jesus came to our world to fully feel the pain and suffering that is an inherent part of our lives. And according to the apostle Paul, there is meaning in our suffering because our experience unites us with the experience of Jesus. He came down to our level and suffered human existence so we could learn from our own suffering and become more like Him.

I'll continue to work on my health, and I'm bound to have many moments of frustration in the future. But it's much easier to bear up under suffering when I realize that a greater purpose is always at work.

O Lord Jesus, You freely chose to share in our suffering. With Your example and help, may I approach my daily difficulties with equanimity. Reveal to me how these trials can move me closer to You. In Your precious name, I pray. Amen.

Using Your Pain?

Praise be to the God and Father of our Lord Jesus Christ . . . who comforts us in all our troubles, so that we can comfort those in any trouble with the comfort we ourselves receive from God (2 Corinthians 1:3, 4).

Scripture: 2 Corinthians 1:3-11
Song: "Cross of Jesus, Cross of Sorrow"

Ruth told me she still had severe knee pain, even though her doctor insisted that the X-rays of her replacement surgery were normal. Her physical therapist questioned whether she was doing her exercises faithfully, but she knew she was doing them exactly as directed. "What am I going to do?" she asked me. "I'll never get rid of this pain!"

Why do some of us have chronic pain? Our Scripture today provides us with one possible explanation. There will be times when we can use our experience to assist others who are in a similar difficulty. As we go through our daily life, we can try to be aware of those situations that call out for our help.

It's rarely helpful to say: "I know just how you feel!" However, if we do, indeed, have an idea of the suffering someone is experiencing, we can be genuinely sympathetic. We can also lift our eyes, together, to our Savior, who chose to suffer the pains of humanity with us. As the writer to the Hebrews put it: "We do not have a high priest who is unable to sympathize with our weaknesses, but One who has been tested in every way as we are" (Hebrews 4:15, *HCSB*).

Heavenly Father, let me never waste the sufferings that come into my days! Keep me alert to others who are hurting too. Show me how to offer just the right compassion and consolation—the kind that sustains me, as well. In Christ, amen.

God Speaks

[Paul and Barnabas] spoke in such a manner that a large number of people believed, both of Jews and of Greeks (Acts 14:1, *NASB*).

Scripture: Acts 14:1-7
Song: "My Soul in Silence Waits for God"

As a teen, I'd often walk up to church and play the piano when no one else was there. In the silence and semidarkness, I would sometimes stop, be completely still, and let a blessed sense of peace wash over me. Then my prayers would flow.

Over the next few years, I learned that prayer involves not just talking to God but listening for Him too. And He speaks "in such a manner" that we can hear, if our hearts are open.

Paul and Barnabas knew that a particular way of speaking in the synagogues would have the best effect. This took some planning and thinking. They'd need to take the time to know their audience and shape their message accordingly.

A few years ago, I took a course in contemplative prayer, in seeking the awareness of God's presence in silence. The motivation issued from the psalmist's words: "Be still, and know that I am God" (Psalm 46:10). As we pursue knowing Him, we can be sure He already knows us thoroughly and shapes His message to our spirit.

In other words, surely God speaks to each of us in ways we can receive. He knows exactly how to reach out to us. Sometimes His voice is most clearly heard in the silence.

Dear Heavenly Father, You speak to us in ways that we can understand. Please help us to hear Your message, and prepare it for others in ways they can hear. I pray in the precious name of Jesus, amen.

Not Easy

We must suffer many hardships to enter the Kingdom of God (Acts 14:22, *NLT*).

Scripture: Acts 14:8-11, 19-23
Song: "How Deep the Father's Love for Us"

A man who worked for the government said to me, "Our new managers took control over the office that I had worked in for many years. They were implementing changes that would hurt the clients we were serving. Because I respectfully disagreed with them, rumors and doubts about my work, reputation, and character began to spread."

In order to fit in with the people in power, most of his fellow workers joined in on those group dynamics. "By the time I left the job," he said, "few people were even speaking to me."

It seems futile for us to even care about what people think of us. After all, their perceptions can change overnight, and their views may draw from gossip and innuendo. Any attempt to "fit in" with that kind of group is bound to lead to continual moral compromises on our part, because the values of the group are constantly changing.

But all of this is a hardship! We all want to be liked, and we want to feel we're accepted by the people around us. But in carrying out Christ's mission, building His church, can we really afford to focus on the crowd's approval? As our Scripture today reminds us: the call to follow Christ will identify us with Him. And His life was anything but easy.

O God, thanks for reminding me of the futility of chasing after the approval of others. Let me focus solely on pleasing You today—and I know that includes loving those around me. Help me, Lord. It's not easy! Through Christ I pray. Amen.

Watching from a Distance

His sister stood at a distance to see what would happen to him (Exodus 2:4).

Scripture: Exodus 1:22–2:10
Song: "Have Thine Own Way, Lord"

When our son was a toddler, he would hold his breath if he didn't get his own way. Terrified that he would pass out, I expressed my fears to my doctor. "Just let him go," he said. "If he passes out, he'll start breathing again automatically."

I recall the first time I did this (and the last time he tried it). Kicking and screaming, his face grew red as he held his breath. I walked away and he did pass out—but only for an instant before he came to.

Years later I had to let go of him again. My husband and I were both in bed when our son came in and asked us to give him a ride to meet a girl that we disapproved of. "I'll take him," my husband said. In days past, I would have stayed awake, tossing and turning, wondering what was happening. Instead, I prayed, "Lord, watch over him. If he does anything he shouldn't, let him know it'll be over his mother's prayers." And I went to sleep.

Perhaps, we can all take a lesson from Moses' sister—stand at a distance and see what happens when we put our family in God's hands. They will be stronger for it. And we can sleep better, knowing He's in control.

Lord God of Mercy, I know You love my family even more than I do, and that You have a plan for each of them. Help me to let go and watch You work. I pray through Christ, my Lord. Amen.

December 18–24. **Donna Clark Goodrich** is a mother, grandmother, freelance writer, editor, proofreader, and conference instructor from Mesa, Arizona.

Chosen of God

You did not choose me, but I chose you (John 15:16).

Scripture: Isaiah 42:1-9
Song: "Whosoever Meaneth Me"

Do you remember standing on the playground, waiting to be chosen for a team? This may bring back unpleasant memories if you were the last one standing, and the captain *had* to choose you.

Maybe you wanted to join a glee club in school but weren't chosen because you sang a little off-key. Or perhaps, as an adult, you watched as someone else was chosen for a position at your work place, a position for which you were more qualified. And it hurt.

I made out OK at our annual church youth camp, as I not only enjoyed playing softball but was also good at Bible quizzing—two things for which our team received points. But I remember other times in my younger days when I was the last one chosen. And later a boy (whom I was certain liked me) chose another girl to date. These weren't pleasant experiences.

In today's Scripture, Isaiah foretells the coming of Christ, God's "chosen one." Later, in the New Testament, we see that now *we* are the chosen ones: "Chosen by God and precious" (1 Peter 2:4), "chosen in the Lord" (Romans 16:13), "a chosen people" (1 Peter 2:9).

Doesn't that have more eternal value than being chosen for a team, a date, or a position at our job? Imagine: chosen by the Lord of the universe . . . to be a member of His family.

O Lord, thank You for choosing me to be one of Your children. In return, help me to choose You in every decision I make in my life today. In the name of Jesus, amen.

He Can Use Any Size

But you, Bethlehem Ephrathah, though you are small among the clans of Judah, out of you will come for me one who will be ruler over Israel (Micah 5:2).

Scripture: Micah 5:1-5
Song: "O Little Town of Bethlehem"

In years to come, the town in Michigan where my husband ministered would become known for a national golf tournament. But during the time we were there, it was just a small suburb of a larger town. Our church was small in comparison to other nearby churches, running between 30 and 40 in attendance on Sunday mornings.

We were there only one year, but in that year we saw the following: a husband and wife reunited; a mother of seven children baptized and the family committed to attending church; an agnostic neighbor who allowed her son to participate in a church talent program; our 2-year-old daughter healed of a kidney disease.

Bethlehem was a small town—a suburb of Jerusalem, so to speak—about five miles south of the great city. It is first mentioned in Genesis 35:19 as the burial place of Rachel. Naomi and Ruth came to the city, David was anointed there, and as Micah had predicted years earlier, Jesus was born there. Thus we see that it's not the size of the place that matters; it's what God causes to *happen there* that's significant.

So, it's not the physical size of a person that counts, it's what we allow God to do in our hearts and lives.

Lord, if we're serving in a place today that's small and little known, or if we feel we're small in the world's eyes, help us to know that little is much if You're in it. In Jesus' precious name, I pray. Amen.

Are You There?

The virgin will conceive and give birth to a son, and they will call him Immanuel (which means "God with us") (Matthew 1:23).

Scripture: Matthew 1:18-25
Song: "O Come, O Come, Emmanuel"

Why was Jesus not called "Immanuel"? The notes in my reference Bible say: "According to Hebrew usage the name does not represent a title but a characterization. The name *Immanuel* shows that He really was [and is] with us." What a beautiful promise we can cling to every day.

· Going through an illness? God is with us.
· Facing financial difficulties? God is with us.
· Grieving a broken relationship? God is with us.
· Watching children leave the faith? God is with us.
· Loving an unbelieving spouse? God is with us.
· Going through a difficult valley? God is with us.
· Crossing over the Jordan River? God will be with us.

I remember a period of time when our family experienced several deaths, including the suicide of a teen. "Are you sure there's a God?" the voice of doubt taunted me. My head said yes, but my heart said, "Where are You? *Are You there?*"

One night while praying I said, without thinking, "Lord, I know You're here for me. You've always been here." Peace returned.

O Immanuel, Lord of all, I know this is a promise I can count on: You have been there with me in the past, and You'll be with me in the future. When I doubt, help me to stop and listen for Your voice. Speak, Lord, your servant hears! In the name of the Father and of the Son and of the Holy Spirit, I pray. Amen.

We Know We Can Trust Him

When [the Magi] had gone, an angel of the Lord appeared to Joseph in a dream. "Get up," he said, "take the child and his mother and escape to Egypt" (Matthew 2:13).

Scripture: Matthew 2:13-18
Song: "Lord, Speak to Me That I May Speak"

I remember our first move as parents—a distance of 750 miles—with three young children, aged three, two, and eight months. Although the trip was somewhat stressful, it helped to know that my husband had a job waiting for him, and we were assured of a place to live. We'd been preparing for this move for several months.

I can't even imagine what I would have thought if my husband had awakened me in the middle of the night and said, "Get the kids dressed. We're moving to another country."

"Where? Why?"

"Well, I had a dream."

"You must be crazy! I have friends here, our kids are young, and you won't even have a job or a place to live when we get there."

"I know, but an angel told me . . ."

From past experience, Joseph knew he could trust God, so when the Lord spoke, Joseph obeyed. And his obedience saved Jesus' life.

God speaks to us in different ways today—through His Word, through godly friends and, perhaps, even through a dream. And from past experiences, we know we can trust Him, so we know it will bring glory to Him and be a blessing to us, if we obey.

Lord, Your commands to us can affect our lives and, ultimately, the lives of our families. Help me to trust and obey Your voice today. In Jesus' name, amen.

Called to Leave

I am the Lord your God, . . . who directs you in the way you should go (Isaiah 48:17).

Scripture: Matthew 2:19-23
Song: "I'll Go Where You Want Me to Go"

Not just new believers but mature Christians often ask themselves: "What is God's will for me? What path shall I take?" We pray, seek counsel from the Bible and friends, and make what we feel is the right decision—only sometimes to discover, after a short time, the choice was wrong for us.

After working in a hospital for two years and enjoying my work, I entered nurses' training. My church gave me a going-away party with nurses' shoes, hose, and a nurse's watch. I left home with excitement. Several months later, however, I knew that career wasn't for me. I returned home, feeling like a failure.

My husband left seminary to accept the pastorate of a small church. Although at the time we both felt it was God's will, a year later—due to myriad family health issues—we felt just as certain it was time to leave.

God knows the future, and His timing is always right. Whether He calls us to a ministry for a few months or several years, He will not allow that time to be wasted. I grew closer to God during my brief time in nurses' school. And I certainly learned skills that helped me later in life. In addition several lives were spiritually transformed during my husband's one-year ministry.

Dear Father God, when You call me to a new place, help me respond in joyful obedience, knowing that the heavenly hand that points the way also provides the way! I am willing to go, Lord, in Your wisdom and strength. Through Christ, amen.

In the Presence of the King

Where is the one who has been born king of the Jews? We saw his star when it rose and have come to worship him (Matthew 2:2).

Scripture: Matthew 2:1-12
Song: "O Worship the King"

In 1994 my best friend and I took a 14-day trip to the British Isles. We saw all the normal tourist sites—Big Ben, Buckingham Palace, and Westminster Abbey. We took boat rides on the Thames River and Loch Lomond. We watched pottery being made at the Wedgewood factory and visited famous cathedrals and ancient tombs.

At that time, the queen of England was staying in Balmoral Castle, and after passing by its entrance, we stopped at Crathie Chapel where the queen attended church on Sundays. Just as we left, a horse-drawn carriage came toward us and turned into the castle drive. "The queen's getting ready to leave," our tour guide told us. "If we had time, we'd wait so you could see her." But we had to keep to our schedule, so we went on.

When my friend passed away in November 2014, the family asked me to tell about some highlights of our 69-year friendship. I shared a few, and then ended by saying, "Kathy missed seeing the queen by a few minutes, but now she's standing in the presence of the king."

The Magi traveled far—about 200 miles, it's believed—until they saw the star that led them to the baby Jesus. But they didn't come to see just any baby; they came to worship the king.

Lord, You deserve our very highest praise and worship. Help me to live my life so that someday I will stand in Your presence without shame. In the name of Jesus, amen.

God's Way Is New

Put on the new self, created to be like God in true righteousness and holiness (Ephesians 4:24).

Scripture: Ephesians 4:17-24
Song: "Away in a Manger"

We join Christians worldwide to celebrate Jesus' birth today. He entered the world in a most unexpected way—as a brand new baby. After all, so many of God's chosen people expected their Messiah to arrive as a warrior to overthrow their Roman captors. Instead, they—and we—got a tiny infant who grew up to save the world in a way no earthly warrior could.

Babies inspire awe as we watch them wriggle and hear them coo. The little fist that locks around one of our fingers stirs our hearts. As children grow, they react with wonder to lights, sounds, and other stimuli. Wide-eyed, openhanded, they remind us how amazing and intricate is God's design for life—an ever-expanding newness of growth.

Today's verse challenges us to keep becoming new selves in Christ. We are to grow more like Him, but what does it take? We can acknowledge our infantile helplessness over sin. We can turn to Jesus with humble, open hearts and receive forgiveness. We can grow as God's children by reading and studying the Bible, spending time in prayer, and joining our Lord's community in worship. As we heed God's guidance, we may go in some unexpected—and blessed—directions. Thanks be to God!

God of wonders and surprises, thank You for the greatest surprise of all: Jesus' love and mercy. Praise You, in His precious name. Amen.

December 25–31. **Jane Heitman Healy**, of South Dakota, is a librarian and writer for adults and children. She enjoys spending time with family and friends, serving her church, and reading.

Walk, Cook, and Serve in Love

Walk in the way of love, just as Christ loved us and gave himself up for us as a fragrant offering and sacrifice to God (Ephesians 5:2).

Scripture: Ephesians 4:25–5:2
Song: "Lo, How a Rose E'er Blooming"

The holiday meal's aroma struck my nose as soon as I stepped inside my hostess's house. A succulent turkey had cooked for hours, and my mouth watered at the thought of the accompanying stuffing, mashed potatoes, and gravy.

The hostess had sacrificed time and money to plan, purchase, and prepare this meal, a "fragrant offering" for her friends. As a guest, I felt honored and thankful for the invitation. Around the table, conversation and laughter flowed as we enjoyed each other's company. We parted with hugs, full of food and friendship.

Jesus often shared meals with His disciples, even stooping to wash their dusty feet beforehand. Those were His friends, but Jesus also loved people that society deemed most unworthy: an adulteress, a tax collector, a Samaritan woman, and others who were changed forever by His touch. Then Jesus' love went far beyond human friendship and hospitality. He gave us His own body and blood so that we could live with Him forever.

As Jesus' followers, we are called to "walk in love." We may not all be great cooks, but we can use the abilities we have to share Jesus with others, bringing them the sweet fragrance of His love and forgiveness.

O Jesus, thanks for coming to live with me, showing me how to love others. Thank You for Your sacrifice, allowing me to live as Your loved and forgiven child, now and forever. Help me to love everyone as You have loved me. In Your name, amen.

Mission Success

Set your minds on things above, not on earthly things (Colossians 3:2)

Scripture: Colossians 3:1-11
Song: "In Heaven Above"

NASA's New Horizons probe thrilled the world in July 2015 when it sent back its first images of Pluto, over 3 billion miles from earth. New Horizons took almost 10 years to reach Pluto. Long before that, teams of scientists at several sites determined how the probe should be built, what scientific instruments the probe should carry, and other logistics. While the rest of us went about our daily business in the world, these scientists set their minds on space. Thanks to their work toward a successful mission, we now know much more about the dwarf planet and its moons.

The writer of Colossians tells us to keep our minds on things above. He refers to things far "above" our solar system in distance and importance. The New Horizons probe had to overcome earth's gravity to reach outer space. We have to overcome our sinful natures to reach eternal life. Jesus alone makes that possible through the grace that comes by His cross.

Attending worship, studying Scripture, and offering daily prayer keep us focused on things above. In fact, setting our minds on things above helps give us God's perspective and priorities. In heavenly fellowship we live our earthly lives in community as Jesus' disciples. That's mission success.

Creator God, I am awed to think that You made the enormous universe and little me. Still You loved me enough to send Jesus to die for me. Keep my heart, soul, and mind focused on things above today. In the name of Jesus, amen.

Unwrap Your Gifts

Now eagerly desire the greater gifts (1 Corinthians 12:31).

Scripture: 1 Corinthians 12:27-31
Song: "We All Are One Mission"

My choir played a gift exchange game in which the player could either choose a wrapped gift from the pile or take a gift that someone else had already opened. We shared lots of laughs as people decided whether to go for the known item or open a new box.

Suspense filled the air when a player chose a wrapped gift. Should the player go for the biggest or smallest box? What might be in that lumpy one? Swaps and switches were made until the very end, because everyone wanted to go home with the gift they thought was greatest.

God has given each of us gifts to use for His purposes. If we're unsure what they are, He will help us discern our gifts. However, unlike my choir game, we don't get to choose. Sometimes our gifts may feel under appreciated or even burdensome. Sometimes we might want to swap for someone else's gift that seems more powerful, public, or important. However, let us trust God's plan. He knows us and sees our great potential for service in His kingdom.

Each gift of every believer is important to God's work in and through the church. Our gifts work together for the good of the whole body of Christ. All we need to do is unwrap our gifts—discover and develop them—and use them for God's glory.

Gracious God, thank You for the gifts and talents You've given me. Help me discern where and how to use them. Show me my place in the body of Christ, and lead me in working with others to serve You. Through Christ the Lord, I pray. Amen.

Together We Stand

If one part suffers, every part suffers with it; if one part is honored, every part rejoices with it (1 Corinthians 12:26).

Scripture: 1 Corinthians 12:12, 13, 22-26
Song: "Blest Be the Tie That Binds"

A school superintendent retired early due to his failing health. Because of kidney disease, he spent much of his time connected to a dialysis machine, but the whole community actively supported the family with help and love as the disease progressed.

When his condition became known, a former student contacted him. He had been her high school principal, a man who had believed in her, encouraging her to follow her dream of becoming a nurse. Now, tests showed that her kidney would be a good match for him.

The community suffered together with their superintendent—students, teachers, parents. And the former student felt honored to be able to give back to her principal, who had given her so much. The old adage that "a sorrow shared is half a sorrow, a joy shared is twice a joy" gets to the heart of today's Scripture, and it was lived out in this small town.

We are all weak and needy at some point, while others are strong. In each situation, the strong are called to help the weak carry their burdens. When the weak become strong, they can help others. So when we experience joy, let's share it with those less joyful, so that more people can be uplifted. In joy and sorrow, we are God's people together.

Thank You, Lord, for the people You've put in my life to double my joys and divide my sorrows. Empower me to help those who need it and to allow others to share my joy. I know this is how we can be like Jesus to one another. In His name, amen.

When Evil Comes

Do not repay evil with evil or insult with insult. On the contrary, repay evil with blessing, because to this you were called so that you may inherit a blessing (1 Peter 3:9)

Scripture: 1 Peter 3:8-12
Song: "There Shall Be Showers of Blessing"

On June 17, 2015, a stranger joined a church prayer group in Charleston, South Carolina. He sat with the gathered Christians for awhile . . . before pulling his gun and killing nine of them. The country mourned and condemned the action, yet the families of the slain did a surprising thing. They forgave the shooter. They said they prayed for him and urged him to repent.

When evil arises, retaliating is just human nature. The Old Testament says, "Show no pity: life for life, eye for eye, tooth for tooth, hand for hand, foot for foot" (Deuteronomy 19:21). But Jesus turned that upside down in His Sermon on the Mount. "You have heard that it was said, 'Eye for eye, and tooth for tooth.' But I tell you, do not resist an evil person" (Matthew 5:38, 39). Jesus even tells His listeners to love their enemies.

In today's Scripture, Peter reminds us of Jesus' call to rise above evil and react with blessing. While this is difficult, the church of Charleston showed us that it is possible. We still hold people responsible for the consequences of their actions. They still owe a debt to society. But God's Spirit helps us release our own bitterness. We can be free, in Him, no matter the actions of others.

O God, I know that evil exists and sometimes touches me personally. In my daily life, I may receive insults and meanness. Fill me with Your Spirit so that I can respond as Peter advised—with blessing. Thank You for Your gift of love! Through Christ, amen.

New Year, Fresh Start

As a prisoner for the Lord, then, I urge you to live a life worthy of the calling you have received (Ephesians 4:1).

Scripture: Ephesians 4:1-16
Song: "Day by Day"

Is it your New Year's resolution to stick to your resolutions? Or have you given up on the idea of making resolutions because you've failed, year after year? Experts recommend writing down goals that are specific, measurable, achievable, relevant, and time-bound (SMART). I've done that—and still failed to meet my goals or keep my resolutions.

Many of us would like to make some life changes, but we lack the discipline to follow through. Clearly, our willpower alone won't ensure success.

Thankfully, each day gives us a fresh start. Though we have to live with the consequences of yesterday's failures, the failures vanish into mist as we confess them to God. God forgives us and helps us start anew to "live a life worthy of the calling you have received," as Paul says. We are called to be God's people, to live in peace and harmony, and to serve God together. The Lord has even given each of us gifts to help us accomplish His purposes.

With God's direction, we can set goals that will build up the body of Christ. With God's power, we can reach those goals. So, greet the new year with confidence, knowing that God Almighty has His own infallible goal: that we will one day be like His Son, Jesus (see 1 John 3:2).

God and Ruler of all time, thank You for calling me to serve You. Show me opportunities to use the gifts You've given me for service in Your kingdom. Thank You for giving me fresh starts, and help me grow in You in the new year. In Jesus' name, amen.